THE MASTER OF LIGHT

Dorothy Michelson Livingston

THE
MASTER OF
LIGHT

A BIOGRAPHY OF

Albert A. Michelson

ILLUSTRATED WITH PHOTOGRAPHS AND DRAWINGS

THE UNIVERSITY OF CHICAGO PRESS
Chicago and London

The University of Chicago Press, Chicago 60637
The University of Chicago Press, Ltd., London

Printed in the United States of America
86 85 84 83 82 81 80 79 5 4 3 2 1
LCN: 72–1178

For Goodhue,

AND FOR MY DAUGHTERS,

Dorothy, Ursula, and Beatrice

*If a poet could at the same time be a physicist,
he might convey to others the pleasure, the
satisfaction, almost the reverence, which the
subject inspires. The aesthetic side of the subject
is, I confess, by no means the least attractive to
me. Especially is its fascination felt in the
branch which deals with light.*

Albert A. Michelson, *Light Waves and Their Uses*

CONTENTS

CONTENTS

ILLUSTRATIONS

DIAGRAMS IN TEXT

ILLUSTRATIONS

ILLUSTRATIONS

THE MASTER OF LIGHT

Introduction: Quest for My Father

IN my memory, Father was always returning home from some glamorous country, laden with exotic presents, long Latin scrolls telling how wonderful he was, and frequently a fat, golden medal. One morning in 1909, when I was almost four years old, he returned from Lima, Peru, where he had delivered a series of lectures. I was still in the bathtub when I heard the front door slam and the welcoming shrieks of joy from Madeleine and Beatrice, my older sisters.

"Dody," they called, "Pahdie is home!" I leaped out of the tub, slipped through my nurse's clutches, and ran naked down the stairs to throw myself into my father's strong arms, covering him with foaming suds.

Father always seemed taller than he actually was. He had

thick black hair rising high off his forehead and graying around the temples. Deep thought wrinkles, a strong nose, and a firm chin gave him a stony, impassive look that could intimidate, but now he was smiling. Under the shaggy eyebrows his deep-set eyes looked down with appealing gentleness. I felt as though I had tamed him.

"Dody, my lammikin," he said, hugging me through the suds, "run upstairs and get your clothes on. I think you children might be interested in something I have in my suitcase."

I slid down reluctantly and went to finish my bath. When I returned, Father was unwrapping some little stuffed hummingbirds, a mounted peacock butterfly, a giant stag beetle, all gleaming with a shimmering blue-green iridescence on their wings.

"What makes them change color?" Beatrice asked. She was six, in her first year of school. Father's face lighted; it was the right question to ask.

"That's just what I've been trying to find out," he answered.

"The rainbow and the halo," he told us, "are the only colors caused by prisms in nature except dew drops and icicles, perhaps. But this little diamond beetle has grown a grating on his back that beats any I can make. He has some two thousand lines on one inch of wing. So the colors you see are caused by interference, not pigment."[1]

"How very clever of him!" Beatrice said.

Father's consuming interest in the behavior of light was contagious. We delighted in the double image and brilliant colors produced by a little prism he brought us from his laboratory. And on evenings when he was in a mood to talk, he would tell us about rainbows, lightning, or the Northern Lights. Sometimes the explanation was longer than a child's span of concentration. Madeleine asked him what sounded like a simple question: Why is the sky blue? But, as physicists know, the answer could fill a book. As Father explained the propagation of light waves, touched on the scattering of particles, and pointed out the virtues of the undulatory theory as against the corpuscular theory of the motion of light, Madeleine's attention began to wander. He became offended when he saw that she was no longer listening, but when she climbed onto his knees and asked to be forgiven, he said, "It doesn't matter if you don't understand it now, as long as you realize the wonder of it."

In the years following my father's death, my feeling of loss at last gave way to a deep curiosity. I wanted to know what he had really been like as a person, not just as my father, and to find out exactly what he had done, what obstacles he had overcome, and what significance his work had for modern science. He had a reputation for aloofness. Harvey Lemon, for many years his research assistant, wrote: "Even those cosmic human forces of love, hate, jealousy, envy, and ambition seemed to move him little. He possessed an astonishing indifference to people in general . . . one knew the surface, little more. . . ."[2]

I found myself totally unequipped for the task I had undertaken—I was not a writer, and certainly not a physicist. In truth, my formal schooling ended without even a high school diploma. At Miss Porter's School, in Farmington, Connecticut, it was enough to carry the daisy chain. What gall to think of interpreting Father! I did not know where to begin.

There was another hazard: Father's reticence and dislike of publicity. He was close-mouthed, confiding in no one, and he would certainly have resented my poking around in his past. For a while, these obstacles held me back. My search consisted mainly of cornering any physicist I chanced to meet at a cocktail party and asking, "Why is it so important to know the exact speed of light?"

Most of the answers only puzzled me. One was that the speed of light is one of the few "constants" in nature, unaffected by the motion of the source of light or that of the observer. What observer, I wondered. I was to hear a lot about this unfortunate creature before I had finished. He was forever on board a train, going toward nowhere in particular, and never even allowed to comment upon the phenomena he observed. Aristotle stood him on the earth, Copernicus and Kepler put him up in the sky, and Einstein had him locked in an elevator, plunging down an endless shaft.

Another answer, however, made its point: If we are ever to have interplanetary communication it will be by means of Michelson's discovery of the length of light waves. He had obtained the one unit of measurement known to be the same on Mars as on the earth.

I learned that the speed of light, represented by c, is one of the elements in Albert Einstein's famous equation $E=mc^2$, the formula that enabled man to make use of atomic energy and eventually to move into outer space.

On December 19, 1952, Case Institute of Technology in Cleveland commemorated the one-hundredth anniversary of my father's birth with a ceremony which I attended. Paying tribute to his memory on this occasion, Einstein sent a message that anyone could understand.

> I always think of Michelson as the artist in Science. His greatest joy seemed to come from the beauty of the experiment itself, and the elegance of the method employed. But he has also shown an extraordinary understanding for the baffling fundamental questions of physics. This is evident from the keen interest he has shown from the beginning for the problem of the dependence of light on motion.[3]

I gathered incentive from this ceremony, but it was not until the winter of 1962 that I mustered up courage to ask for an interview with the distinguished physicist and secretary of the American Physical Society, Dr. Karl Darrow, who had been a pupil of my father from 1912 to 1917.

Talking to him on the telephone, I scarcely knew what questions to ask.

"You knew my father . . ." I began, but he stopped me.

"Although I was his pupil for five years, I never would presume to say that I knew him." As a student, Dr. Darrow had evidently been as frightened of Father as I now was of him. However, he consented to see me and agreed to let me bring a tape recorder to his office. The tape recorder, I thought, would remember exactly what he said, even if my own memory failed. Although it was an antiquated model and so heavy I could hardly lift it, the clumsy instrument gave me confidence.

On a cold December morning in a heavy snowstorm I found my way to Dr. Darrow's room in Pupin Hall, one of the older buildings of Columbia University. He greeted me with polite reserve and gave me permission to plug in my tape recorder. The instant of contact created a sudden explosion. Searing sparks destroyed the delicate mechanism and an acrid yellow smoke filled the office. Dr. Darrow, through a fit of coughing, motioned me toward the large plate-glass window. We each grasped a handle, straining in unison, but there was no budging it. "One, two, three—lift"—we tried again, redoubling our efforts, and this time it flew up. An icy blast blew every paper off his desk. I fell on my hands and knees, clutching at the whirling sheaves.

I caught sight of a clock and realized that the half-hour allotted me was nearly over. Clutching my charred tape recorder and muttering apologies I beat a retreat. I learned later that I had plugged in my AC recorder in one of the few buildings at Columbia University that were still using direct current.

After that experience, some two years elapsed before I dared attempt another interview. Meanwhile I had discovered the Science Section of the New York Public Library and, even more useful, the Niels Bohr Library of the American Institute of Physics. I took a course on the history of science at the New

School for Social Research, as well as a course in non-fiction writing. From the Michelson Museum at the Naval Weapons Center, China Lake, California, I procured a complete set of my father's papers. When, in 1966, I saw Dr. Darrow again, I had a host of questions ready, and he was kind enough to tell me where to find the answers.

Part of my curiosity about Father's past arose from the mystery surrounding his first marriage and subsequent divorce. The subject was forbidden in the house while I was growing up. The taboo involved not only his first wife but the children of that marriage, two sons and a daughter, born in 1878, 1879, and 1881, respectively. Occasionally, some friend would ask about them; Father always replied that he knew nothing about their activities, not even their whereabouts.

It therefore came as a surprise, tinged with a pang of jealousy, to learn that Margaret Heminway, whose name I had never heard, had been Father's wife for more than twenty years, during the time in which he had achieved the most brilliant successes of his long career in physics. Those other children had been growing up in his home during those vital years. He became *my* father only toward the end of his life.

Both sons were dead by the time I began my search, but in 1966 I discovered that my half-sister, Elsa, then eighty-five, was living quietly in Nassau. I wrote that I was anxious to talk with her about Father and her childhood. It was a bitter disappointment when she excused herself from seeing me, saying she feared our meeting would upset her. I wrote again, pleading that she was the only person in the world who actually remembered Father at the time of his greatest experiment. Finally I coaxed her into answering my questions by letter.

"My father was like a very important guest in the house," Elsa wrote.[4] A provocative answer. The fog of mystery shrouding my father's relationship with her mother was not cleared up. If anything, it thickened. Curiosity overcame discretion and reticence. I set up a file with the papers I had gathered, a card index from 1852 to 1931, and in 1968 I began to fill it with notes.

Searching the records of Father's life I looked for clues to a pervading inner conflict or encounter with frustration which might have made him shun ordinary family life and turn to the haven of abstract thought. But my subject refused to cooperate. He kept enjoying himself when he was supposed to suffer. Perhaps the secret lay in depending, not on others, but only on himself. He once said: "It is the pitting of one's brain against bits of iron, metals, and crystals and making them do what you want them to do. When you are successful that is all the reward you want."[5] Again, when someone asked why he spent his whole life on the behavior of light, I saw his glowing smile as he replied, "Because it's so much fun."

This quest for my father has obsessed me for many years. At moments he has emerged vividly before my mind, only to dissolve mysteriously into a world I have only begun to understand. Without the careful interpretations of his work given me by scientists who knew him, many of them now dead, I could have provided only a one-sided view of the man. I ask indulgence from those readers who are already familiar with the simple problems in physics that I have tried to explain, as well as from those who ordinarily shun the world of science. My wanderings in the dawn of modern scientific endeavor have brought me a delight I hope to share.

CHAPTER 1

Strzelno to the Golden West

SUNLIGHT filled the village square of Strzelno, Poland, dressed in garlands and bunting for a celebration, and shone upon the faces of the men and women standing near the town hall and on the many children lined up in orderly rows. They had gathered on that July day in 1963 to hear the speeches of the Mayor, the local Commissar, and the Dean of Science of Copernicus University in Torun at the dedication of a plaque to the memory of a man born in their village on December 19, 1852, who had won the Nobel Prize.

"Strzelno is proud of her son," said the Mayor, "And although his life was spent far away from us, we will remember that his genius came into being here among our people. It is a great moment in Polish science. He has put us into history."[1]

The leader of a small band of musicians had made a special effort to procure the music for the United States national anthem, not readily available in Iron Curtain countries. As the band struck up the unfamiliar strains of "The Star Spangled Banner," the Mayor unveiled a tablet marking the birthplace of Albert Abraham Michelson. When the speeches were over, a procession formed and moved down the road to Ulica Michelsona (Michelson Street), followed by the band and all the children.

Albert's mother was born Rosalie Przylubska, the second of three daughters of Abraham Przylubski, a Polish businessman from Inowroclaw near Strzelno.[2] The family name and a picture of her mother suggest that she came from typical Polish peasant stock. Her older sister Auguste married a doctor, and perhaps it was at their wedding that Rosalie first met Samuel Michelson, a young merchant of Jewish descent, who had come to live in Inowroclaw. He had little in the way of financial security to recommend him as a husband; he had no store of his own and probably sold his wares from a pushcart. Since Rosalie certainly did not marry him for money or position, he must have had a generous amount of personal charm. He was twenty-five and Rosalie just a year younger when they married and moved to Strzelno, and there Samuel opened a shop of his own. No doubt he had some help and plenty of advice from his father-in-law, the distance between the villages being 30 kilometers, less than a day's ride on horseback.

Albert was their first baby, born on December 19, 1852. He was a healthy boy and much loved. Two little girls, Pauline and Johanna, followed shortly. Pauline lived to a ripe old age, but poor Johanna seems to have been ill-starred from the beginning. Her birth was registered under the wrong name and Samuel had to have the entry in the register corrected several months later. After that, there is no further mention of her. Probably she died in infancy. Her brother never spoke of her.

The Michelson family seems to have left Strzelno late in 1855. (The last date related to their affairs in the local register is August 21, of that year.) Their decision to emigrate was probably influenced by the political situation in the Prussian-dominated section of Poland. The abortive "revolution of 1848" had left conditions very unsettled. Anti-Semitism was rife, and purges of Jews were frequent in the towns and villages around Strzelno. Curfews were enforced and the ghettos became intolerable.

After working their way across northern Europe, Samuel and Rosalie and their children embarked on a steamer sailing between a North Sea seaport, probably Hamburg, and New York. For emigrants, the crossing in steerage was a mixture of joy and terror. There was triumph in having extricated themselves from a hopeless past, regret at leaving their relatives and the familiar way of life, and fear of the vast ocean tossing their ship on its waves. Rosalie, pregnant again, had need of all her courage to withstand the discomfort of the crowded vessel and to gather her forces against the unknown life ahead.

The crossing took almost three weeks. Upon landing in New York, the Michelsons went to the house of Rosalie's relatives, the Friedenburgs, on the lower East Side, where they stayed to refresh themselves from the long sea voyage. Here they heard talk of the wild adventures and the sudden fortunes made overnight in the growing rush for California gold. Among the "forty-niners" were Samuel's sister Belle and her husband, Oscar Meyer, who had made a quick success at Murphy's Camp in Calaveras County. This news spurred the Michelsons to follow.

There were three routes by which they might continue their journey to San Francisco, all dangerous and expensive: by covered wagon across the continent; by ship around Cape Horn; or by a combination of ship and mule wagon to Panama, across the Isthmus, and up the West Coast. The last was the route they finally chose.

Samuel booked passage on a small ship to Porto Bello, on the Isthmus, where a vessel might be warped beside the pier. The alternative was to risk disembarking in the shark-infested waters of a shallower harbor such as Chagres. Porto Bello hardly lived up to its name. It was a tropical slum known as the "grave of Europeans." Many inhabitants, black, white, and Indian, lived there in squalor; many were ill with "brain fever," malaria, or smallpox. Apathy lay upon the town like a shroud. Money was useless even to those who had it to spend. Thieves and robbers looted the dead, the sick, and the unarmed passengers. There were no police.[3]

The Michelsons escaped the perils of Porto Bello and set forth on their journey across the Isthmus, traveling in canoes paddled by natives, through swamps and lakes. Gaudy parrots sitting in the mango trees protested the intrusion, while flocks of herons and cranes rose from the river bank as they progressed. Changing to muleback on the higher land, they passed Indian villages perched on the crests of low, rounded mountains.

The next stage of their journey was probably made on the pioneer railroad completed in 1855 between Aspinwall (now Colon) and Panama City, a distance of less than fifty miles. Here fresh discomforts awaited them. Drinking water was available only at exorbitant prices, because it had to be carted several miles in barrels. Raw sewage flowed down steep and narrow streets lined with saloons, gambling halls, and brothels. Violence was common and sensible people armed themselves to the teeth, looking like brigands to avoid being taken by them.

In this tropical hell, Samuel and his family waited for passage to San Francisco. Although Albert was not yet four years old, the horrors of this trip across the Isthmus, often retold by his parents, remained in his memory as long as he lived. Several weeks passed before cabin space was obtained on a ship of the Aspinwall Line. After sixty days at sea, the Michelsons reached the Golden Gate.

Clipper ships lying at anchor crowded San Francisco harbor. Many of these stately square-rigged vessels were deserted; their crews had gone to the "diggings" seeking gold. Samuel, however, did not have the prospecting fever. He felt safer in his own familiar trade and so bought supplies that would be needed by the miners. As soon as he was able to get accommodations, he and his family climbed into a stagecoach for the last lap of their journey to Murphy's Camp in the foothills of the Sierra Nevada, some 150 miles east of San Francisco.

Murphy's Camp, or Murphy's Diggings as it was first known, had been founded in 1848 as a trading post with the Indians. John Murphy and his brother Daniel were among the first to begin panning for gold in the stream. They hired some Indians for this work, and in one year, it is said, they took out two million dollars in gold, simultaneously creating a land boom in the area of Calaveras.[4]

By 1856, when the Michelsons arrived, Murphy's had grown into a flourishing mining town, fairly well settled. Here they were greeted by Samuel's sister and her husband. Oscar Meyer was engaged in a mining operation. With his help, Samuel set up a little store, stocked with picks and shovels, pans for gold-panning, pot-bellied stoves, heavy boots and jackets, blankets, bedding, and canvas tents.

The rough life of the camp and town made a vivid impression on Albert. He acquired here some of the tenacity and toughness of mind that he brought to his mature life as a scientist. The atmosphere was exciting. For a few lucky ones money was rolling in—the claims at Murphy's were the richest of any in Calaveras County. Five million dollars was taken from just one four-acre placer area. An ounce of gold dust to the pan was rather common, four or five ounces was not unusual, and many claims paid sixteen ounces to the pan. In a period of ten years, during the 1850s and 1860s Wells, Fargo and Company shipped fifteen million dollars' worth of gold dust from Murphy's. Individual claims were restricted to 80 square feet. Arguments were usually settled with fists, knives, or bullets, and the women and children were safer behind locked doors after sundown because the men of the town then became gun-happy from gambling and whisky.

During Albert's second year in Murphy's, work began on a great suspension flume, an aqueduct across the canyon at the lower end of the valley. It connected with a supply of water brought from the Stanislaus River some fifteen miles higher up in the mountains. The water was brought to the Central Hill Mine, on a ridge a mile south of Murphy's, to wash out the miners' gravel. The construction of this flume, completed in three months' time, was one of the great engineering feats of the early miners. The watertight boxes, suspended on wires, zigzagged overhead amid a network of struts and stays, carrying the main force of the stream across the valley.

Narrow wooden houses with two-story balconies lined both sides of Murphy's unpaved street. No one had time to paint them. Bret Harte describes a hotel, modeled after the one in Murphy's, in "The Luck of Roaring Camp":

> It was designed with an eye to artistic dreariness. It was so much too large for the settlement that it appeared to be a very slight improvement on outdoors. It was unpleasantly new. There was the forest flavor of dampness about it, and a slight spicing of pine. Nature, outraged, but not entirely subdued, sometimes broke out afresh in little round resinous tears on the doors and windows.[5]

Harte's character, Perthonia, whom he describes as "dirty, drabbled and forlorn," told how she had given up little by little what she imagined to be the weaknesses of her early education. Now, transplanted to a backwoods society, she was hated by the women and called "proud" and "fine." Such epithets may well have been thrown at Rosalie Michelson when she insisted that her son begin his schooling, mind his manners, and even start lessons on the violin at a time when he was hardly able to reach out far enough to hold the fiddle or stretch his fingers on the strings. Rosalie set a high standard for her children. To be sure, there was no lack of gaiety or fun, but it was always after the work was done. No child of Rosalie's failed to absorb an enormous respect for literature and a love of beauty in one form or another. The effect on Albert of his mother's values is clear. Her training made him able to resist the lure of easy money all his life.

Across the street from the Michelsons lived the blacksmith, Dave Baratini, and a few houses farther away the apothecary, Dr. William Jones, who did everything from probing for bullets, to dispensing pills and arnica to the miners. A young girl, Bee Matteson, operated the first telegraph office in Murphy's. Her father, T. J. Matteson, was the surveyor who had laid out the route of the canal from the Stanislaus River. He also operated the pioneer stagecoach line daily from Murphy's to Angels, a nearby town.

The stagecoach usually came into town dreadfully overloaded, with fifteen or more people clinging to the top-heavy vehicle. When time came for departure, Matteson's drivers often had trouble in preventing more men from climbing aboard the coach than it could safely hold.

Murphy's provided more sinister forms of excitement. Public hangings took place frequently, in the hope of intimidating outlaws. One of the outlaws, a "handsome, fancy dresser," was a Spaniard named Joaquin Murieta, the three-fingered bandit whose raids of revenge upon the men who had flogged him kept the whole town in terror during the early 1850s.

On Sundays, the villagers enjoyed a quieter diversion. They could board a coach in front of the Sperry and Perry Hotel (next door to the Michelson house) and ride twelve miles to the Big Trees in Calaveras Grove. These were the first *Sequoia gigantea* to be discovered, and they attracted people from all over the world. Among them were Ulysses S. Grant and Mark Twain.

THE MASTER OF LIGHT

Albert attended the first public school built in Murphy's. It was furnished with handmade desks, built by the local carpenter. In 1857, there were fifty-five children enrolled under a Mr. Jaquith, the principal, and his assistant, Isaac Ayers. Albert's first-grade teacher was Mary Anne Conway, an Irish girl of only fourteen who had come around the Horn to California in 1847 on the *Susan Drew*, one of the first ocean-going steamships built in the United States. Mary Anne had been educated in Spanish at the Convent of Monterey and had almost forgotten her English.

On a Sunday afternoon three years after the Michelsons had arrived in Murphy's, the great fire of 1859 demolished the town. In forty minutes everything was in ashes except Peter Travers' General Store and the sagging walls of the Murphy Hotel. Since the residents of Murphy's had no title to their property except pre-emption or "squatters' rights," the fire caused a good many arguments over boundaries. Albert's family luckily escaped personal injury. Along with the others, the Michelsons soon began to rebuild, and out of the ashes a new town was born, marking a new and more opulent era. The crowning feature of the new Murphy's was Putney's Opera House, on the site of the old Smith's Saloon and the office of Judge Putney, Justice of the Peace.

Albert was eight when the Civil War broke out. It took some months for the news to reach Murphy's, but when they heard it, the miners sided unanimously with the Union. Money poured out of their coffers and almost every man who had two legs to walk—and some who did not—joined the Calaveras Light Guard, as they called themselves. They drilled up and down the street, preparing for the conflict.

Excitement ran riot in the town when a captain with a company of 300 men passed through Murphy's in 1862 on his way over Ebbett's Pass to the battlefields of the East. Many of the miners left their claims to join the Union Army. When news finally came that Lee had surrendered and the war was over, the whole population became frantic. Bells tolled, guns roared, and for days no one, not even Samuel Michelson, was sober. But Murphy's was a town of extremes. The residents' exuberance in victory was equaled by their despair in mourning Lincoln's assassination. Out of love for the late President, the Michelsons gave Albert the middle name of Abraham.

During these lively years, the Michelson family expanded. Julie, Benjamin, Bessie, and Miriam were born in Murphy's while the gold rush rose to its peak.

When Albert reached the age of twelve, his parents felt that he had exhausted the slender opportunities for education at Murphy's. It was time, they thought, to send him to a "proper" school in San Francisco. The decision was made easier by the departure for that city of Belle and Oscar Meyer, with their sons Mark and young Oscar, in 1864. Albert was sent along with his cousins and spent the next two years living with the Meyers and attending Lincoln Grammar School.

In September of 1866, Albert transferred to the San Francisco Boys' High School (now called Lowell High School). The principal, Theodore Bradley, was so much impressed with him that he took him into his own home and gave him the job of setting up experiments for the science class and helping with the chores. In the evening, when Albert's studying was finished, Bradley encouraged him to practice the violin.

It was Bradley also who taught Albert the "manly art of self-defense," instilling in him the knowledge that he need never tolerate insults or be afraid to fight with his fists. The boy took to boxing with pleasure; his quick coordination compensated for his slight build. Albert was fortunate in his teacher. Bradley believed in developing his promising student into a well-rounded man rather than a prodigy.

After his first year of high school in San Francisco, Albert went home to spend the summer of 1867 with his parents at Murphy's. The town was in complete decline; empty shacks and abandoned mine shafts were everywhere, and it was impossible to earn a living. The center of prospecting had shifted to Virginia City, over the mountains in Nevada, where, in 1859, silver had been found in the Comstock Lode. Though still sparsely populated, the former Nevada Territory had been declared a state by President Lincoln in October of 1864.

The difficulty of supporting his large family caused Samuel to follow the miners to Nevada. He and Rosalie piled their belongings and their six children into a mule wagon and joined the procession of wagons and freight teams winding their way past Lake Tahoe and Carson City toward their new home in the silver-mining town, Virginia, as the city was often called. Samuel, profiting from his ten years of experience in supplying miners' needs, sank all his resources into a vast stock to be shipped once he had settled himself in a suitable spot.

Virginia, an overcrowded town of 30,000 people, sprawled over the side of Mount Davidson. Gold Hill and Silver City, originally separate villages, had been absorbed by the expanding town. On the outskirts grazed a herd of Bactrian camels, remnants of an experiment of 1861 to introduce the two-humped beasts from China to carry salt over the mountains. Although more useful than mules on desert ground, the animals were unsteady on precarious mountain trails where the rocks cut into their soft feet. Travelers were terrified when they first came upon the camels, and horses often broke into a stampede at the mere smell of them. Consequently, the poor creatures were penned up in the daytime and allowed to graze only after dark.

At the foot of Mount Davidson lay the Chinese section of Virginia, the result of another unpopular experiment in transplantation. The miners both envied and disliked the Chinese laborers who toiled sixteen hours a day, successfully reworking the discarded mine dumps. The pungent odor of burning opium hovered over the entire quarter.

Higher up, clinging to the steeper slopes, were the squalid shacks of the Piute and Washoe Indian tribes, now thoroughly subdued. Livery stables and feed stores lined the road along the outskirts of Virginia, but in the town itself brick and stone houses had replaced the wooden shacks of yesterday's pioneers. At night the streets were lighted by gas, and at crossroads every corner boasted a thriving saloon. In one year a million dollars' worth of liquor was consumed in Virginia City, and that year was said to have been rather a dry season; in bonanza periods three times as much "tangle leg," "sheepherder's delight," or "tarantula juice" went down the miners' throats. Men were said to fall asleep in the road crossing from one saloon to another.

The Michelsons settled in a new house at 24 South C Street, where Samuel kept his store on the first floor. Somewhat intimidated by the struggle for survival in this gilded jungle, Rosalie watched over her family closely, barring the shutters at night against burglars or stray bullets. The children's enjoyment of their life in the mountains was later expressed by Albert's sister Miriam, when she became a successful novelist.

> They all came, mothers or mothers-to-be of those boys born to the town trade, to the miner's lot; and of those girls who graced the firemen's engines in the Fourth of July procession, bare-armed, bare-necked with crimped tresses flying, glowing goddesses of red, white and blue liberty. . . .
>
> But if nothing ever came to Virginia City in that season, but spring itself, 'twould be enough . . . there would be air fit for the hierarchy of heaven to breathe, honey-strained through infinite planes of crystal clear sky. Air, and a rare, ineffable odor breathing over the sunned-through purity, exhilarating, intoxicating, of white sage perhaps, of Heaven knows what!
>
> No wonder we believed in the season's intangible, incredible, maddening promise. No wonder we lost hold

of prosaic possibilities and, betting on the radiant future, gambled with life itself."[6]

Below the road, the track of the Virginia and Truckee Railroad, the richest, most picturesque line in the history of the American West, was being laid from Carson City up the steep grade to Virginia. The ascent was over 1,600 feet in 13½ miles, spanning ravines and tunneling through the mountains. Day after day the Michelson children, along with most of the child and adult population of Virginia, watched the giant construction winding up the valley. When it was finally completed in 1870, the railroad became a symbol of the spirit of Western adventure.

While the silver mines roared with activity, the Michelson family flourished. Albert's brothers and sisters were swept into the drama of Western life. They reveled in the exciting gossip about fortunes won or lost, the uninhibited feelings displayed, and the joyous abandon of everyday life in this boom town. Some of this raucous spirit and much of the vitality were to be imbibed by Charlie Michelson, born in 1869 in Virginia City.

But Albert, who graduated from high school the year of Charlie's birth, had acquired a different set of values. He could see no prospect of continuing his studies, as he wanted to do. A paper he wrote on optics had drawn favorable comment from Bradley and he hoped to explore the subject further. A possibility opened when Samuel Michelson spotted in the *Territorial Enterprise* of April 10, 1869, a letter from the Honorable Thomas Fitch, Nevada Representative in Congress, stating that he proposed to appoint a candidate to the Naval Academy from the State of Nevada. The appointment, open to all Nevada boys from fourteen to eighteen years of age, would be subject to the results of an examination judged by a board of examiners. If he could win it, Samuel told his son, his family would be proud of him. Bradley also encouraged Albert, pointing out that he would have splendid instruction in the natural sciences, including physics and chemistry. Albert agreed to take the examination. He brought with him a letter of recommendation from his teacher:

> To whom it may concern:
>
> This certifies that the bearer, Albert Michelson, has been a member of the San Francisco Boys' High School during the last three years; that he has graduated with honor from the same; that in character as well as scholarship he is worthy of great commendation; and that he exhibits great aptitude for scientific pursuits.
>
> Very Resp'y,
>
> Theodore Bradley
> Principal
>
> San Francisco
> June 1869[7]

The examination took place on June 10. Albert was one of three who tied for first place. His rivals were James Wilson Blakely and William Gifford Cutler. The examining committee passed on this information to Congressman Fitch and left it to him to decide which of the boys would get the appointment. Fitch selected Blakely for three reasons: his parents could not afford to give him a good education, he was the son of a man who had lost his right arm (some said in the Civil War) and "with whom fortune has not always dealt kindly," and his appointment was strongly recommended by the Honorable D. R. Ashley, Fitch's predecessor in Congress.

"I hope the numerous friends of the other candidates will be satisfied with my settlement of this vexed question, and will receive this as a reply to the one hundred and thirteen letters and telegrams on this subject I have had the honor to receive during the last four days. I return my thanks to the committee

for what they did and forgive them for what they left undone,"
Fitch wrote to a local paper.[8]

After this announcement, Fitch no doubt received another inundation of mail protesting the injustice of his choice.
If he followed Blakely's record at the Naval Academy, he
would have been forced to recognize that his candidate
proved to be very poor material indeed. His first academic
tests show him listed well below passing, he was unable to
retrieve his standing in the following year, and on November
16, 1871, he was dropped from the Academy.[9]

Whether from the pricking of his conscience or, more
likely, because of the threats of a powerful section of his con-
stituency, Fitch did not abandon Albert. He was prevailed
upon to write to the recently elected President, Ulysses S.
Grant, stating the reasons he hoped young Michelson could be
given another chance.

> Hamilton, White Pine County, Nevada
> June 17th, 1869
>
> Sir
>
> I respectfully solicit your personal perusal of, and at-
> tention to, the communication I now have the honor to
> address you.
>
> Having been notified by the Secretary of the Navy of
> the [sic] a vacancy in the Naval Academy from this State,
> I determined to submit the appointment to competition,
> and did so by public advertisement—a copy of which I
> have annexed hereto. A number of boys competed for the
> prize, and after an examination of unusual length and
> severity, the committee reported three of the candidates
> as equal in scholastic attainments—I annex a copy of the
> committee report. I also annex a copy of the reasons I
> have given for selecting the lad who has received the
> nomination for Midshipman.
>
> The object of this communication is to solicit from

you the appointment of Midshipman for one of the three who received the Committee's endorsement—Master A A Michelson.

Had I felt at liberty to be governed by considerations of political expediency, I should have selected him. His father is a prominent and influential merchant of Virginia City, and a member of the Israelite persuasion, who by his example and influence has largely contributed to the success of our cause, and induced many of his co-religionists to do the same. These people are a powerful element in our politics, the boy who is uncommonly bright and studious is a pet among them, and I do most steadfastly believe that his appointment at *your* hands, would do more to fasten these people to the Republican cause, than anything else that could be done.

I am sure that young Michelson could pass even a severer examination than that made at the Naval Academy, and that he would be an ornament to the service, and a credit to his nominator, and if you can give him the place you will never regret it.

The Union people of Nevada are proud and grateful for the recognition they have received at your hands in the manner of appointments and will demonstrate to you hereafter, that the "strong box" of the nation will be the stronghold of your administration on this coast. I know you can greatly please them and strengthen us by making this appointment, and I take the liberty of expressing my deep solicitude that it may be made.

Very Respy. Yours

Thomas Fitch

To the President[10]

Michelson never saw this letter or knew of its existence, because it was mailed to the White House. At the same time,

he was dispatched to Washington with another letter of introduction, full of praise but minus the political implications.

He set off alone across the continent, riding one of the first
trains of the transcontinental railway. Only a month before his
departure, the Central Pacific had raced the Union Pacific to
a rendezvous midway, each trying to see which could build the
farthest and fastest, for a prize of vast government land grants
and bonds, allotted on a mileage basis. The attention of the
nation was focused on this meeting at which the last rail was
laid on a tie of California laurel, fastened with a "golden spike,"
while the two locomotives faced each other on a single track.

Albert saw the breadth of the country for the first time.
Crossing the Continental Divide, the train descended from the
Rocky Mountains, scattering great herds of buffalo as it crossed
the broad plains. Armed guards were posted on every car
because of the danger of an Indian attack or a holdup by
bandits.

When Albert announced himself at the White House,
President Grant, slumped in his chair, received him and listened with kindness and interest to his story. Drinking had
coarsened Grant's face and rounded his belly so that he no
longer looked like the pictures Albert had seen of him as a
general charging into battle. But his voice was gentle as he
broke the news to Albert that he could not help him, having
already filled the ten appointments-at-large that were allotted
the President.[11]

Albert concealed his disappointment with difficulty. He
thanked the President politely, bowed, and left his office with
one of Grant's naval aides. This officer, admiring the boy's
determination, advised him to go to Annapolis on the chance
that a vacancy might occur if one of the President's ten appointees failed to pass his examination.

On his arrival at Annapolis in late June, 1869, Michelson
went straight to the office of the Commandant of Midshipmen,
Captain Napoleon B. Harrison. He waited three days before he

finally was granted an interview, was examined, and then told there was no vacancy. Embittered and discouraged, his money almost gone, he returned to Washington and boarded a train for San Francisco. Just as the train was about to leave, a messenger from the White House came aboard, calling out his name. For the second time, Michelson was taken to see the President, who had been persuaded by Vice Admiral David D. Porter, Superintendent of the Academy, and one of Michelson's examiners, to make an exception in his case. Brushing regulations aside, Grant gave him the nomination for an eleventh appointment-at-large, which he received on June 28.[12]

Michelson, telling this story in later years, chuckled over beginning his naval career by what he thought was "Grant's illegal act." But having once exceeded his quota, Grant went on to appoint two more midshipmen-at-large, a total of thirteen, in 1869.[13]

CHAPTER 2

Appointment to Annapolis

UNDER Vice Admiral Porter's command, the Naval Academy had developed rapidly. It was no longer confined to the informal, haphazard cluster of small wooden houses that had been converted to its use in 1845, the year of its founding. Grounds had been enlarged and several new buildings added.

Porter's influence on the men at the Academy was even more effective than the physical changes he had wrought. He treated the midshipmen[1] as human beings, and recognized that they were young (some were barely fourteen) and needed the outlet of athletic sports. He set a precedent by boxing with the midshipmen himself. Baseball clubs were organized, and dancing was added to the curriculum, much to the distaste of the old-guard admirals, who spoke scathingly of "Admiral Porter's Dancing Academy."[2]

Only a few years earlier, Admiral John Adolphus Bernard Dahlgren and his Board of Visitors had come storming down to Annapolis in high dudgeon over Porter's increase in "high science" (higher mathematics). They had advocated the immediate abolition of instruction in astronomy, mechanics, and physics; moral science; naval, international, and constitutional law; history and composition.[3] Calculus was deemed "obnoxious." But Porter was able to defeat these conservatives because he maintained a higher degree of efficiency in seamanship, gunnery, and naval tactics than had ever been reached before. This was partly because his cadets were more lively and healthier than those in former classes. The visitors disapproved of his introduction of sports on the grounds that if the midshipmen were being trained on taxpayers' money they should not be out playing games. But Porter insisted that the midshipmen who were to represent the United States in all the seaports of the world were to be, in effect, ambassadors, gentlemen with impeccable manners, in perfect physical condition, with a wide cultural background of languages, history, science, and literature. Although Porter resigned in December 1869 his improvements were retained and Michelson's education had the advantage of his standards.

Shortly after the examinations were over on June 30, Michelson was issued two navy blue uniforms, one fatigue suit, two caps, one overcoat, six white shirts, socks, drawers, handkerchiefs, one black silk handkerchief or stock, one mattress, bedding, towels, and two pairs of boots, all of which he had to pay for out of his salary of $500 a year. He moved his new belongings into a room that he shared with one other boy in a new five-story building completed in 1869.[4] He was then ordered to make ready for the summer cruise.

Michelson set sail on the sloop *Dale* with fifty-two of his classmates.[5] Among them were young Blakely from Nevada and several fourteen-year-olds, who had a hard time doing anything right. Michelson felt at home on the water and soon ranked eighth in the class in seamanship. The *Dale* returned to Annapolis in time for the midshipmen to prepare for the fall term which began October 1.

Michelson's courses in the Fourth Class (as the first-year class at the Academy was designated) included mathematics, grammar, geography, history, French, drawing, and fencing. He stood seventh in the order of general merit in a class of ninety-two, second in mathematics, and first in drawing.[6] The drawing classes featured perspective and draftsmanship. On cruises each cadet was required to keep a notebook with sketches of the various parts of a ship and its rigging. Michelson was assigned to participate in a topographic survey for planning coastal defenses. Although his maps were beautifully accurate, he incurred the censure of his superiors because the borders were illustrated with pictures of local scenes that had caught his eye.

Following reveille at 6 A.M. the midshipmen's daily routine consisted of three two-hour periods. Classes were followed by drilling and an hour or so of recreation before dinner. Evenings they spent in reading and studying until the evening gun fire and tattoo at 9:30. Taps and lights-out followed at 10.

Michelson divided his spare time between Old Fort Severn, a circular building converted to a gymnasium, where he learned "the arts of defense" taught by two sword masters, a boxing master, and a gymnast, and the house of a former governor of Maryland, which contained a library of 17,000 books. Fire drills were frequent. The Academy operated one steam fire engine and one hand engine. As most of the houses were of wood, the danger of fire was considerable.

A conduct report was read out at the roll call before breakfast. Michelson took his turn with the others as officer in charge of discipline for twenty-four hours at a time. He seems to have fitted into the system well enough. In the first eight months he received 130 demerits, not an unusual number[7]—another presidential appointee received 1,086. During his four years as cadet-midshipman Michelson was reprimanded for, among other transgressions, skylarking and whistling in the corridor, laughing on guard, reading a novel on duty, playing a musical instrument on Sunday, introducing wine into the Academy, disorderly and very inattentive at fencing, receiving visits after taps, smoking in his room, and visiting the cake stand during study hour.

Very little of the $500 remained after Michelson had paid for his food and lodging, laundry, and clothing, including his dress uniform. However, there were comparatively few opportunities to spend money; the normal routine of training and study took up most of the time.

The summer cruise of the Third Class began on June 16, 1870, on the practice ship *Savannah,* under Commander Samuel P. Carter. Michelson and forty-nine of his classmen sailed to Plymouth, England, visited Funchal, Madeira, and returned to Annapolis Roads on September 15.

As a third classman at the Academy, "Mike," as his friends called him, ran into trouble with his instructor in physics and chemistry. The occasion was a physics recitation, for which he had not bothered to prepare, although most of the class had been up all night cramming. There was mild irritation that Michelson usually drew top grades without opening his "Ganot" (the physics textbook, *Elementary Treatise on Physics . . .,* by Adolphe Ganot, 1863), and some hoped that he would be called upon for one of the difficult problems and they would have the pleasure of seeing him "come a cropper."

They had their wish. Michelson was the first to be called up to the blackboard and was asked by the instructor (who may have been Lieutenant Commander Caspar F. Goodrich) to outline the steps in the resolution of a complicated optical problem from the textbook. The problem was not difficult for Michelson; as he later said, "Optics was my favorite subject."

After studying the problem for a moment, he began to resolve it in his own original manner, which in no way resembled the method in the textbook. His solution was nevertheless correct. Rather pleased with his work, he started back to his seat.

Suspicion had mounted in the instructor's mind as he watched the blackboard. Cheating was not to be tolerated; the reputation of the United States Naval Academy was at stake. If necessary, he would make an example of Michelson, expose him before the board of officers, keep him on the griddle until he confessed, and then disgrace him. Openly, before the class, he accused Michelson of cribbing, then, his voice rising to a roar, demanded that he hand over the "pony" or "trot" he was hiding.

Michelson was completely astounded by the accusation. "I don't have anything on me, sir," he finally said. He was searched and nothing was found. The instructor then asked another cadet to proceed to the blackboard and, without erasing Michelson's work, to describe the "proper" steps as taught by Ganot. This fellow had studied his lesson and Michelson watched with interest as the steps were set down. Only the answers agreed. After class there was a good deal of excitement among the cadets. Even those who envied Mike's obvious facility in the subject were one hundred percent behind him when it came to a showdown with the authorities.

The story of Michelson's tangle with the instructor spread rapidly throughout the Academy. Michelson was ordered to appear before a board of officers and professors selected to investigate the charge brought against him.

On the appointed day, Mike timidly attempted to explain how he had arrived at the answer to his problem without using the recommended method. The professors warned him that he would be severely punished if he had cheated in any way, but said that, if he had some reasonable explanation, he should give it.

Michelson asked to be assigned a similar problem. One of

the professors opened the textbook and picked one out. Michelson began covering a large section of the blackboard with his solution. The board of officers carefully followed his reasoning and calculations. Then they compared his conclusion with that in the book. Once more, with his own original method, he had arrived at the correct answer. The board, finding the exposition in order, rendered a verdict of not guilty and the Commandant dismissed the case.[8]

In the summer of 1871, on the sloop *Saratoga*, the Second Class visited the New England coastal towns, including Narragansett Pier and Newport, Rhode Island, two of the pleasantest and most hospitable ports for young naval officers. By the time the *Saratoga* returned to Annapolis on September 15, Michelson had had a total of eight months at sea and had begun to feel more at home on board than ashore. His marks in seamanship and the practical exercises in seamanship fell off somewhat, but he still maintained a high average, standing sixth in the order of merit.

The least popular of Michelson's teachers in 1871–1872 was Lieutenant Timothy Lyons, assistant instructor in ethics and English studies. Lyons, just back from two years of sea duty, was salty, toughened, and unusually hard on the cadet-midshipmen (so designated since 1870). The smallest irregularity in syntax was reprimanded, and the culprit had to recopy the assignment. The cadet-midshipmen often met in the evenings to enjoy a little music and to let off steam. On these occasions they sang a ditty directed at Lyons. Michelson accompanied them on his fiddle. The chorus ran as follows:

> Oh, Daniel in the lions' den
> was put there for correction,
> but that was not one-half as bad
> as a plebe in Lyons' section.[9]

By the time he reached the First Class, Mike had become well liked and popular. His skill at boxing and his talent with the fiddle drew the admiration of his fellow students. One of them, Bradley A. Fiske, later to become a rear admiral, provided some engaging anecdotes. Fiske was a year behind Michelson.

The events of my second-class year that stand out the most clearly in my memory are my fight with Michelson and the trip of the midshipmen to Washington to take part in the parade on Grant's second inauguration, March 4, 1873.

My fight with Michelson was caused by what I thought to be an affront to my official dignity. I was a "double diamond," or sergeant, as was Michelson; but one evening, due to the absence of the cadet petty officer of his company, which was the first company, it devolved upon Michelson to give the order right dress after we went left face into line. While we were gradually easing back or moving backward in order to form a straight line, Michelson sang out, Dress back, Mr. Fiske.

So I met him after dinner and challenged him to fight, a challenge that he accepted with promptness and apparently with pleasure. . . .

The details of the fight were very carefully arranged; in fact the arranging of the details took more time than did the fight itself. That I had not the slightest chance became evident in about one minute; but I hammered away the best I could until the referees saw that I couldn't see out of either eye and declared that the fight was finished. I was put on the sick list by the surgeon for "contusions," and I stayed on the sick list for eight days.[10]

The parade that Admiral Fiske remembered stood out clearly in Michelson's mind as well, and he loved to recall it in later years. The cadet-midshipmen were awakened at 4:30 on the morning of March 4, 1873, for Grant's second inauguration. They were crowded into a very cold train for Washington.

Upon arrival they began their march through the city to the point where the parade was to start. The wind was very sharp and bitter cold, and the men shivered as they marched, squinting to prevent snow from blowing in their eyes.

At the destination, they broke ranks to enter a house where they warmed themselves. Here they heard a rumor that the West Point cadets were to march without topcoats. Not to be outdone by the Army, every Navy cadet peeled off his overcoat before they lined up. The West Pointers, in the meantime, had arrived wearing their long blue capes. Seeing the midshipmen's hardy appearance, they hastily stripped off the capes and fell in line. As a result, President Grant was accompanied on his second inaugural down Pennsylvania Avenue by the shivering contingents of his service academies, blue with cold but too proud to admit it.

Out of a class which had numbered ninety-two in 1870, only twenty-nine completed the rigorous training to graduate as midshipmen on May 13, 1873.[11] By the time Michelson reached his final examinations it was easy to see where his real interests lay. He led the class in optics and held second place in heat and climatology (thermodynamics). But seamanship and its practical application had been sadly neglected, for in these two studies he was number twenty-five. In the over-all order of merit, however, he ranked ninth.

As an advanced student in physics, Michelson had received special training with laboratory instruction. However, in the eyes of the Superintendent of the Naval Academy, Rear Admiral John Lorimer Worden, who had commanded the *Monitor* in its victory over the *Merrimac* in 1862, Michelson's skill in the physical sciences in no way excused his shocking lack of interest in the all-important naval exercises of seamanship and gunnery. He gave Michelson a piece of his mind in a private talk: "If in the future you'd give less attention to those scientific things and more to your naval gunnery, there might come a time when you would know enough to be of some service to your country."[12]

Michelson never forgot this admonition. He was fiercely patriotic, and his pride was cut to the quick. But in later life, after he had achieved fame and national honors, he was able to laugh at Worden's advice.

His years as a cadet-midshipman had on the whole been happy ones. He had developed as a human being, able to make warm friends, to give or carry out orders as the occasion arose, to make quick decisions, to concentrate his attention on the important matters, ignoring trivia. His love of sports had kept him in fine physical condition and he never cringed from competition. He had acquired a fair command of French and Spanish and felt thoroughly at home with the arts of music and painting.

Michelson did not sail on the summer cruise in 1873. Instead, he chose to take a furlough and visit his family before going to sea for two years, as was customary after graduation. He found Virginia City a virtual metropolis in comparison to the small town he had left four years ago. The Virginia and Truckee Railroad brought him all the way up the valley right into town. New buildings had sprung up everywhere and the Michelsons had moved from C Street into a more elegant house on A Street.

Samuel and Rosalie overwhelmed their son by the effusion of their greeting. "Al is home! Al is home!" the younger children screamed as they danced about him. Charlie was now a mischievous four-year-old; the two oldest girls were already teaching school. There were seven of them in all.

During his furlough, Rosalie and Samuel begged Al to put on his dress uniform so that they could see him in all his naval glory and show him off to their friends. Reluctantly he agreed.

Several gangs of small boys flourished in Virginia City. The members of the Con-Virginia gang, named for a nearby mine, were passing down A Street when Albert stepped out of his father's house, resplendent in his uniform and wearing his sword. The gang resented this apparition of cleanliness and military bearing invading their territory. Teasing and good-natured curiosity turned into taunts and threats and a "battle" began. Handing his sword to Miriam, whose loyalties were strained between her brother and her hometown heroes, Albert fought off the gang with a long, heavy can of ice cream which he held by its stout wire handle. "He swung that can and laid about him," said Miriam, until both Albert and his tormentors were covered with great gobs of ice cream. Miriam refused to say who won, but there was no question that Albert's uniform was ruined.[13] Rosalie must have been furious.

When his leave was up, Albert was not altogether sorry to leave Virginia City. On his return to Annapolis he probably heard of the lecture tour of the British physicist John Tyndall and may have attended those delivered at Johns Hopkins University in nearby Baltimore. Tyndall is better remembered for his devotion to "pure" science than for his own researches in the fields of light and sound, although those were original and deserving. One of his statements was: "The scientific man must approach nature in his own way; for if you invade his freedom by your so-called practical considerations, it may be at the expense of those qualities on which his success as a discoverer depends."[14] Acting on his own principles, he put the full amount of his earnings from his American lecture series in 1872–1873 (several thousand pounds) in trust for the benefit of American science.

Michelson realized that his studies would be interrupted for at least two years by the training cruises required of all Annapolis graduates. On September 18, 1873, he was ordered on board USS *Monongahela,* the first of the five sailing ships on which he served during this period. The others were the *Minnesota, Roanoke, Colorado,* and *Worcester.* The cruises took him from Portsmouth, New Hampshire, to Rio de Janeiro, with calls en route at many ports in the Caribbean. Some of the ships on which Michelson trained had auxiliary steam, but such power was used only going in and out of port. Cruising was done under sail, and Michelson was made to understand that his reputation depended almost wholly on his ability to handle sailing ships.

This dependence on sail was surprising in view of the success of steam power during the Civil War, when every naval battle was fought under steam alone. This may have been because the battles were fought in inland waters, rivers and harbors, rather than on the open sea. Steam enginery, or "steam," as the department has always been called, had been established at the Academy by Admiral Porter in 1867, at the suggestion of Lieutenant Commander Eban Hoyt, Jr., chief engineer, who fitted up a steam launch with sails and engines as a miniature brig for the training of midshipmen. Hoyt took his craft out on a trial run using only her engines. Porter had been invited to go along, but, fortunately for him, he was ill and unable to go. The boiler of the ship exploded, killing Hoyt and mortally wounding the helmsman and two seamen. Thus, "steam" lost its ablest representative, and the accident itself set back for a time the Naval Academy's preparation for the age of steam power.

Some officers and men regretted the decision and feeling over the issue ran high. Similar controversies raged among strategists over the use of air power in the 1920s and more recently over the adoption of nuclear weapons and fuel. But Michelson did not allow himself to be drawn into this kind of controversy. His interests lay in testing the theories of pure science rather than in practical applications. Besides, he enjoyed the ship's movement under sail. His fine handwriting occurs frequently in the logs of these ships: "Weather clear and pleasant—bright moonlight, slack water at twelve." On another occasion he watched a total eclipse of the moon in the soft, tropical sky.

During the quiet evenings while he had the watch, he had

ample opportunity to reflect and to wonder about the motion of the ship as she glided noiselessly through the waters of the Caribbean. Standing on the deck, he could feel the breeze on his cheek, watch the stars rising or setting, and guess at the speed by timing the rate at which a dark headland disappeared from view. But he began to consider whether, when he was relieved and had returned to his quarters below decks, there was any way to determine the ship's motion.

Galileo had asked himself a similar question and answered it in a most imaginative way:

> Shut yourself and a friend below deck in the largest room of a great ship, and have there some flies, butterflies, and similar small flying animals; take along also a large vessel of water with little fish inside it; fit up also a tall vase that shall drip water into another narrow-necked receptacle below. Now, with the ship at rest, observe diligently how those little flying animals go in all directions; you will see the fish wandering indifferently to every part of the vessel and the falling drops will enter into the receptacle placed below. . . . When you have observed these things, set the ship moving with any speed you like (so long as the motion is uniform and not variable); you will perceive not the slightest change in any of the things named, nor will you be able to determine whether the ship moves or stands still by events pertaining to your person.[15]

He advises his friend also that if he should try jumping toward the stern of the ship, he will cover no more space than he could cover jumping forward even though the ship is moving quite rapidly. And should he throw something to his friend, it would need no more force to travel forward than aft.

> And if you should ask me the reason for all these effects, I shall tell you now: "Because the general motion of the ship is communicated to the air and everything else

contained in it, and is not contrary to their natural tendencies, but is indelibly conserved in them."[16]

Michelson found it disturbing not to be able to tell where
the ship was going, and it was always a satisfaction to emerge
from the cabin to see the night's progress written into the
ship's log.

His last cruise, aboard the *Worcester,* was along the
Colombian coast. The ship spent nearly two months in port but
the midshipmen were seldom allowed to go ashore. Michelson
and some others were suspended from duty for twenty-four
hours on one occasion when they failed to return to ship all
night, in violation of a squadron order.

Sailing down the Colombian coast the *Worcester* passed
the harbor of Porto Bello, where the Michelson family had
landed eighteen years earlier. Albert remembered how, as a
small boy clutching his little sister's hand, he had followed the
stream of frightened passengers down the gangplank. He and
his parents, once bewildered immigrants, had come a long way
in the new country.

When the cruise was over, the *Worcester* docked at Nor-
folk, Virginia, where orders were waiting for Michelson. He
was to proceed to Annapolis to be examined for promotion. On
July 16, 1874, he was commissioned Ensign, although for some
reason this commission was not signed until later.

Ensign Michelson never resented naval discipline, and as
a subordinate he took his punishments with good grace. He
was also capable of employing severe disciplinary measures,
when required, with men under his command. This was demonstrated during his first year as an instructor, when he lived
on the ground floor of a dormitory.

At midnight, on April 1, 1875, the entire Naval Academy
was awakened by the reverberating echo of a huge cannonball
rolling slowly down the inner stone steps of the midshipmen's

new quarters. Michelson sprang out of bed to investigate the disturbance.

The cannonball had come to rest after bouncing down the stairwell. He thought he detected a scuffle overhead as though some of the men were hiding to enjoy the effect of their joke. Doors and windows were opening around the quadrangle, and lights went on in the house of the superintendent, Rear Admiral C. R. P. Rodgers. Curiously, there was no sound or sign of disturbance in the sleeping quarters; every bunk was filled.

"Sir, is something out of order?" one of the men asked, rubbing his eyes as though waking from a sound sleep. "I thought I heard an explosion."

Michelson asked the man who was responsible for the offense to come forward and take his punishment. No one responded. He then ordered every man in the section to get dressed immediately and report to the recitation hall.

Although he was secretly amused with the audacity of the joke, he showed no trace of this. Maintaining order was not easy, and Michelson felt that his newly acquired authority was at stake. As the men appeared, he addressed them with severity.

"Gentlemen, you will all stand at attention until the culprit shows spirit enough to confess."

Heels snapped together as the men drew themselves up smartly in a double rank, eyes front and arms pressed closely to the seams of their trousers, but no one spoke. Minutes stretched into hours but Michelson refused to relent. He paced up and down in front of the men for four hours. The midshipmen remained motionless.

Toward morning, shoulders drooped and bodies swayed as the men fought off sleep and exhaustion. At 5:30 A.M., with no further comment, Ensign Michelson dismissed his men. He had made his point and they, to be sure, had also made theirs![17]

Michelson had begun to have serious doubts regarding his future in the Navy. Admiral Worden's words at the time of graduation still made him smart with indignation. Although Worden had been relieved in 1874, the service had not kept pace with the times. Promotions stagnated. After the Civil War, twelve lieutenants remained in that grade for twenty-one years. The Academy, like the Navy itself, was undergoing a difficult period. In Congress, warring factions disputed the value of naval power, while, within the Navy, the importance of science in training officers was much questioned. The basic problem was lack of funds.

In spite of these uncertainties, Michelson decided to continue with his naval career. It may have been the opportunity of working under Lieutenant Commander William T. Sampson that weighed in favor of remaining. The period of training was over and sea duty from now on was limited to the summers. On December 16, 1875, he became an instructor in physics and chemistry at the Naval Academy.

Sampson, later to command the squadron blockading Santiago, Cuba, during the Spanish-American War, and the man for whom Sampson Hall is named, had been head of the Department of Natural and Experimental Philosophy and was responsible for maintaining the high standard of instruction in the sciences that had first attracted Michelson to the Naval Academy. But he was absent from the Academy when Michelson took physics and chemistry, and they began to know each other only in the spring of 1875, when Sampson returned to the department. He was to play an important role in Michelson's professional career and also in his private life.

Michelson saw a good deal of Commander Sampson, who often invited his young colleague to come to his home for dinner in the evening. Gradually their acquaintance grew into a warm friendship that came to include Sampson's whole family. When Mrs. Sampson's niece, Margaret Heminway, came to Annapolis for a visit, Michelson was introduced to her as a matter of course. She was an imaginative girl and she seemed to have been immediately attracted to Michelson. In a letter recalling the meeting, she described him as the handsome young officer with the "brilliant eyes."[18]

Margaret had just returned from a finishing school in Paris. Her background provided her with an innate self-confidence. Her father, Albert Gallatin Heminway, had been trained for a legal career but had retired early after conspicuous success on Wall Street. To reflect his new eminence, he built The Towers, an impressive house in New Rochelle, New York. This was a massive edifice of gray granite, with crenelated towers imitating an English castle of Norman style. At the rear, a terrace opened on a formal garden surrounded on three sides by orchards.

By the end of the summer of 1876, Margaret and Albert were secretly engaged, and eventually he went to New Rochelle to ask Heminway's permission to marry his daughter. On this visit, Michelson must have become acutely aware of the wealth and elegance of the family into which he hoped to marry. The world of these fashionable New Yorkers, with their town and country houses, clubs, and frequent trips to Europe, was far removed from that of his immigrant parents, who had struggled to keep their drygoods business from failure in the raw towns of the new West. But the Naval Academy training had equipped him with some sophistication and polish, and there was a Navy tradition in the Heminway family. Although Heminway could scarcely have been enthusiastic about the match, he gave his consent; he must have seen that his daughter was deeply in love.

On April 10, 1877, when Margaret was eighteen and Albert twenty-four, their wedding took place. Michelson had favored a marriage by a Justice of the Peace, but for Margaret's sake he acceded to Mrs. Heminway's wishes for an Episcopalian service. The ceremony was performed at the Towers by Dr. Charles Canedy, rector of Trinity Church in New Rochelle, where the Heminways were parishioners.

The large bay window in the drawing room was banked

high with flowers. Margaret wore a long, fringed wedding dress of heavy white satin, and a veil crowned with orange blossoms. Michelson was resplendent in his full-dress uniform.[19] Commander and Mrs. Sampson, as well as a number of other officers and their wives, came up from Annapolis to toast the bride and groom at the reception. The dancing continued long after Albert and Margaret had left on their wedding trip.

CHAPTER 3

The Speed of Light

ETURNING from his honeymoon, Albert received orders to report as watch-officer on board the U.S. frigate *Constellation*, to sail June 26 for Buzzards Bay on the annual summer cruise with the cadet-midshipmen. Older than the Navy itself and a veteran of seven wars, the *Constellation* had been launched in Philadelphia in 1797. She was, in fact, America's oldest ship.[1] This added to her interest historically but left much to be desired in the way of comforts. Michelson slept in a hammock strung between overhead beams, in which it was impossible to stretch out. Whenever he turned over in his sleep, he found himself dumped on the deck. Below, there was only one small washroom with nine washbasins and no ventilation, something of a nightmare when many of the crew were seasick.

After a supper of dried apples at five o'clock the men were given nothing to eat until the next morning at eight. In fact, dried apples comprised the major part of their diet at sea. Their hopes for a change of food rose on one occasion when the *Constellation* put into port and the paymaster went ashore to buy provisions. The midshipmen were ordered to hoist the boxes of provisions aboard. They examined these with intense curiosity, trying to distinguish markings which would reveal the contents. All were marked "Dried Apples."[2]

Sunburned and toughened by his summer cruise, Michelson returned to Annapolis, where his young wife joined him. Margaret was pregnant. The coming winter of 1877-1878, which was to see the birth of his first son, was also a turning point in his career. For it was at this time that Michelson began his serious preoccupation with the mysterious phenomenon of light.

This turning point came about almost by accident. Commander Sampson called him in for a briefing on the physics course which he was to teach the advanced students. Lecture demonstrations were a new teaching method at this time and Sampson suggested that Michelson begin with a demonstration of the experiment on the velocity of light made with a rotating mirror by the French physicist Jean Bernard Léon Foucault. Michelson protested that he did not know enough, but he was told to brush up a little and take over the class.

In spite of his modesty, Michelson was already fairly well versed in this subject. In his final physics examination as a First Classman, for which he had received a top grade, the second question on light had read: "Describe Foucault's apparatus for determining the velocity of light. What results are obtained for media denser than air? Show from the physical explanation of single refraction that these results are agreeable to the undulatory theory."[3] Now he hurried to the library to "bone up" on the behavior of light, already fascinated by the phenomenon that was to be so important in his life.

The first to ask "What is light?" were the Greeks. The Pythagoreans, sometime about 530 B.C., developed the early principles of mathematical physics to explain the universe. They believed, as did Aristotle about two hundred years later, that an object was seen because it emitted particles of light that bombarded the eye of the observer. However, Aristotle's teacher, Plato, the geometer Euclid (c. 300 B.C.), and the astronomer Claudius Ptolemy (second century A.D.) all held that, on the contrary, rays of light emanate from the eye and extend to the object. The great Arabian scientist Alhazen, who, about A.D. 1000, was the first physicist to give a description of the human eye, supported Aristotle's view. But in all these speculations, light was assumed to be instantaneous. Not until 1638 did the idea that light might have a finite speed find expression. That was the year in which Galileo attempted to measure the speed of light.

Galileo made his experiment with nothing more reliable than two lanterns placed on hilltops less than a mile apart. First the shutter of one lantern was uncovered, and when the attendant of the second lantern saw its beam he uncovered his lantern. Galileo observed no time lag between flashes but he realized that the naked eye was incapable of catching it. He stated that "if not instantaneous, it is extraordinarily rapid."[4] Measurement would have to await far more sophisticated and accurate means of observation.

In the 1670s Ole Römer, a Danish astronomer, studying the cycle of Jupiter's nine moons at the Paris Observatory, measured the period of the "first satellite," Io, as it passed into Jupiter's shadow, eclipsed by the planet. Continuing his vigil, Römer made a table predicting the time of future eclipses. As time passed, Io lagged behind schedule to the point where it was 8 to 10 minutes late at the rendezvous. This lag occurred while the earth was in the part of its solar orbit farthest from Jupiter. Römer explained to the French Academy in 1676 that the discrepancy was not due to any irregularity in the little moon's habits, but rather to the time, which he calculated at 22 minutes, that light takes to cross the earth's orbit. (This

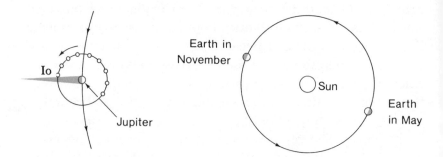

Römer's discovery
(Adapted from Henry Crew, *General Physics*, 3rd ed., rev., New York: Macmillan, 1916, p. 521)
Observations of the eclipse of Jupiter's satellite Io, at six-month intervals, gave the data needed to determine the speed of light across the diameter of the earth's orbit.

value is now calculated to be 16 minutes and 36 seconds.) This was the first experimental evidence that the passage of light is not instantaneous.[5]

Thus Römer was the first to calculate the speed of light; his figure was 138,000 miles per second. Fifty years later the British astronomer James Bradley verified Römer's theory. Bradley made the first determination of this velocity by observing the aberration of light from a star—that is, a small periodic change in the star's apparent position.

Bradley, like Galileo, learned something about physics from experience in a sailboat. He went out with friends on the Thames one September day in 1728 and noticed that each time the boat put about, the little pennant at the top of the mast seemed to change position, although the wind remained steady. In his mind, he compared the wind to the starlight, the sailboat to the earth in orbit, and the pennant to his telescope. In a flash of insight, he understood that the aberration of light from a star is caused by a shifting of the earth's position in relation to the direction from which the light comes to us from that star, as well as by the speed of light itself. The angle of his telescope depended on the ratio of the velocity of the earth to that of light.

Knowing the angle of aberration and the earth's velocity in orbit, Bradley estimated that light reaches the earth from the sun (half the earth's orbit) in 8 minutes 13 seconds,[6] a closer guess than Römer's value of 11 minutes.

All these attempts to measure the speed of light were based on astronomical observations. Because the speed is so rapid, it had been considered impossible to clock it over a short distance on the earth's surface. In the early nineteenth century the French scientist Dominique François Arago first suggested making a terrestrial measurement by relating the distance which a beam of light travels to the rotation of a mirror or the intervals of space on a toothed wheel. But Arago's eyesight failed before he could put his idea to the test.

Aside from Galileo's brave attempt, before Michelson turned his attention to the problem, only three men, all nineteenth-century French physicists, had tried to find the speed of light by using a terrestrial measurement. These were Armand Hippolyte Louis Fizeau in 1849, Fizeau's arch rival Foucault who made a similar experiment one year later, and Marie Alfred Cornu, in 1874.[7]

Foucault was already famous for his invention of the gyroscope and for his pendulum to prove the rotation of the earth. The three Frenchmen had each used a different means of reflecting and diverting the beam of light so that it could be measured. Fizeau chopped it off into small quantities with a rotating toothed wheel. Foucault, following Arago's lead, achieved his purpose with a rotating mirror. Cornu adapted Fizeau's method with some success. Of the three, Foucault, in 1862, found the most accurate value for the absolute velocity of light, 185,200 miles per second.[8]

His method was not altogether different from Galileo's, but it was more sophisticated. Instead of a second lantern and observer on the distant hill, Foucault placed a concave mirror to reflect the flashes of light directed at it from his "first observer" by means of a rotating mirror.

Foucault encountered trouble with this arrangement because a good deal of light was lost sweeping across the face of the concave mirror. The larger the distance between mirrors, the larger M had to be to reflect the same amount of light that it received. In his attempt to remedy this difficulty, Foucault tried using five giant concave mirrors, but even then the greatest distance over which he could flash the beam was only 20 meters (65.62 feet).[9]

To measure the speed of light only two ultimate measure-

Foucault's method of measuring the speed of light
(Diagram A is from Michelson, "Experimental Determination of the Velocity of Light made at the U.S. Naval Academy . . ." , 1878; diagram B is reproduced from Leon Foucault, *Recueil des Travaux Scientifiques*, Paris, Gauthier Villars, 1878; this work was not available to Michelson when he wrote his paper, but he illustrated this arrangement in *Studies in Optics*, 1927.)

A. Light travels from S, the source, to R, a revolving mirror, through L, a lens, where it is focused on the concave mirror M. By the time the light is returned to R, the revolving mirror will have rotated enough to deflect the returning light beam through a measurable angle.

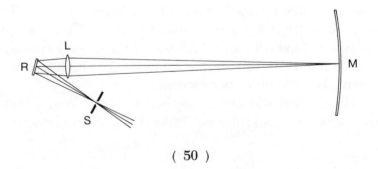

ments were required: the distance, and the time for light to travel that distance. The real difficulty lay in acquiring and applying the skill necessary to achieve significant precision of measurement.

In the course of demonstrating Foucault's method, its faults, already pointed out by Cornu, became obvious to Michelson. The returning beam was displaced only about 0.8 millimeters, a distance too small to measure accurately. "In November, 1877," Michelson said, "a modification suggested itself."[10] With this inspiration, he redesigned the experiment, replacing the concave mirror with a plane mirror, altering the lens position, and lengthening the path of light to 500 feet so

B. Light from the source *a*, passing through the glass *g*, falls on the lens *£*, is focused on the revolving mirror *m*, and is transmitted to *a'* and *b'* on the concave mirror *M*. It is also reflected to *a"* and *b"* and to *a'''* and *b'''* on the concave mirror *M'*. Returning along these paths, the beam is deflected at *m*, so that it arrives at *b* instead of at *a*, its source. This deflection, which reveals the speed of light, is observed in the telescope at α (alpha) and β (beta). In this arrangement Foucault has placed the lens *L* between the source *a* and the revolving mirror *m*.

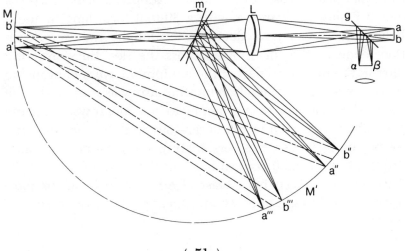

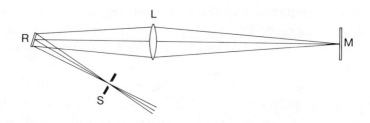

Michelson's modification of Foucault's method
(Adapted from "Experimental Determination . . . Made at the U.S. Naval
Academy . . .," 1878)
Here the lens L is placed in the light path between the rotating mirror
R and the plane mirror M, the distance LM being equal to the distance
LRS. This change made possible the use of a much greater distance
between mirrors without too great a loss of light intensity. As a result
Michelson achieved an accuracy 200 times that obtained by Foucault.

that the returning beam would be deflected at a wider angle.
A beautiful simplification had taken place.

Michelson was able to assemble most of his equipment
from pieces available at the Naval Academy: a plane mirror, a
lens 5 inches in diameter with a 39-foot focal length, and a
heliostat, a device for reflecting the sunlight in a fixed direction, even as the sun moves across the sky. But a rotating
mirror, the most vital part of the equipment, was not available
there. By this time Michelson's enthusiasm was so great that he
spent $10 of his own scarce money to buy one. It was "of plane
glass about one inch in diameter—silvered on one side, and
supported by two screws, terminating in needle points, which
fitted into two small conical holes in the edge of the disc."[11]
This mirror, driven by a blast of air from a hand- or foot-
operated bellows, rotated about its axis at about 130 turns per
second.

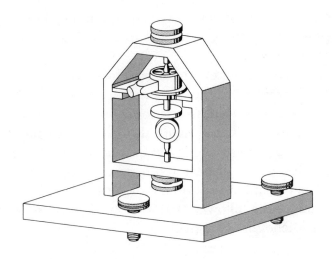

Michelson's rotating mirror of 1878
(Adapted from "Experimental Determination . . . Made at the U.S. Naval
Academy . . .", 1878)

By late spring in 1878 Michelson was ready to make a preliminary test.

Knowing the speed of the rotating mirror, the distance traveled by the light beam, and the amount of deflection of the returning beam, he could use simple mathematics to calculate the speed of light. Taking the mean value of the results of the ten final observations, Michelson arrived at the figure 186,508 miles per second in air. (It is usually given *"in vacuo"*; light moves a trifle faster in a vacuum.)

Formula, $V = \dfrac{4\pi r n D}{\delta}$

V = the velocity of light
r = the radius of measurement
n = the number of turns per second
D = twice the distance between mirrors
δ = the displacement

(53)

The displacement was twenty times that found by Foucault.[12] This accounted for the greater accuracy of Michelson's Annapolis measurement.

Unknown to Michelson, the astronomer Simon Newcomb, an eminent member of the National Academy of Sciences, president of the American Association for the Advancement of Science, and director of the Nautical Almanac Office in Washington (where he investigated physical phenomena for the aid of navigation), was also interested in measuring the speed of light. He had planned experiments long before Michelson's attempt and, as the following letter shows, had been kept up to date on Michelson's progress.

> Department of Physics and Chemistry
> U.S. Naval Academy
> March 25, 1878

Prof. Newcomb
Dear Sir,

Thinking you would be interested to know how Michelson's plan for measuring the velocity of light is coming on, I can tell you it promises entire success. The original plan has been considerably changed so that *any* distance can be used. The arrangement admits of such precise adjustment that I think that when we have arranged to count the revolutions of the mirror the results will be good. The large photo-heliostat silvered on its front face is used as the fixed mirror. The rotating mirror, also silvered on one face, is a little more than one inch in diameter. At a preliminary trial on Saturday with a distance of about 250 ft and about 125 revolutions we obtained a deviation of 1/25 inch. The fixed mirror is now placed at a mile distance and the mirror will be given a velocity of 200 turns. . . .[13]

Only part of this letter has been preserved and the signature is missing.

About this time, Michelson, learning of Newcomb's interest, wrote to him:

> U.S. Naval Academy
> Annapolis, Md.
> April 26th, 1878

Professor Newcomb:
Dear Sir,

Having read in the "Tribune" an extract of your paper on a method for finding the velocity of light, and hearing through Capt. Sampson and Capt. Howell that you were interested in my own experiments, I trust I am not taking too great a liberty in laying before you a brief account of what I have done. [Here Michelson describes his experiment, adding that the distance between mirrors might be considerably increased.]

Unfortunately, as I was about to make an accurate observation the mirror flew out of its bearings and broke.

It would give me great pleasure, dear sir, if you could honor me with an interview, in which you could advise me how to arrange some of the details so as to insure good results.

> Believe me, sir,
>
> Your Obedient Servant
>
> Albert Michelson
> Ensign U.S.N.[14]

Four days after receiving Michelson's news, Newcomb answered with a warm letter of approbation.

To have obtained so large a deviation from apparatus so extremely simple, seems to me a triumph, upon which you ought to be most heartily congratulated. So far as I know, it is the first actual experiment of this kind ever made on this side of the Atlantic.[15]

He responded to Michelson's request by hurrying down to Annapolis to see at first hand the remarkable results that Michelson had achieved despite the fate of the mirror.

Thus began Michelson's long association with the distinguished astronomer. The relationship between the older man and the rising star was apparently devoid of any petty jealousies, though Newcomb might well have resented the young scientist who had accomplished with primitive equipment at a cost of $10 what he was not able to do as well with the thousands of dollars later appropriated by Congress for his own experiments.

Upon examining Michelson's arrangement, Newcomb advised him to use a concave mirror as had Foucault and to place the rotating mirror in a vacuum to avoid the vortex produced by rotation. But he was very open-minded: "Still, I am not at all sure but that your plan is better than mine. Certainly it is simpler and cheaper," he wrote.[16]

Furthermore, Newcomb made a very favorable report to Rear Admiral Daniel Amman, Chief of the Bureau of Navigation. On June 5, 1878, he wrote:

> I have the honor to report that in obedience to your order of the 9th Ultimo [sic] I have made an examination of the apparatus for determining the velocity of light devised by Ensign A. A. Michelson at the Naval Academy, under the direction of Commander Sampson, and believe the experiments to be well worthy the encouragement of the Department and of Congress. . . .[17]

The possibility of Congressional support had already been suggested to Michelson. W. W. Johnson, professor of mathematics at St. John's College, Annapolis, told him that Alexander H. Stephens, former Vice President of the Confederacy and at present a member of the House of Representatives, might bring the matter before Congress. Michelson suggested that Newcomb call on Congressman Stephens to "inform him about the particulars," and give the needed push. But the gesture, if Newcomb made it, produced no result. Nor did the Senate Appropriations Committee look upon these ideas with favor; it failed to earmark any funds in the Naval Appropriation Bill for the purpose of measuring light.

Newcomb decided to make his next move through the National Academy of Sciences, communicating his own plan for measuring the velocity of light and at the same time mentioning that ". . . Recent trials of a still different and more simple apparatus have been made at the Naval Academy by Ensign Albert A. Michelson, U.S.N. . . . To prevent any misapprehension, I will say that his apparatus has been entirely of his own devising. . . ."[18]

In the end, since Newcomb had submitted his own proposal before Michelson came on the scene, the Appropriations Committee decided that Newcomb's plan be the one put into execution.[19] Newcomb received a $5,000 appropriation from Congress to carry out his experiments, while Michelson had to look elsewhere for money.

In May of 1878 Michelson published his first abstract of the experiment in a letter to the editors of *The American Journal of Science and Arts.*[20] Shortly after this letter appeared he was invited to present a paper to the American Association for the Advancement of Science. The paper was given at the meeting held in St. Louis, Missouri, in August 1878, at which Newcomb presided.[21] None of the awards of his later years would cause Michelson the same kind of elation as this first taste of success and the scientific recognition.

Earlier in 1878 another joyful event had occurred in the Michelson family. On January 16 Margaret gave birth to a son, who was christened Albert Heminway Michelson in honor of his maternal grandfather. The Heminways visited Annapolis that spring, and undoubtedly Albert Heminway was given a thorough indoctrination into the paths of light, reflected and refracted, in and out of heliostats, lenses, and mirrors. He responded with the promise of $2,000 for carrying out further measurements on a larger scale.

Counting on this windfall, Michelson went "shopping" to the best instrument makers he knew, Alvan Clark and Sons of Cambridge, Massachusetts. The bulk of the money was spent on a revolving mirror (1½-inch diameter) which had to be optically true, and an 8-inch lens with a focal length of 150 feet. The cast-iron frame for the mirror with three leveling screws was made by Fauth & Co. of Washington.

Michelson was promoted to the rank of Master in February of 1879. In the spring of that year the instruments were ready, and through the early summer Michelson spent all his time, outside of teaching duties, on preparations for the new experiment. He chose a couple of promising students to help him and selected a section of the old sea wall on the Severn River for running the tests. His instruments were housed in a little shed built on the pier of the ferryboat slip. From this point, where he placed the revolving mirror, he had an unimpeded line of vision for some 2,000 feet along the river bank to the stationary mirror, mounted in a brass frame surrounded by a heavy wooden case to shield it from the sun. The first step was to measure the distance between the mirrors as accurately as possible. This was done by means of a calibrated steel tape resting on the ground and stretched by a constant force of 10 pounds. Square lead weights were placed along the line at intervals of approximately 100 feet, and measurements were taken from the forward side of one to the forward side of the next. Michelson, with characteristic caution, made repeated measurements forward and backward, each corrected for temperature variation which caused the tape to contract or expand. The average or "true" distance between the mirrors was 1986.23 feet. The next task was the fine adjustment of the instruments themselves. The revolving mirror had to be perfectly balanced, an extremely delicate process. As the speed of rotation was increased, any irregularity in the little mirror's shape would produce a tortured vibration and rising scream of protest. By dint of grinding, repolishing, and continual testing, a wonderful symmetry was finally achieved and the mirror spun noiselessly on its axis.

To measure the speed of rotation (128 revolutions per second), Michelson used an electric tuning fork with a steel mirror mounted on one of its prongs. When the rotating mirror and the tuning fork were both at rest, the image of the revolving mirror could clearly be seen reflected in the tuning fork's mirror. When the fork commenced to vibrate at a given pitch, determined by Michelson's fine musical ear, the image appeared drawn out into a band of light. Then, as the mirror began to rotate, the band appeared as a number of images of the revolving mirror. As the mirror and the fork were synchronized to make the same number of revolutions as vibrations, these multiple images were again reduced to one sharp image.

Measurements were taken at intervals all through the day. Toward noon Michelson found that the sun's heat caused "boiling," a disturbance in the atmosphere when the light appears to shimmer, to such a degree that observations were impossible. At twilight or early in the morning he could usually get good results. Matching wits against the possible errors of his primitive equipment—(primitive, that is, in comparison with modern electronic machinery), he played with his instrument as one might with a beautiful toy, coaxing it into perfect performance in spite of itself.

His figure from this experiment was 299,940 kilometers, or 186,380 miles, per second.[22] Three years later he corrected two small errors which reduced the final result of this series at Annapolis to 299,910± 50 kilometers per second,[23] or 186,355 miles per second, with the last mile somewhat uncertain (as scientists write it, 186,355±31 miles per second.)

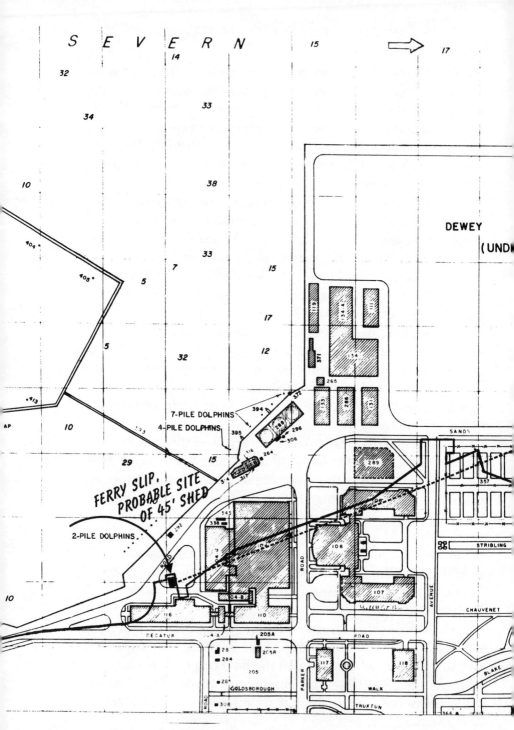

The line of sight along the Severn River at Annapolis, used in Michelson's 1878 experiment

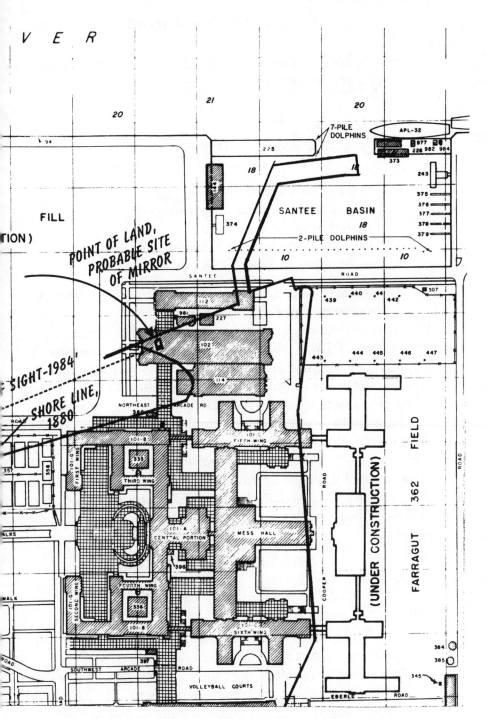

(Sketched by Professor Emeritus Earl W. Thomson of the U.S. Naval
Academy)

The formula that he used in his 1880 report to the Nautical Almanac is the following:

(1) $\tan \varphi = \frac{d_1}{r}$

(2) $V = \dfrac{2592000'' \times D \times n}{\varphi''}$

φ = angle of deflection
d_1 = corrected displacement (linear)
r = radius of measurement
D = twice the distance between the mirrors
n = number of revolutions per second[24]

One cannot help marveling at the astonishing freedom given Michelson, a regular officer in the Navy, to work out these problems, which could hardly be called relevant to the curriculum of 1879. This was largely due to the backing of Commander Sampson, Simon Newcomb, W. W. Johnson of St. John's College, and Captain John Adams Howell, head of the department of Astronomy and Navigation at the Academy.

News of their son's accomplishments reached Samuel and Rosalie from time to time, but on May 14, 1879, the readers of the Virginia City [*Evening*] *Chronicle* were given the full story, most of it picked up from *The New York Times*. Next to an account of the acquittal of the man who had shot Mrs. O'Leary's goat for devouring his flowers, the *Chronicle* featured:

THE VELOCITY OF LIGHT

A YOUNG COMSTOCKER'S CONTRIBUTION
TO THE WORLD OF SCIENCE

Ensign A. A. Michelson, a son of S. Michelson, the dry goods merchant of this city, has aroused the attention of the scientific minds of the country by his remarkable discoveries in measuring the velocity of light. *The New York Times* says:

"It would seem that the scientific world of America is destined to be adorned with a new and brilliant name. Ensign A. A. Michelson, a graduate of the Annapolis Naval Academy, and not yet 27 years of age, has distinguished himself by studies in the science of optics which promise the discovery of a method for measuring the velocity of light with almost as much accuracy as the velocity of an ordinary projectile. . . ."[25]

On reading this account of their son's achievement, the family was certainly bursting with pride, and Congressman Thomas Fitch must have been rather pleased to have the boy he had recommended at sixteen come through so well within ten years.

When the heat of summer bore down upon Annapolis, Albert sent his wife and baby north to New Rochelle. Margaret was expecting her second child. From time to time Michelson visited the Heminways, but for the most part he stayed in Annapolis toiling over his instruments, oblivious to the heat.

The second baby was born on August 11, 1879, and Margaret named him Truman after one of her uncles. Truman was less sturdy than his brother and more sensitive, and this continued to be true as they grew up.

The time was now drawing near when, in the logical course of his naval career, Michelson would again be sent to sea. He realized that this could put an end to his career in scientific research. The astonishing success of his very first venture fired him with a longing for further direct encounters with the secrets of physics. As desperately as he had longed to enter the Navy, he now longed to extricate himself from its rigid routine.

Margaret implored him to get out of the Navy, but there was as yet no alternative. In this agonizing dilemma, Simon Newcomb came forward with a brilliant, if temporary, solution. He arranged to "borrow" Master Michelson from the

Academy and in the fall of 1879 set him to work for the Nautical Almanac on further determinations on the speed of light.

Newcomb explained that preparations for his own method had progressed so far at this time that to change over to Michelson's plan would be impractical.[26] Michelson was therefore detailed to assist in carrying out Newcomb's experiments.

This was no doubt a disappointment but there were compensating factors. He had an opportunity to watch closely the methods of an outstanding mathematical astronomer at work. Newcomb had attended the Lawrence Scientific School at Harvard. A true "Renaissance man," he had a finger in every scientific pie of the 1880s. He organized an expedition to Africa to view an eclipse and appeared shortly thereafter in California with his own designs for the new Lick Observatory on Mount Hamilton. Renowned as an economist as well, he lectured frequently and wrote articles on a wide range of subjects.[27]

During the winter of 1879–1880, Michelson spent a good deal of time in New England checking out equipment that Newcomb had ordered from Alvan Clark and other instrument makers. He was often in touch with Professor Alfred Marshall Mayer at the Stevens Institute of Technology in Hoboken, New Jersey, who helped him determine the rate of the tuning fork, an essential part of the apparatus. Margaret was living with her family in New Rochelle, and Michelson made the Heminway house his headquarters so that he could be with her and the little boys. In the spring the four of them returned to Annapolis. There Michelson found time to make an experiment "On the modifications suffered by Light on passing through a very narrow slit," and this was the title of the paper he read before the National Academy of Sciences at the April Session of 1880. He concluded, first, that light on passing through a very narrow slit is partially or completely polarized in a plane at right angles to the length of the slit; and, second, that such a slit allows rays of short wavelength to pass more readily than those of greater wavelength.[28]

Still based in Annapolis, the Michelsons spent much of their time in Washington that spring, and there they enjoyed the company of Simon Newcomb. The eminent astronomer cut a dashing figure, driving his own high-spirited horses in a somewhat reckless fashion. Narrowly grazing the carriages of others at one moment, he was apt to drive right up onto the sidewalk the next.[29] Meanwhile, he chatted nonchalantly with his frightened passenger, who might be one of President Rutherford Hayes's cabinet members, or a visiting dignitary with a beautiful wife or daughter.

Through Newcomb, Albert and Margaret met a wide variety of people. Michelson's life, which had been confined by the boundaries of the Naval Academy, began to expand. He relished the exchange of thought, the banter, and the chance to sharpen his wits among men of the world. Margaret charmed everyone she met. But Michelson recognized that this pleasant existence was only temporary. He needed to establish himself permanently somewhere.

From New York, in between errands for Newcomb, he wrote at the end of a report: "Have you heard anything further in reference to the Professorship; and have you any idea how much longer we will be in suspense?"[30]

Wolcott Gibbs, a Harvard professor of Applied Science, wrote to Julius Hilgard (later a superintendent of the United States Coast and Geodetic Survey) on July 19, 1880, probably at Newcomb's suggestion:

Dear Hilgard:

Can't you do something to help Michelson to get one of the two vacant professorships of mathematics in the Navy? His letters of recommendation were sent in long ago and were very strong as he is a most brilliant fellow. If he does not get this place he will have to go to sea for some years and will be lost to science. All that is necessary I believe is to get the President to say a word to the Secy of the Navy who does not seem to be able to make up his mind. I consider it a matter of real importance to the country to keep such a man and give him a chance to work. . . .[31]

The President does not appear to have said the magic word, and even before Gibbs's letter was written Michelson had said in a letter to Mayer at Stevens Institute that he had abandoned the idea of a professorship of mathematics in the Navy because of the law requiring an examination which he doubted he could pass, "as I make no pretense of being either an astronomer or a mathematician."[32] On June 28 he began working steadily in Washington on the tests for Newcomb's experiments.

Newcomb used two different locations in taking measurements. In the first experiment, the one on which Michelson worked during the summer of 1880, the observer was stationed at Fort Myer, southwest of Arlington Cemetery, with the fixed mirror placed on the grounds of the Naval Observatory, then located on the Potomac Rver. In the second experiment, the fixed mirror was placed at the base of the Washington Monument.

On September 13 Michelson left Newcomb's employ. Either he had grown restless working on a project he had not originated, or perhaps he craved a change of scene because other more exciting ideas were brewing in his head.

CHAPTER 4

~~~~~~~~~~~~·•◦∞◦•·~~~~~~~~~~~~

The Luminiferous Aether

MICHELSON'S success in measuring the speed of light led him to explore further the theory of the "aether" (as it used to be spelled), a hypothetical substance through which light waves were said to travel. From Ganot's *Elementary Treatise on Physics* he had learned of the subtle, impalpable, and imponderable fluids occupying all space, even that occupied by solid matter.[1]

The term "aether" was first used by Plato, and Aristotle had said that light was an energy of a diaphanous medium filling all space. The nature of the medium had baffled the best scientific minds of the seventeenth, eighteenth, and nineteenth centuries. The inconsistencies were manifold. A "tenuous jelly" or an "elastic fluid," it could penetrate steel or

permeate a vacuum. Yet the planets rolled through it undeterred, without friction or loss of speed. Devotees of the
theory, and Michelson became one of the staunchest, argued
its virtues against all denials, with such conviction that belief
in it has endured in one form or another even to this day. It
is now called "space."

The seventeenth-century French philosopher René Descartes imagined light to be a "pressure transmitted by an infinitely elastic medium which pervades space."[2] "Light," he
said, "in luminous bodies is only a certain movement, or a very
lively motion which passes toward our eyes . . . in the same way
that the movement of resistance of bodies which a blind man
meets passes to his hand by the medium of his stick."[3]

The classical theory of the nature of light, generally supported by Sir Isaac Newton and widely accepted, was the emis-
sion theory, according to which light consisted of material
particles that were thrown off from luminous bodies at tremendous velocities and moved in straight lines through space. In
1665 the English experimental philosopher Robert Hooke
challenged this concept with his presentation of the first wave
theory of light. The Dutch physicist and astronomer Christian
Huyghens in 1678 developed the idea since known as Huyghens' Principle, which states that a wave is propagated
around a vibrating center and borne along by an all-pervading
medium, the aether.[4] The proponents of both theories maintained a belief in the existence of some kind of aether, though
their definitions of its nature varied. None of the scientists of
those days could conceive of action at a distance—such as that
of gravity, for instance—without some sort of contact between
the bodies. It was inconceivable, Newton thought, that brute
matter should, without the mediation of something, even
though it were not material, operate on and affect other matter.

As time went on, the disciples of Newton and Huyghens,
less open-minded than their idols as is often the case with the
followers of great men, divided into factions, passionately sup-

porting one theory or the other. In 1799, Thomas Young, a doctor of medicine in London, developed the wave theory against strong opposition from the conservative Newtonians. Young first described his theory of light waves in a letter to the Royal Society, drawing an analogy between the movement of light and that of sound.[5] Convinced he was right, he openly challenged Newton's objections to the wave theory. In 1801 he gave the Bakerian Lecture before the Royal Society "On the Theory of Light and Colours," in which he explained the phenomena now called interference.

No one has ever actually seen the crest or the trough of a light wave because it is far too small to be visible even with the most powerful microscope. Light waves vary in length according to their source, and some are so small that a hundred million of them would fit into a meter. But, when sunlight is allowed to pass through a pinhole (or slit) onto a screen it makes a pattern of rings strongly suggesting the circular waves caused by dropping a stone into smooth water.

When two pebbles are dropped into a pond, circular waves from each of them invade the waves of the other, causing a pattern of "interference" (see diagram on page 70). (This is a misnomer, Michelson later said, because in no sense do the waves actually interfere with each other but rather pass unaffected on their separate ways.)

In a similar fashion, Young proved, sunlight passing through a pinhole or slit is diffracted—that is, it emerges in a pattern of spherical waves. If it is then passed through two pinholes, these waves interfere as they cross each other. Whenever the trough of one wave hits the crest of another, they cancel out, and a dark band appears. On the other hand, when two crests arrive "in phase," the light is doubled and shows up as a white band. (See diagram on page 71.) These are the bands or fringes of interference that Michelson was later to observe and measure by means of the "interferometer" that he devised for the purpose.

In 1870 the ether was defined as an elastic solid, not rare

THE MASTER OF LIGHT

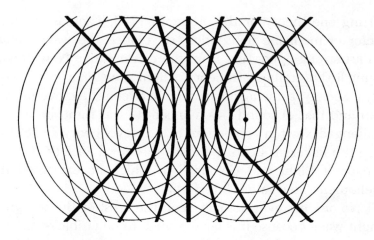

Pattern of interference
(From Michelson, *Light Waves and Their Uses*, 1903, p. 12)

but extremely dense. This medium, however necessary it might be theoretically to carry light waves, proved difficult if not impossible to visualize. There is nothing known on earth that behaves in the manner required to fulfill its functions. The basic assumption was that this ether was stationary or that, if it were dragged along by the moving earth it would be at a calculable rate, known as the "Fresnel dragging coefficient," after the French physicist Augustin Jean Fresnel, who measured it in 1818.[6]

As the idea of light-carrying ether, pervading the intervals between all atoms of matter and the vast distances of interstellar space, gained credence, physicists began to look for a way in which they might detect it. One possibility was to try to measure the speed of the earth as it moved through the stationary ether.

In the search to find this figure, the speed of light could become a measuring rod. It would be affected by the motion of the ether and thus might be used to detect the ether drift. Many physicists carried out experiments to see if this were

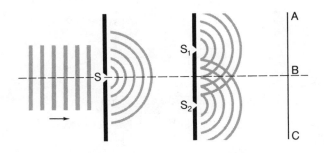

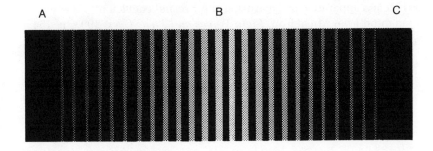

Young's double-slit experiment
(Adapted from F. A. Jenkins and H. E. White, *Fundamentals of Optics*,
New York, McGraw-Hill, 1957, p. 234)
S—single slit or pinhole
S_1, S_2—two slits
A-C—screen where interference fringes appeared
B—central white fringe where crests of light arrive in phase

possible. Arago proposed the use of light from a star to see if light moved at the same speed through ether whirling with the earth as through ether whirling against it,[7] but testing with the light of a star proved to be impractical.

Fresnel contended that the speed of light would be slightly affected by the motion not only of the ether but of any medium through which it was traveling. His theory was re-

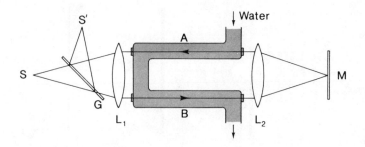

Fizeau's apparatus for measuring the Fresnel coefficient
adapted from Michelson, *Light Waves and Their Uses*, 1903, p. 154.
Light from S is split into two beams which pass through the tubes A
and B. These contain water flowing rapidly in opposite directions.
On reflection from the mirror M the beams interchange, so that
when they return to lens L_1, one has traversed both tubes in the
same direction as the flowing water while the other has traversed the
tubes in the opposite direction. The lens L_1 then brings the beams
together to form interference at the eyepiece S.

ceived with skepticism until, in 1859, Fizeau devised a method
for testing the effect by passing light through two tubes of
moving water.[8]

Michelson later called Fizeau's arrangement "one of the
most ingenious experiments that has ever been attempted in
the whole domain of physics."[9] The result showed that light
waves were accelerated by a fraction of the velocity of the
moving water, clearly less than the full amount.

Another attempt to find the effect of motion of a medium
on the velocity of light was made in 1871 by George Airy, the
British Astronomer Royal. Testing for the aberration of light in
a telescope filled with water, Airy expected that the angle of
aberration of light traversing the water, which was moving
with the speed of the earth in orbit, would increase by one-
third. Yet no such increase was observed.[10]

Fresnel proposed an explanation for this difficulty: that

the light-carrying ether might be carried along by the water in the telescope, not by the full amount of its speed, but by the dragging coefficient. Fizeau's test with the moving water seemed to bear out this opinion.

In 1873, the year Michelson graduated from the Naval Academy, James Clerk Maxwell, first professor of Experimental Physics at Cambridge University, published his monumental treatise on electromagnetic theory. On the assumption that light and electricity travel with the same speed and are both vibrant disturbances in the ether, Maxwell created the field equations to describe the electromagnetic behavior of space. ". . . The undulatory theory of light," he said, "has met with much opposition, directed not against its failure to explain the phenomenon, but against its assumption of the existence of a medium in which light is propagated."[11] He set forth his picturesque vision of the great ocean of ether, some of it possibly even inside the planets in motion, carried along with them, or perhaps passing through them as the "water of the sea passes through the meshes of a net when it is towed along by a boat . . ."[12]

Before Maxwell's discovery, the speed of light was just a measurement. But when he worked out his electromagnetic equations it became apparent that this value represented an important relationship between electricity and magnetism. Therefore an accurate value for this speed might lead to other constants, might even help to reveal the nature of the universe.

On March 19, 1879, shortly before his untimely death at the age of forty-eight, Maxwell wrote to David Peck Todd, Director of the Nautical Almanac Office, with a question about the possibility of a celestial measurement of the ether drift. In this letter, Maxwell stated that it would be impossible to measure "a quantity depending on the square of the ratio of the earth's velocity to that of light."[13] He had observed that the velocity of light in ether, accelerated by the earth's motion in orbit, would differ by an extremely small amount from its speed in an ether at rest. Being of the order of the square of this ratio, or one part in one hundred million, he feared it would be too small to measure.

Michelson thought otherwise. Experiments to detect ether drift up to this time were all "first-order effects,"—that is, measurements of the ratio of the speed of the earth to that of light. As each of them failed, it became an accepted fact that no first-order effect could succeed. But since Michelson's refined figure for the speed of light gave him a distinct advantage over his predecessors he thought he might contemplate a second-order effect: the square of the speed of light, c^2, in relation to the square of the earth's speed, v^2.[14]

Intrigued by the problem, he began to think about how to devise an instrument that could count and measure light waves with an accuracy no one had yet attained. With such an instrument he hoped to measure not only the speed of the earth through the ether, but also the speed of the whole solar system on its way, supposedly toward the constellation Hercules. It was more reasonable to expect the ether to be at rest in relation to the fixed stars than in relation to the solar system. But before he could begin, he felt a need for additional study in order to answer the question Maxwell had raised.

At that time there was no college or university in the United States where students of science could do graduate work. Johns Hopkins was beginning to offer such courses, but most of the scientists of the period received their training abroad. Michelson decided to take some basic courses at the University of Berlin and to study theoretical physics there with Hermann von Helmholtz, the leading physicist of Germany. Among Helmholtz's American students who later distinguished themselves in their various fields were Asa Gray, the botanist; Ira Remsen, the chemist; G. Stanley Hall, the psychologist; and Michael Pupin, the inventor, to name only a few.

Having requested and been given a year's leave of absence from the Navy, Michelson, with his family, sailed for

Germany in the fall of 1880. With their two little boys, Albert and Truman, aged three and one, the Michelsons found living quarters with Frau Doktor Landmann at 54 Königgrätzer Strasse, and Michelson enrolled at the University of Berlin.

The city, at that time, was lighted by gas and used horses for transportation, but the Institute was a splendid new building, the best-equipped and the most modern in the world.

Shortly after beginning work at the university, Michelson wrote to Newcomb:

Berlin, Nov. 22nd, 1880

Dear Sir,

Your very welcome letter has just been received. It will give me much pleasure to let you know how I am progressing.

At present the work in the laboratory is very elementary, and I am trying to get over that part somewhat hurriedly.

Besides this work I attend the lectures on Theoretical Physics by Dr. Helmholtz, and am studying mathematics and mechanics at home.

I had quite a long conversation with Dr. Helmholtz concerning my proposed method for finding the motion of the earth relative to the ether, and he said he could see no objection to it, except the difficulty of keeping a constant temperature. He said, however, that I had better wait till my return to the U.S. before attempting them, as he doubted if they had the facilities for carrying out such experiments, on account of the necessity of keeping a room at a constant temperature.

With all due respect, however, I think differently, for if the apparatus is surrounded with melting ice, the temperature will be as nearly constant as possible.

There is another and unexpected difficulty, which I

fear will necessitate the postponement of the experiments indefinitely [namely] that the necessary funds do not seem to be forthcoming. . . .[15]

Newcomb promptly brought Michelson's need to the attention of Alexander Graham Bell. Before patenting his telephone, Bell had also been pressed to find financial backing. He took an immediate interest in Michelson's idea and arranged to make him eligible for a grant from the Volta Foundation, which Bell had recently established for such a purpose with French prize money he had won. Dr. C. A. Bell, a relative of the inventor, was in charge of the Volta grants. Michelson wrote to him in December 1880:

Dear Sir,

Your welcome letter has just been received.

I took the liberty of questioning the prudence of the offer which Prof. Bell was kind enough to make, for as I then said, I was young and therefore liable to err, and my entire reputation as a "scientist" was based upon a single research, which fortunately was successful.

Since, however, he was pleased to differ with me, I gratefully acknowledge the generous gift.

I have not however undertaken this work without consulting several prominent scientific men. The answer they all give is that if successful the success would be grand; but that it is at present impossible to say whether the experiments are practicable or not. All, however, advise me to try. So that, with this assurance and that of Prof. Bell, that in either case he will consider the money well spent, I shall begin the work with greater confidence.

Very truly yours,

Albert A. Michelson
Master, U. S. Navy[16]

When the funds arrived, Michelson, working in the basement of the University of Berlin, began designing his instrument. From Schmidt and Haensch, an excellent German firm of instrument makers, he ordered the optical flats (slabs of glass ground to precisely equal dimensions) that he needed. He referred to the instrument as his interferential refractometer. Not until the 1890s was this formidable name changed to interferometer.

The idea of the experiment Michelson planned was to project a beam of light in the direction in which the earth is traveling in its orbit, and one at right angles to this. The first beam, he thought, would naturally be retarded by the flow of ether passing the earth. The second beam, crossing this current at right angles, although the distance is the same, should arrive ahead of the first by a length of time determined by the velocity of the earth.

As he later explained to his children: "Two beams of light race against each other, like two swimmers, one struggling upstream and back, while the other, covering the same distance, just crosses the river and returns. The second swimmer will always win, *if there is any current in the river.*" It was crucial to the success of the plan to split a single light beam, send the two parts off at right angles, and, by means of mirrors, rejoin them to observe the fringes of interference and thus determine the "winner" and measure by what length of time "he" had won.

Michelson was familiar with an instrument credited to Jules Celestin Jamin, director of the Physical Laboratory in Paris. It was an assemblage of mirrors and lenses designed to measure the refractive indices of gases by the interference of light waves. Michelson rearranged these pieces into the shape of a cross, placing the "beam splitter," a half-silvered mirror, in the center. The half-silvered mirror allows some light to penetrate it, while the rest is reflected to the plane mirrors which, in turn, bring the two separate pencils of light together again at the eyepiece where they may be examined to see if the waves are "in phase."

Michelson's interferometer was so sensitive that the slightest sudden motion would cause an immediate shift of the fringes, throwing the calculations out. Traffic vibrations made it impossible to work during the day, even though the instrument had been mounted on a heavy foundation with the hope of eliminating these disturbances. Professor Helmholtz was acquainted with H. C. Vogel, the director of the Astrophysikalische Observatorium at Potsdam, and through this friendship Michelson was permitted to move the whole operation to this secluded spot some thirty miles from Berlin. The Observatory was beautifully situated on a hill overlooking the town of Potsdam. Only the main building, begun in 1878, was ready for use when Michelson began his experiment. He arranged his delicate instrument on the stone base of the circular room beneath the central tower.

As Michelson described his equipment:

The source of light [is] a small lantern provided with a lens . . . the two mirrors were made approximately equal by a pair of compasses. The lamp being lit, a small hole in a screen placed before it served as a point of light. . . .

It frequently occurred that from some slight cause (among others the springing of the tin lantern by heating) the fringes would suddenly change their position, in which case the series of observations was rejected and a new series begun.[17]

In Potsdam he was able to observe the fringes, undisturbed. He was astonished himself at the beauty of the interferometer's performance.

Here, the fringes under ordinary circumstances were sufficiently quiet to measure, but so extraordinarily sensitive was the instrument that the stamping on the pavement about 100 meters from the observatory, made the fringes disappear entirely![18]

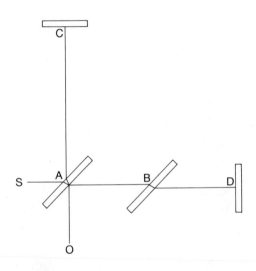

Plan of the ether-drift experiment of 1880 at Potsdam
(Adapted from Michelson, *Light Waves and Their Uses*, 1903, p. 40)
The source of light, *S*, was a lantern. The lightly silvered mirror *A* (the "beam splitter") reflects some of the light to the mirror *C*, while the remainder passes through it to the mirror *D*. These two beams are reunited at *A* and transmitted to *O*, where the fringes may be examined in the eyepiece to see if the waves are "in phase." The two paths are equal. If the leg *AC* is parallel to the earth's motion in orbit, the beam traveling with it might be affected to a greater degree than the beam moving at right angles to it. If the instrument is turned 90 degrees, the path *AC* would be the one experiencing the greater change. Michelson hoped to find a total shift of the interference fringes of 8/100, the distance between adjacent fringes—an amount he knew he could measure. Because the ray of light *SACA* is refracted by the double passage through the beam splitter, a compensating plate of glass *(B)* was inserted between *A* and *D* to equalize the journey. The beam splitter *A* is silvered on its lower edge, while the mirrors *C* and *D* reflect the light from their faces.

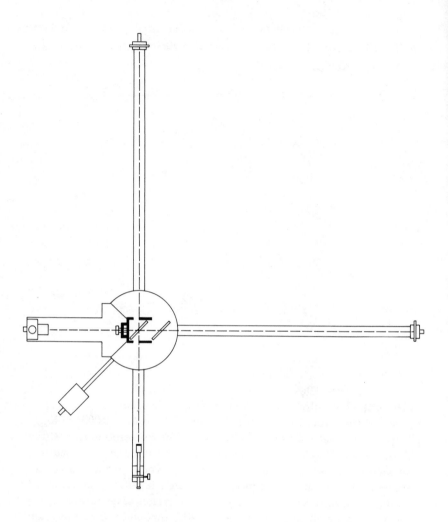

Michelson's first interferometer, 1880
(*Above*) A bird's-eye view; (*opposite*) in perspective
(Adapted from Michelson, "The Relative Motion of the Earth and the Luminiferous Ether," 1881)
As in the diagram on page 79, the source of light is at the left.

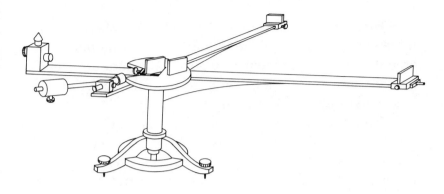

Today, when such devices have long been mechanized, it is difficult to realize the incredible accuracy of which this delicate, hand-operated instrument was capable. According to the English astronomer Arthur Stanley Eddington, it could detect "a lag of one-ten-thousand-billionth of a second in the arrival of a light wave."[19]

Margaret Michelson had to spend more time alone as the fever of work devoured her husband. She was expecting another baby, and this time Michelson hoped for a daughter. He asked Margaret to let him name the baby if it proved to be a girl, inasmuch as she had named both the boys. At Christmastime, he took his wife to see a new production of Richard Wagner's opera *Lohengrin*, which had caused a furor of enthusiasm at Bayreuth. Margaret enjoyed the evening, the first she had spent with her husband in months, and Michelson was carried away by the sensuous music, which haunted him for days.

When the birth took place, Margaret stoically refused anesthesia and bore the pains in silence. Afterward, she called her husband to show him the baby. Michelson had his wish. It was a beautiful little girl, and he named her Elsa, after Lohengrin's bride.

Throughout the winter of 1880–1881 Michelson continued his careful preparations, taking very little time for rest or recreation. To prevent changes of temperature from expanding or contracting the brass arms of the interferometer, he covered them with long paper boxes. He had every reason to believe that he would be able to detect a difference in the speed of light along these two arms—minute but enough to establish it as a fact. Yet after six months of careful work, when he looked at his results, the fact loomed indisputably: there was no evidence of any shift in the fringes. He summed up the result:

> The interpretation of these results is that there is no displacement of the interference bands. The result of the hypothesis of a stationary ether is thus shown to be incorrect, and the necessary conclusion follows that the hypothesis is erroneous.
>
> This conclusion directly contradicts the explanation of the phenomenon of aberration which has been hitherto generally accepted, and which presupposes that the earth moves through the ether, the latter remaining at rest.[20]

In considering possible reasons for his negative result Michelson now turned to the theory set forth by Sir George Stokes, a Fellow of Pembroke College, Cambridge, and the oldest of the famous trio of Stokes, Kelvin (William Thomson, Lord Kelvin), and Maxwell. Stokes's views on the ether were in direct opposition to those of Fresnel. He believed that the ether in the interior of matter moved along with that matter; that the earth carried the ether along inside itself, even that ether which immediately surrounds it, to a lesser and more gradual degree, decreasing as the action of rotation becomes remote. At the end of his paper on the result of his Potsdam experiment, Michelson wrote:

It may not be out of place to add an extract from an article published in the *Philosophical Magazine* by Stokes in 1846.

"All these results would follow immediately from the theory of aberration which I proposed in the July number of this magazine; nor have I been able to obtain any result admitting of being compared with experiment, which would be different according to which theory we adopted. This affords a curious instance of two totally different theories running parallel to each other in the explanation of phenomena. I do not suppose that many would be disposed to maintain Fresnel's theory, when it is shown that it may be dispensed with, inasmuch as we would not be disposed to believe, without good evidence, that the ether moved quite freely through the solid mass of the earth. Still it would have been satisfactory, if it had been possible to have put the two theories to the test of some decisive experiment."[21]

If, as Stokes proposed, the ether were carried along with the earth, all optical phenomena on the earth would then occur exactly as if the earth were at rest. This theory appealed to Michelson because it explained his negative result without doing away with the ether.

Michelson reported the outcome to Alexander Graham Bell. He seemed to derive some satisfaction from the belief that, although he did not find what he was looking for, at least he had proved Fresnel and others wrong about the ether being at rest.

> Heidelberg, Baden, Germany
> April 17th, 1881

My dear Mr. Bell,

The experiments concerning the relative motion of the earth with respect to the ether have just been brought to a successful termination. The result was however *negative*. . . .

At this season of the year the supposed motion of the solar system coincides approximately with the motion of the earth around the sun, so that the effect to be oserve [observed] was at its maximum, and accordingly if the ether were at rest, the motion of the earth through it should produce a displacement of the interference fringes, of *at least* one tenth the distance between the fringes; a quantity easily measurable. The actual displacement was about one one hundredth, and this, assignable to the errors of experiment.

Thus the question is solved in the negative, showing that the ether in the vicinity of the earth is moving with the earth; a result in direct variance with the generally received theory of aberration. . . .

N.B. Thanks for your pamphlet on the photophone.[22]

If the ether were in motion with the earth, it would be quite impossible to perceive any motion. The interferometer was not at fault in being unable to perceive it. Galileo had experienced a similar failure when trying to measure the speed of light. He knew it was finite, but he could not prove this with his lanterns. The interferometer had performed with marvelous accuracy, and its beauty consoled Michelson to some extent for the negative result. He began to think of new fields where this technique might apply. Like Pygmalion, he became enraptured with his own creation. Theoretical physicists as a rule do not experience this emotion and are therefore inclined to belittle it. But Galileo knew the feeling and voiced his exultation over the marvels of his telescope with a similar joy:

"O telescope, instrument of much knowledge, more precious than any sceptre! Is not he who holds thee in his hand made king and lord of the works of God?"[23]

When spring came, Michelson realized that he needed a change of scene and a chance to refresh himself after encountering this impasse. To Margaret's joy he suggested a trip through the Schwartzwald. Folding easel and watercolors went into his satchel, and for a little while they replaced his instruments, as the sunlight and summer landscape replaced the basement room of the observatory where he had been imprisoned with his insoluble problem. Sometimes on foot, sometimes by carriage, Michelson and his wife explored the German countryside like a later generation of *Wandervogel*. It was a peaceful interlude.

In the summer of 1881, the Michelsons moved to Heidelberg. Margaret had not been well after the third baby's difficult birth, and it was hoped that the pleasant climate and the distractions of music and the theater in the beautiful old university town would hasten her convalescence.

At Heidelberg University, Michelson attended lectures on optics by Professor Georg Hermann Quincke. He also studied with Robert Wilhelm Bunsen, a researcher in chemistry and spectroscopy, popularly known for the burner he invented. Bunsen had made great sacrifices to his work. He lost the sight of an eye in an explosion of acids and later almost died of arsenic poisoning in a search for its antidote, which, in the end, he found.

In Bunsen's class, Michelson learned that the vapor from each element gives off its own unvarying spectrum, which can be recognized as clearly as experts now identify the signature on a check or the fingerprint on a weapon. It may have been in Bunsen's laboratory that Michelson perfected the art of producing the "half-silvered mirror," that vital organ at the heart of his interferometer.

Michelson enjoyed his studies, and the atmosphere of Heidelburg was relaxing after the strain and the disappointment he had undergone. He made some charming watercolors of the river bank with the great castle dominating the valley of the Neckar from its overhanging crags. He was infected by the lively atmosphere in the town. Students went down the street arm in arm, sometimes singing gaily, or gathered in animated groups at the coffee houses and beer halls. Dueling with swords, although forbidden by the authorities, was an accepted ritual and many students bore the fashionable slashes across their cheeks.

The summer passed pleasantly and Michelson would have lingered in the congenial surroundings at the university if he had not begun to worry about securing a position after his return to America. No firm offer had materialized.

In the interim, Michelson turned his mind to opportunities at hand. He was well aware that the French were making important strides in the field of optics, and Paris was becoming the center of important work in several scientific fields. He had long been anxious to meet with the eminent Frenchmen whose work had originally brought him to a career in physics, and he made arrangements to leave for a winter's study in the French capital.

Foucault was dead, but there were others who had carried on the study of optics. Michelson felt that he could learn much from a winter of study at the Collège de France and the École Polytechnique. There were three men in particular with whom he wished to study: Cornu, Mascart, and Lippmann.

Marie Alfred Cornu, who had measured the speed of light in 1874, was something of an eccentric. He had curious theories about music. Minor keys were abhorrent to him and he wrote at length about Beethoven who, he said, seldom used the minor harmonies and if he had to, always returned quickly to the major. Cornu carried a tuning fork with him at all times to test his own ear, which was extremely accurate, as well as to check the pitch of any sound he might hear.

Éleuthère Élie Nicolas Mascart was professor of physics at the Collège de France. He had constructed a spectograph for the mapping of spectra by photography and had investigated ultraviolet rays. Mascart had also made an ether-drift experiment, which had produced only the negative first-order effects that were an accepted result. Gabriel Lippmann, only seven years older than Michelson, had also been a pupil of Helmholtz. When Michelson arrived in Paris in the fall of 1881 he found that his reputation had preceded him. His accurate determination of the speed of light, followed by his daring challenge to the received theory of astronomical aberration as Fresnel had established it, made his French colleagues eager to meet him. When he presented himself at the École Polytechnique, he was asked if he were by chance the son of the famous Michelson. When he laughingly replied that he was himself that Michelson, invitations were pressed upon him to meet the other professors of the science faculty. Discussion soon turned to the new instrument he had devised.

Cornu was extremely skeptical about the whole idea. Patting Michelson condescendingly on the back, he said: "My dear friend, that experiment was tried fifty years ago by the celebrated Fresnel and it does not work."

"But, Professor, I have seen these fringes," Michelson replied.

Cornu asked for a demonstration, and Michelson set up the interferometer so that it would perform, though only imperfectly. The optical flats were held in place by wax and the source of light was probably a candle. The fringes of sodium light are monochromatic and therefore far more easily visible than white light, but Michelson did not know this at the time. Using white light, he worked for three days without success. Cornu smiled indulgently whenever he came to the laboratory and saw the effort it was taking. Finally he offered to "call it a draw." Michelson begged for a little more time. Suddenly the fringes appeared. Handing a glass to Cornu, he asked the professor to see for himself. When the glass was inserted in the path of one of the divided rays, this ray was slowed up in entering the denser medium and thus arrived out of phase so that the fringes vanished.

"My friend, you have it," exclaimed Cornu. He congratulated Michelson warmly and called his colleagues to witness another demonstration.[24] Michelson did not mention the real purpose for which he had designed this delicate apparatus. He preferred to show them the tricks it could perform rather than its failures.

M. André Potier, a former pupil of Cornu, called Michelson's attention to an error in his calculations in neglecting the effect of the earth's motion on light traveling in the arm of the interferometer at right angles to that motion, which Potier said would reduce the fringe shift to zero. Michelson acknowledged his error at the February 20, 1882, meeting of the Paris Académie des Sciences but pointed out that the fringe displacement would be reduced only by half, not to zero—using his Potsdam figures, from 0.08 to 0.04. This merely emphasized the negative result, but Michelson was considerably discomfited to find that, after taking such infinite pains, he had overlooked so simple an error.

The same error was discovered by Hendrik Antoon Lorentz, professor of mathematical physics at the University of Leiden. Lorentz was at work on a problem concerning the relations between light, magnetism, and matter, for the solution of which he, with his pupil Pieter Zeeman, would win the Nobel Prize in 1902. Lorentz was probably one of the first to react to the implications of the negative result of Michelson's ether-drift test, because it differed from his theory of electrons moving in an ether at rest. Although the two exchanged some letters, they did not meet until many years later.

Margaret had remained in Heidelberg because the baby was too young to travel. But as time went by and her husband failed to send for her, she began to feel neglected. Communication between them had been at a low ebb during the months when he had been almost completely absorbed in his work. An understandable resentment built up in her, along with a feeling that her love and talents were not appreciated. On his part, Michelson found he could accomplish much more when he was alone. He also preferred not to take her with him to the gatherings he attended, even when they were not of a scientific nature, because she frequently tried to take over the limelight and to give the impression that she had "created" him. Her loneliness during the past year had made her doubly garrulous when she found an audience, and she could talk rings around him in three languages. Besides her fortune, which she spent freely, Margaret had considerable charm and beauty, all of which she used as weapons, forcing Michelson into a bitter struggle to maintain his individuality.

Eventually he did find living quarters for her in Paris, the children were entered in French schools, and Margaret settled down. But their lives were developing independently and they seldom discussed any subject other than the trivia of everyday living.

In the spring of 1881, a great weight was lifted from Michelson's mind—he received an appointment on the faculty of a university. He had a powerful friend in George F. Barker of Philadelphia, editor of *The American Journal of Science*, which had published his first paper on the velocity of light. Barker had influence with John Stockwell, chairman of the faculty of the recently founded Case School of Applied Science in Cleveland, the only independent technological college west of the Alleghenies. Barker initiated a lively correspondence with Stockwell, calculated to whet the appetite of the board of trustees and persuade them into making a firm offer to his young friend.

March 22, 1881

. . . I mailed at once the enclosure to Mr. Michelson and also cabled him to the effect that the intentions of the

Cleveland people were good. I have also mailed him your letter to me received today. I can appreciate his position. He is now deriving his support from the Navy. He cannot afford to resign from that position until he has a positive certainty to fall back upon. While it may be very true that the trustees of the Case School are favorably disposed toward him, that favorable disposition would not in my opinion warrant his resigning from the Navy. If he does not do this however he will be sent to sea.

The chance to secure him for the Case School I regard as one not to be trifled with. He doesn't ask any salary and will expect to wait until such time as may be necessary before beginning his duties. But he asks (and I think rightly) that he be elected something even Instructor in Physics as you and Dr. Taylor are if not a full Professor right away, with the understanding that he is not to go on duty until wanted. I [c]an see no reason why some such guarantee cannot be given him. One on which he can have the courage to resign from the Navy and spend another year or more in Europe in special study. Then he can s[e]lect and bring home his apparatus and be ready to go at once at [sic] work. I have not heard a word from him since I wrote to you, So I say all this on my own responsibility. With best wishes,

Cordially yours,

George F. Barker[25]

At a meeting of the Case Board of Trustees a few days later, it was resolved that Albert A. Michelson be appointed Instructor in Physics, with a salary of $2,000 per annum to take effect September 1, 1882. The trustees also gave him permission to finish his studies in Paris before taking up his duties in Cleveland. In addition he was provided with the sum of $7,500

(Barker had suggested $10,000) for the purchase of instruments for the new laboratory at Case. He was in the perfect position to carry out this assignment, for at that time the French excelled in the construction of instruments.

Michelson resigned from the Navy, and in April of 1882 he and his family sailed for the United States.

CHAPTER 5

Foundations Tumble

T HE Case School of Applied Science in Cleveland, at which Michelson taught for seven years, was founded in 1881 with the purpose of training men in science and engineering for the steel, oil, and mining industries of Ohio. (It later became Case Institute of Technology and is now part of Case Western Reserve University.)

Leonard Case, Jr., the founder, was the son of a Cleveland pioneer, who left him a fortune. He graduated from Yale and became a lawyer, mathematician, and poet. He traveled widely in Europe before returning to Cleveland, where in 1877 he deeded a valuable piece of land, including the Case homestead, for the founding of The Case School of Applied Science. He was known to his Cleveland friends as "a scholar and original thinker, shrinking from public notice, modest to a fault, retiring in disposition, generous, manly, benevolent and humane."[1] Judge R. P. Ranney was president of the Case

School's first board of trustees. In 1882, when Michelson arrived, there were five men on the faculty and a student body of seventeen. Classes were held in the old Case homestead at Number Seven, Rockwell Street, near the Cleveland public square. The quiet dignity of the mansion's exterior gave no indication of the beehive of activity within. Classrooms filled the first and upper floors while the Physical Laboratory used the rooms in the cellar.

John Stockwell was professor of mathematics and astronomy and leader of the faculty at Case. Stockwell, a self-educated farm boy, had developed into an accomplished astronomer, whose reputation as an original thinker was widespread. He had followed Michelson's work with keen interest and was chiefly responsible for bringing the young physicist to Case.

Stockwell was sitting in his office surrounded by an enormous number of papers and books when Michelson appeared in July of 1882 to make his report on the instruments for the physical laboratory he had ordered in France and Germany with the money provided by the trustees. The instruments were to arrive in November. During their talk, the two men discussed a plan to repeat the experiment on the velocity of light, using funds that Newcomb had promised for the purpose.

Stockwell passed Michelson on to the architect John Eisenmann, who held the chair of civil engineering and drawing. He had designed the Case Main Building and was later to design the Old Arcade, a magnificent structure of steel and glass. Eisenmann suggested as a location for the velocity of light experiment a tract of land that lay along the Nickel Plate Railroad and offered to survey it.

On his return from Europe Michelson had been greatly disappointed to find that the mountings for the apparatus he had used at the Naval Academy had been completely destroyed. There remained no vestige of the stone pier or of the building that had housed the instruments. Another blow was the disappearance of one of the revolving mirrors, which he had left in his father-in-law's house. When it turned up again, he wrote to Newcomb:

New York June 15th 1882

. . . The mystery is solved and the revolving mirror found!

I mentioned at the dinner table that I was to repeat my experiments, and that naturally led to the subject of the lost instrument.

Mrs. Heminway asked what I intended to do with the other instrument. "What other?" I asked. "The one down stairs." I knew immediately that the mirror was found. Mrs. H[eminway] knew that I had two instruments in New Rochelle—and *did not* know that I had left one of them (the micrometer) at the Steven's [*sic*] Institute, and has been thinking (not knowing a "revolving mirror" from a great equatorial), that *that* was the missing instrument.[2]

Michelson gave Newcomb full reports of his work in Cleveland. He had secured the services of an able machinist for thirty dollars a month, and a little house on the grounds of Case School had been built to cover the instruments. Few trains were running on the Nickel Plate tracks when Michelson did his work, and those only at long intervals. In his report to Newcomb on September 6, 1882, he wrote:

I have succeeded in making some fifty observations of extremely varying degrees of accuracy and the result thus far is 299810 (vacuo).

I think it quite possible that the final result may vary from this as much as 100 kilometers—but not much more.

My arrangements are as yet far from perfect and unfavorable skies have prevented my doing much work.

I have attempted to suppress the bellows which I used in my previous work as a regulator but find now that they will be necessary.

The mirror turns now so smoothly that it is with difficulty that any sound can be heard even when the ear is but two or three inches away. . . .[3]

Michelson's experiments had a way of costing far more than had been originally expected and he was worried because Newcomb was soon to go to Africa for an extended period in order to chart the transit of Venus across the sun's disk. Newcomb's elaborate documentation of the paths of all the planets back to the earliest records in astronomy had earned him the reputation of being a human calculating machine. He was a member of the Bache Fund committee that made money available to Michelson through the National Academy of Sciences, but Michelson did not know what funds would be forthcoming during Newcomb's absence. Fearing that he would be caught in a pinch at a time when Newcomb could not be reached, he added:

Could you give me an idea of how much we have spent thus far?

When do you expect to return from your trip, and will you pay a visit to Cleveland?

Have on hand but $20 of the fund you sent—can you let me have more before you go? . . .[4]

And later, "Money has given out."[5]

Newcomb came to his financial rescue again, and with patience and time the experiment was brought to its conclusion.

Michelson's Cleveland figures on the speed of light, 299,-853±60 kilometers per second *in vacuo* (186,320±37 miles per second) became the accepted standard for forty-four years until they were superseded by his own measurements made in 1927 between Mount Wilson and Mount San Antonio in California.

Margaret and the children joined Michelson in Cleveland in September. She did not take kindly to existence in this provincial manufacturing town, which she found filled with hardship and boredom. She made frequent trips to New York, once she had finished unpacking, settled the servant problem, and put the boys in school. They too had an adjustment to make after two years abroad. Their picturesque Bavarian jackets and lederhosen were somewhat conspicuous in Cleveland. Elsa, at eighteen months, was her father's favorite. This was the age he preferred and he wished she need never grow up. On Sunday mornings he sometimes took her with him down to Wade Park to see the ducklings dabbling in the water.

In July of 1883, Michelson went to visit Alexander Graham Bell in Washington. The disappointment of the negative result in Berlin made him all the more anxious to explain the experiment fully to Mr. Bell and to stress the many other important uses he foresaw for his instrument.

Bell described Michelson's visit in a letter to his wife on July 25, 1883:

> The only thing that prevented me from fleeing to Oakland on Wednesday was the fact that I expected Mr. Michelson as a guest—and I guessed he would come. [Bell enjoyed his frequent puns.]
>
> Wednesday was pretty hot too—but I managed to keep comfortable in the draft of the laboratory fanwheel and in the evening my visitor arrived. It was perfectly delightful to meet a man with whom I can talk my thoughts—and with whom I can discuss intelligently all the questions that interest me. I think that Mr. Michelson is enjoying his stay with me too. I am very glad to have

this opportunity of knowing more of him—for I have a very high respect for his abilities—(though I rather suspect from his manner that he has too). Well, if a man has great natural abilities I don't see why he should be blamed if he recognized the fact. . . .

I am enjoying Michelson's visit *very much indeed*— and I feel that he too is not altogether disappointed. Since I came to America I have made a great many acquaintances but very few "friends." Michelson is one of the few *young men* towards whom I have felt drawn naturally. There seems to be a natural sympathy between our minds —and we have been discussing the affairs of the *Universe!* with a vengeance.

Gravitation—Electricity—Magnetism—Meteorology —Chemistry—Moleculars, Atoms, "Points of Matter"— Education—and I don't know what else—Evolution and Religion—are a few of the topics. Don't wonder therefore that I have had to wait for this opportunity of writing you.[6]

Michelson gave an exhibition for Mr. Bell and his guests, making the interferometer perform much as it had done for Cornu. George Barker, who had secured the Cleveland professorship for Michelson, wrote that he was very disappointed not to be able to attend the dinner or "witness the exhibition."[7]

Michelson returned to Cleveland refreshed and exhilarated by his visit with Bell. The trustees had raised his salary to $2,500. He joined the new East Side Tennis Club and played there frequently. The three dirt courts on Bell Avenue, surrounded by bleachers, were kept in excellent condition. To whiten the lines, Michelson built his own marker in the instrument shop at Case. The club's president, Charles A. Post, and Michelson were opponents in the opening tournament on May 31, 1885. The games were evenly fought and made a fine spectacle for the 200 people who filled the grandstand. Michel-

son won his match in straight sets, partly because he had perfected a loffard shot—a kind of lob with a spin on it—which
caused trouble for his opponents. Post and Michelson became
regular partners and later in the summer went to Newport,
Rhode Island, to play in the international tennis tournament.
According to a pupil of this era, there was a legend that Michelson loved tennis so much that whenever a good player invited
him to play a match, he would dismiss his classes and make off
for the courts, to the delight of the student body.[8]

After this exhilarating exercise, Michelson would appear
in the classroom looking remarkably neat and rather formal in
his black square-cut morning coat, stiff high collar, and knife-
edged, pin-stripe trousers. According to the students, his lectures were "most elegant, absolutely clear and finished."[9] No
loose ends remained to puzzle or confuse them. He was, however, an exacting teacher, and most students found it necessary
to put in long hours of reading in order to keep up with his
pace. He continued the naval routine of giving two tightly
packed lectures each week, plus one period of recitation.
There was trouble in store for any student who was inattentive.

In class, Michelson described various experiments on the
velocity of light, ending with a detailed explanation of the
method and figures he had achieved along the railroad tracks.
He never mentioned himself as the experimenter, preferring to say, "it was discovered that," "An experiment took
place . . .," "results showed . . .".[10]

Michelson had a far closer relationship with his students
of this period than with those of later years. The Case students
spoke reverently of the inspiration they received in his classes.
Two who later became successful in industry were Albert W.
Smith, professor of chemistry at Case, and Herbert H. Dow,
founder of the Dow Chemical Company. Michelson was always sorry to lose a promising physicist to applied science, but
the rewards of the machine age were so great that this often
happened.

As a teacher, he generally attempted to present the problems of physics without revealing his personal bias. But in one controversy, that involving the corpuscular and the undulatory theories of light, he had difficulty maintaining an impartial position.

Physicists today have learned to live with the dual personality of light; they accept the corpuscular and the wave theories as different aspects of the same complex phenomenon. But those of Michelson's generation were not so tolerant. They were passionately devoted to the wave theory because it involved the basic conceptual tools with which they worked. To his students Michelson cited the 1859 experiment of Fizeau on the velocity of light passing from air to water. If light were made up of corpuscles, it was believed, these would be attracted to the densely packed particles of water and the motion of light would be accelerated. The reverse was proved true. Light waves were deflected or retarded upon entering the denser medium. Fizeau's result was widely regarded as a *coup de grâce* for corpuscles and a triumph for waves.

But the corpuscular dragon had many heads and Michelson thought it was time to slay it again. Redesigning Fizeau's experiment, he built a 10-foot tube, filled it with distilled water, and with the mirrors of an interferometer especially assembled for the purpose measured the refraction of light as it entered the water. Not only did he prove that light slows down when it goes into water, but he fixed the ratio for this refraction at 1.33.

Regarding the ether, Michelson told his students only that "the luminiferous ether is to some extent a hypothetical substance and if it consists of matter at all, must be very rare and elastic. *It entirely escapes all our senses of perception.*"[11] He never mentioned his 1881 experiment in Berlin.

On the surface, he seemed to have put the problem of ether drift out of his mind. It was far more satisfying to apply himself to a measurement like the velocity of light to which he could find a definite answer. But lying awake at night, as he did now more and more often, he tossed and kicked loose the bedding around his feet, as he reviewed the steps of his Potsdam experiment, trying to find another way. He was not alone in being haunted by the insoluble riddle. The failure of this crucial test alarmed all who knew of it. Maxwell had warned:

> There are no landmarks in space; one portion of space is like every other portion, so that we cannot tell where we are. We are, as it were, on an unruffled sea, without stars, compass, soundings, wind, or tide, and we cannot tell in what direction we are going. We have no log which we can cast out to take a dead reckoning by; we may compute our rate of motion with respect to the neighboring bodies, but we do not know how these bodies may be moving in space.[12]

Haunted by similar thoughts, Michelson longed to discuss the problem with some of the older men in the field. The chance came later in the summer of 1884. He received an invitation to attend the meeting of the British Association for the Advancement of Science in Montreal in August. This meeting was significant because the British had previously regarded Americans and Canadians as hardly able to understand scientific matters.

En route to Montreal, Michelson met an acquaintance from Cleveland, Edward Morley, the distinguished chemist of Western Reserve University. Morley was fourteen years older than Michelson. He had been a student of astronomy, and like Michelson he had a lifelong dedication to accuracy. Unlike his younger colleague, Morley was a man of deep religious convictions, having originally studied for the ministry. As a teacher, he not only insisted on a mastery of the principles of chemistry but also inculcated into his students good manners, the proper use of the English language, and clear methods of expression. He later became widely known for his work in establishing the weight of various chemical atoms, using hydrogen as a unit.

The new president of the British Association for the Advancement of Science, Lord Rayleigh, was typical of nineteenth-century British scientists. A gentleman of good family and ample means, he had excellent connections and the time to work out his schemes in his own laboratory. In that period scientific research was still largely a gentleman's hobby since only a man of wealth could afford to indulge in it. Lord Rayleigh's life was enlivened by gay dinners and cruising parties with Sir William Thomson and Hermann von Helmholtz on Thomson's yacht *Lalla Rookh.*

Lord Rayleigh and his wife arrived in Quebec on the SS *Parisian*, a special sailing having been arranged to accommodate them. About a thousand scientists from the United States and Canada attended the meeting, concerning which the London *Times* announced: "The Canadians will be brought face to face with the flower of our aristocracy of science. So brilliant a concentration of British talent of a specific order has never before been witnessed out of England." The French-Canadian press was less cordial. The gathering was attacked as a meeting of "Protestants and Free Masons," on the grounds that such a meeting in Canada, if it had any significance at all, could only be detrimental to religious interests. The struggle between religion and science was still unresolved.

The first meeting that Michelson attended took place in Queen's Hall of McGill University. Sir William Thomson, as retiring president, opened the meeting, then handed over the gavel to Lord Rayleigh, who made the opening address.

These two giants of British achievement in the physical field were the stars of the occasion. It was Michelson's first glimpse of the "establishment" in action, and no syllable was lost on him. Rayleigh was the more sophisticated and suave of the two, handling the meeting with perfect tact, skill, and aplomb. George Howard Darwin, son of Charles Darwin, read the first paper, "The Remote History of the Earth."

Throughout the sessions, Simon Newcomb, who had

secured the invitation for Michelson, steered his protegé from group to group, first giving him a brief sketch of the various notables' accomplishments and then introducing him to them with obvious pride. Wolcott Gibbs, the Harvard chemist who had tried to get Michelson a professorship in the Navy, was present, and Michelson had an opportunity to tell him how things were developing at Case. Professor Henry Rowland of Johns Hopkins read a paper on "Recent Progress in Photographing the Solar Spectrum," which created a favorable stir. Rowland had developed a method of ruling extremely fine diffraction gratings and he showed examples of his glass plates that contained as many as 20,000 grooves to the inch. The gratings were much admired as the sunlight playing on the grooved surface broke into all the beauty of the purest spectrum colors. Rowland, who was justifiably proud of his accomplishment, scored a hit with the British scientists. He handed out several small sample gratings, and Lord Rayleigh pronounced them " . . . magnificent . . . a new power in the hands of the spectroscopist . . . triumphs of mechanical art . . . little short of perfection."[13] Gratings became in great demand among astronomers studying the chemical composition of the sun and the stars, since spectroscopy enhanced the study of atomic matter in the distant giants of the sky as well as in small bodies near at hand.

George Forbes, a British physicist, had been experimenting for some time with the velocities of different colors of light. In collaboration with J. Young he had published an article on the subject in *Nature*.[14] In response to this article, Michelson had expressed his opposing views in a letter to the editor.[15] Facing Forbes for the first time in Montreal on September 2, he rose to call Forbes's statements in question. Many scientists agreed with Forbes, including the well-known Scottish physicist George F. FitzGerald, who read a paper in which he stated that blue light traveled faster than red in air and *in vacuo*. But to Michelson's great satisfaction, Lord Rayleigh backed him up:

The great optical constant, the velocity of light, has been the subject of three distinct investigations by Cornu, Michelson, and Forbes. As may be supposed, the matter is of no ordinary difficulty, and it is therefore not surprising that the agreement should be less decided than could be wished. From their observations, which were made by a modification of Fizeau's method of the toothed wheel, Young and Forbes drew the conclusion that the velocity of light *in vacuo* varies from colour to colour, to such an extent that the velocity of blue light is nearly two per cent greater than that of red light. Such a variation is quite opposed to existing theoretical notions, and could only be accepted on the strongest evidence. Mr. Michelson, whose method (that of Foucault) is well suited to bring into prominence a variation of velocity with wave length, informs me that he has recently repeated his experiments with special reference to the point in question, and has arrived at the conclusion that no variation exists comparable with that asserted by Young and Forbes. The actual velocity differs little from that found from his first series of experiments and may be taken to be 299,800 kilometers per second.[16]

Michelson's own paper was "On the Velocity of Light in Carbon Disulphide." The meeting ended with Rayleigh's adieu:

If I had any criticism, it would be this: The time was too good a one. What with science from ten to three, even the most interesting kind, and I agree with Thomson, never in my experience have the discussions been more interesting. What with the general meetings, garden parties and other enjoyments, I have not seen Montreal.[17]

At Lord Rayleigh's invitation Michelson met him in Washington in October of 1884 and accompanied him to hear Sir William Thomson's lectures in Baltimore. Sir William, known affectionately as England's great "electrician," delivered a series of twenty lectures at Johns Hopkins.

Thomson's lectures were open to the public, and in spite of inordinate heat and humidity which nearly prostrated the British visitors, the enrollment taxed the capacity of the small classrooms in which the lectures were held. Before the lectures began some thirty scientists gathered at a reception in Hopkins Hall. President Gilman and the faculty welcomed the guests, and Michelson had a chance to meet the men he wanted most to see. Almost all of them had been trained in Germany, and many were former pupils of Helmholtz.

One man whom Michelson found especially sympathetic was Thomas Corwin Mendenhall. He had a strong interest in scientific matters, particularly in electricity. Well traveled both in Europe and the Orient, he had spent three years teaching physics at the Imperial University of Japan. He later became superintendent of the Coast and Geodetic Survey.

John A. Brashear, a self-made man with little formal education, was highly regarded for his contributions to astronomy, physics, and aeronautics. As the best maker of instruments and optical parts at a time when physicists had to design their own, Brashear was courted and sought after by scientists and industrialists alike.

Newcomb and the spectroscopist Henry Rowland were much in evidence. Both were on the faculty of Johns Hopkins, as was G. Stanley Hall, head of the Department of Psychology. Michelson had hoped, between lectures, to see Rowland's engine for ruling diffraction gratings, but Rowland was extremely secretive about his invention. He never published any complete description or diagram of it.

Rowland had unusual tastes for a physicist; his favorite pastime was riding to hounds, not only through the Maryland countryside but with several of the famous British hunts when he visited Lord Rayleigh. He was not noted for modesty. Once when he was involved in a lawsuit he was asked on the witness stand to state his occupation. "I am the world's greatest physicist," he is reported to have said. Later a friend asked if it was necessary to make such a boast. "I had to tell the truth, you know, I was under oath," he replied.[18]

Michelson was introduced to one of Rowland's graduate students, Henry Crew. Crew, a recent graduate of Princeton, was writing his thesis on the variations of the sun's movement on its axis. He shared with Michelson an interest in spectroscopy, and a warm friendship sprang up between them. Crew, who later edited both of Michelson's books, kept an interesting diary of the Baltimore lectures.

Sir William's first lecture was on "Molecular Dynamics and the Wave Theory of Light." He began with a discussion of the medium through which the waves move and dwelt on the difficulties of determining the properties of the luminiferous ether. He described it as an elastic-solid, a body that undergoes certain displacements in its parts under the action of an external force, as a rubber band does when stretched, but returns to its original state upon release of the force. The general energy equation of a stressed elastic-solid involves twenty-one constants or coefficients. Noting that there were twenty-one persons present, he affectionately dubbed them, "my twenty-one coefficients."[19]

In order to allow the planets to continue orbiting at a constant rate of speed, the ether would have to stretch as they pass and flow together again in their wake, Thomson said. He also referred to the "overwhelmingly great difficulty of finding a field of action for the ether among the atoms of ponderable matter." Could the ether move through a glass lens, through flesh and blood, through the mass of the earth itself? But, if the ether were discarded, what then? The light waves would have nothing to wave in. Can a fish swim without water?

My object in undertaking the Baltimore Lectures was to find how much of the phenomena of light can be ex-

plained *without going beyond the elastic-solid theory.*
We have now our answer: Every thing non-magnetic;
nothing magnetic. The so-called "electromagnetic theory
of light" has not helped us hitherto.[20]

Maxwell's electromagnetic theory, which Thomson lightly
dismissed, involved the concept that electric and magnetic
pressures and tensions in the ether were carried through it in
the form of waves. Maxwell further proposed that these electromagnetic waves traveled at the same speed as light waves
and had similar properties. His theory, however, was still unproven. At Helmholtz's suggestion, Heinrich Hertz, whom
Michelson had met in Berlin, had begun work on ways and
means of testing Maxwell's equations, and in 1887 he produced
from an electric oscillator artificial waves of the kind predicted
by Maxwell, but of a much greater wavelength. These were
later recognized as radio waves.

In 1884, however, Thomson could not bring himself to
accept Maxwell's theory. His strict Scotch-Presbyterian up-
bringing and his austere childhood, much of it spent on the
isolated island of Aran off the Irish coast, contributed to his
conservative outlook.[21] He did not readily accept radical
changes. Before commencing his daily lectures on Natural Philosophy at the University of Glasgow, Thomson recited a passage from the New Testament with closed eyes. His faith in the
Bible and in constant mass, absolute space, and absolute time
remained steadfast until he died.

Rayleigh was more tolerant. An Anglican with agnostic
tendencies, he avoided direct questions as to his religious be-
liefs but when pressed would admit that he thought of Christ
as a gifted man who could see further and truer than he. But
he liked the idea of a power beyond what men see and an
afterlife in which they may hope to take part.

On the religious question, Michelson disagreed with both
these men. He had renounced any belief that moral issues

were at stake in the behavior of the universe. The heavenly bodies revolved with symmetry and grandeur, but without any relation to what is good or bad for human beings. He was inclined to accept Maxwell's theory as long as it acknowledged the role of the ether.

Many of the younger men thought Thomson too conservative. Rowland, whose own experiment on the magnetic effect of electric convection[22] had contributed to Maxwell's discovery, found the views of the aging Englishman outdated and expressed his boredom by sleeping shamelessly throughout the series of lectures. Henry Crew noted in his diary that Sir William "is very confident in his assertions as to the reality of a luminiferous ether." He called the lectures a "grand failure," deploring the inadequate mathematical expositions.[23] It was true that, having prepared his notes in haste, Sir William sometimes found himself in difficulty with mathematics. At one point he appealed to Lord Rayleigh to verify a statement, but Rayleigh merely shook his head, leaving his friend to extricate himself from the dilemma. Edward Morley, the "shark" of the group, helped Sir William over some of the difficulties. In particular, he worked out a complete solution of the dynamical model of a molecule.[24] Some of the "coefficients" thought it was no longer necessary to build an elaborate mechanical model in order to explain optical phenomena. But for Thomson, seeing was believing.

On October 15, Sir William lectured on "Rigidity of the Earth." Physicists had often speculated about conditions beneath the earth's crust. They knew that the temperatures were high, but they were in doubt as to whether the contents were molten or solid. Sir William demonstrated rigidity with an interesting collection of raw and hard-boiled eggs. The rigidity of the interior of the egg had a direct effect on its motion. The hard-boiled egg could be spun standing on its axis while the raw egg flopped around horizontally. He also used cups of sand, molasses, oil, and water to simulate the interior of the earth and its tides. It was known that the earth had only a slight nutation, like the nodding of a top on its axis. From this he deduced that, like the hard-boiled egg, the earth had a high degree of rigidity.

Thomson's listeners did not have to agree with their "teacher" to be stimulated by his thinking. By making a statement, he often prodded them into trying to prove him wrong. This kind of worrying of a subject went on when Helmholtz came to visit Thomson in Scotland or when Rayleigh invited them both to Terling, his estate near London. Students were often asked to sit in on the meetings. These three men inspired most of the significant thought along physical lines of the generation that followed them.

The lectures came to an end on October 17. Michelson had initiated a plan to give Sir William one of Rowland's gratings and had collected three dollars from each of the scientists for this purpose. At the final lecture, Mendenhall presented it along with an album containing the signatures of the "coefficients."

In retrospect all the "coefficients" felt warmly toward Sir William, and they wrote him a letter in 1896 to tell him so. "What we saw and heard at that time, in the halls of Johns Hopkins University, was for each of us an inspiration. . . ."[25] In the history of science the gathering marked a turning point, particularly as regards the United States. American scientists had won British respect.

After the lectures were over, Michelson and Morley left together by train. Talk flowed between them all the way home. It was a great joy to Michelson to find a man like Morley with whom he could share the intricate problems of work and the many tastes they had in common. One of these was chamber music; both were accomplished musicians. Morley was a lovable man, very simple and loyal in friendship, as Michelson would learn when theirs was put to a severe test. He and Mrs. Morley were great readers and shared Michelson's fondness for frivolous thrillers. Among the topics Michelson discussed with Morley on the train was Lord Rayleigh's suggestion that he repeat his Potsdam experiment. That he soon began making plans to do so is indicated by a letter written in December 1884 to Josiah Willard Gibbs of Yale. Gibbs was the only major American physical scientist of Michelson's era who had not attended Thomson's Baltimore lectures. He led the life of a recluse, working in a shed at the back of his sister's house in New Haven and modestly teaching his few pupils at Yale without salary. From time to time he would send off papers on the theory of thermodynamics for publication in *Transactions of the Connecticut Academy of Science.* Yale did not stress the sciences, and most of the faculty were unaware of recent advances and even of the remarkable work being done on their own campus.

There is a story that an emissary arrived from the University of Berlin and announced to President Noah Porter that Berlin University was conferring its highest honor on Professor Willard Gibbs. "Gibbs?" said the president, racking his brain, "We have no Gibbs; I've never heard of him."

Michelson, however, knew that Gibbs existed and wrote to consult him:

> I had the pleasure of talking with Sir William Thomson and Ld. Rayleigh, on the subject of influence of motion media on propagation of light, and they both seemed to think that the first step should be to repeat Fizeau's experiment.
>
> I have accordingly ordered the required apparatus and hope to be able to settle the question within a few months.
>
> Meanwhile, I should very much like to have an opinion from you concerning the feasibility of the experiment which I described to you rather hastily at our last meeting, namely:
>
> 1st. Granting that the effect of the atmosphere may be neglected, and supposing that the earth is moving rela-

tively to the ether at about 20 miles per second would there be a difference of about one hundred-millionth in the time required for light to return to its starting point, when the direction is parallel to earth's velocity—and that when the direction is at right angles?

2nd. Would this necessitate a movement of the interference fringes produced by the two rays?

3rd. If these are answered in the affirmative, provided the experiment is made so far above the surface of the earth that solid matter does not intervene, what would be the result if the experiment were made in a room?

Trusting that I am not imposing on your good nature by propounding these conundrums and hoping to hear from you. . . .[26]

Unfortunately, Gibbs's answers to these "conundrums" have been lost.

There were preliminary experiments to perform before the final one and the expenses would be considerable. Morley volunteered his assistance. He had already given generously of his time and the wisdom of his greater experience. Michelson had come to rely on him.

In full collaboration for the first time, and working in the basement laboratory of the Main Building at Case, Michelson and Morley undertook to repeat Fizeau's 1851 experiment on the velocity of light in moving water,[27] which had been based on Fresnel's accepted theory of a stationary ether. Since Michelson had challenged this theory, he wanted to repeat the experiment with the aid of the interferometer to see if the result would be different. Light was to be projected through two tubes of rapidly moving water to determine if its speed were affected by this motion. It was hoped that Fizeau's results would be proved correct, that the velocity of light would be affected by the motion of the medium through which it

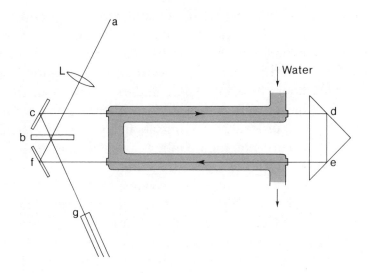

Light in moving water: a variation of Fizeau's experiment
(Adapted from Michelson and Morley, "Influence of Motion of the
Medium on the Velocity of Light," 1886)
Light from a source at *a*, passing through the lens *L*, falls on a half-
silvered mirror *b*, where it divides; one part follows the path *bcdefbg* and
the other the path *bfedcbg*; *c*, *d*, *e*, and *f* are plane mirrors. Water is
circulated in two tubes as indicated by the arrows.

moved. If, however, the new test proved Fizeau wrong, this
would presage another negative result, and Michelson and
Morley might have to give up the whole idea.

Before the test could be made, however, Michelson's par-
ticipation was abruptly arrested.

Every human being has a breaking point beyond which he
cannot push himself without danger. The body must sleep and
the brain must rest. But scientists sometimes try to ignore
these rules and suffer temporary defeat as a consequence. Al-

most every great scientist has been subject to deep depressions, and Michelson was no exception. He became obsessed, forgetting to eat or sleep. Albert and Truman grew frightened of their father, and his laboratory assistants protested at the unreasonable hours he kept. A less understanding man than Morley might have taken offense at his overbearing manner in the laboratory, his ordering everyone about and berating them for errors that were not their fault. Finally he was entirely unable to work. Morley wrote at that time:

"I can only guess at the stresses which brought about his illness. Overwork—and the ruthless discipline with which he drove himself to a task he felt must be done with such perfection that it could never again be called into question."[28]

Margaret was eventually driven to committing her husband to the care of Dr. Allan Hamilton, a nerve specialist who treated his patients at the Hotel Normandie in New York. Before Michelson was taken away on September 19, 1885, he asked to see Professor Morley. He had only seventy-six dollars left of the money from the Bache Fund. Adding one hundred dollars of his own, he pressed the money upon his friend, begging him to finish the experiment without him. Morley agreed. He was thoroughly convinced of the seriousness of Michelson's condition, which he described to his father on September 27, 1885:

. . . Mr. Michelson of the Case School left [a] week ago yesterday. He shows some symptoms which point to softening of the brain; he goes for a year's rest, but it is very doubtful whether he will ever be able to do any more work. He had begun some experiments in my laboratory, which he asked me to finish, and which I consented to carry on. He had money given him to make the experiments, and he gave me this money; the experiments are, to see whether the motion of the medium affects the velocity of light moving in it. I made some trial last week, and found that a good deal of m[o]dification in the apparatus would be necessary, and made drawings for some parts of the apparatus. As soon as these are done, I shall try again. When everything is ready, it may not take more than a week to make the experiment.[29]

Michelson's doctor, a grandson of Alexander Hamilton, had specialized in the treatment of nervous diseases following his graduation from the College of Physicians and Surgeons and was considered one of America's leading authorities in the field. His discoveries led to a radical change in the treatment of the insane and laid the foundations for modern therapy. Under Hamilton's treatment, Michelson began an astonishing recovery. On October 12, 1885, he wrote to Morley:

> I am here under the care of Dr. Hamilton, who assures me that my trouble is not serious, and that he hopes that in a month or two I shall be quite recovered.
>
> My treatment consists principally in amusing myself in whatever way I like—which, by the way, is not so trying as one might imagine, and when one gets used to it—and in a course of "massage" twice a day. The latter is not quite so enjoyable but I shall become accustomed to it in a short time.
>
> Have you had time yet to experiment with the "fringes?"
>
> Let me know how everything is going on and how the two institutions agree, in short anything and everything that may interest us both.
>
> With kind regards to all mutual friends . . .[30]

When this letter reached him, Morley was almost ready to run the experiment. He needed only a new pump which he had ordered from Chicago. In answering Michelson's letter he gave him all the details but also told him the devastating news that the trustees of Case had found someone to take his place on the faculty. This was a cruel blow, and Hamilton felt that an injustice had been done his patient.

. . . his [Michelson's] wife has urged me to shut him up in an asylum which I promptly refused to do.

Mr. Michelson is one of the brightest men of this country if not of the world in his chosen study. He is an accomplished man, very popular with those who know him. . . . Professor Michelson's most temperamental fault is a tendency to emotional acting, but I cannot say that it is unduly expressed, or that he ever acts without proper and adequate stimulus. . . .[31]

This letter, although of a later date, explains the coldness that existed between Michelson and his wife during the rest of their married life. In one sweeping blow, he had, as he thought, lost home, family, freedom, position on the faculty at Case, and the means to carry on his research. Justifiably or not, he came to hate Margaret.

However, Dr. Hamilton's therapy and his belief in his patient were soon justified. In December of 1885, Michelson was released from the doctor's care.

During his stay in New York, he had written to Henry Rowland:

> Hotel Normandie, N.Y.
> Nov 6th 85

My dear Professor Rowland,

Your very welcome letter duly received—many thanks for your kind wishes

The trustees of the Case School have, I am sorry to say, added another to the mistakes they have made, in appointing to fill my place (temporarily, however) a man who has had "twenty years' experience as a teacher" but who has no particular specialty!

Now that my physician assures them that I will be able to resume work in a few weeks they wish to have me return; but in as much as their man has been appointed for a year they wish me to "take into consideration the

strained condition of their finances"—which strained condition results from the very action they were forewarned
against,—namely,—"putting their money into bricks instead of brains."

It looks to me as tho this condition will last indefinitely, and taking into consideration the inconvenience of
being so far removed from scientific centers, I would
much prefer a position farther East. Please do give me
your advice in the matter, and if anything fitting my
capabilities should turn up elsewhere be kind enough to
let me know.[32]

Returning to Cleveland, he faced the ordeal of renewing
contact with his students and the Case faculty, all of whom had
heard rumors of his "insanity." More difficult still was the adjustment with Margaret. He needed her desperately, but at
the same time he felt she had betrayed him. Although their
marriage endured another thirteen years, Margaret was never
forgiven. When he reached home, Michelson instructed Joseph, the Negro valet, to put his bags in a single room at the
rear of the house. Than he went to report for work to the new
administration building that Eisenmann had designed on a
piece of land well out in the country, about four miles east of
the Cleveland Public Square. He walked up the dirt road
through the trees and underbrush toward the new school.
There were deer tracks in the snow and a startled rabbit
bounded away as he approached Main Hall. In an interview
with the secretary of the Case Board of Trustees Michelson was
told that his previous salary would have to be cut in order to
pay the man who had been hired to replace him.

A change came over Michelson's character after his illness. His youthful confidence in people was replaced by cynicism. He grew afraid of being caught off guard, and he kept a
tight rein on the emotional side of his nature. Taking comfort
in the high ceilings and thick walls of his new laboratory, he
plunged into work.

CHAPTER 6

The Michelson-Morley Experiment

I N the last week of 1885 Michelson received permission
from Newcomb to use the Bache funds for the repetition
of Fizeau's experiment. During his absence Morley had
improved the apparatus by installing in the attic a large tank
from which distilled water was to flow through two brass tubes
in opposite directions.

In the months that followed, Michelson and Morley made
sixty-five recorded trials. They found that the moving water
accelerated the speed of light to the degree of Fresnel's dragging coefficient, but not to the extent that they could simply
add the speeds together for a new combined velocity.[1]

They reported their findings to Sir William Thomson:

Cleveland, Ohio
Mar. 27, 1886

Dear Sir William,

You will no doubt be interested to know that our work on the effect of motion of the medium on the velocity of light has been brought to a successful termination. The result fully confirms the work of Fizeau. The factor by which the velocity of the medium must be multiplied to give the acceleration of the light was found to be 0.434 in the case of water, with a possible error of 0.02 or 0.03. This agrees almost exactly with Fresnel's formula $1-1/n^2$.

The experiment was also tried with air with a negative result.

The precautions taken appear to leave little room for any serious error, for the result was the same for different lengths of tube, different velocities of liquid, and different methods of observation. We hope to publish the details within a few weeks.

Very respectfully, your obedient servants,

Albert A. Michelson

Edward W. Morley[2]

Thomson responded immediately:

Dear Profs. Michelson and Morley,

Thanks for your letter of the 22nd. ult. I am exceedingly interested in what you tell me, and am more eager to see in print your description of your experiments. The result is clearly of the greatest importance in respect to the dynamics of the luminiferous ether and of light. I hope before the volume [*The Baltimore Lectures*] is completed to have results from you that can be incorporated as an appendix.[3]

The result of their experiment proved, they concluded, that "the luminiferous ether [is] entirely unaffected by the motion of the matter which it permeates."[4] So far, Fizeau had been proven right. And there the question remained until Michelson and Morley attacked it again in a different way.

On June 15, 1886, the first commencement of the Case School was held in the new building. Dr. John Stockwell addressed the class. The faculty now numbered eight; Charles Mabery and Albert W. Smith had been appointed as assistants in the Chemistry Department. Seven bachelor of science degrees were given out by Dr. Cady Staley, president of the faculty, who was also head of the Civil Engineering Department. Enormous pride in achievement characterized these first ceremonies.

In this same June of 1886, only six months after his recovery from mental illness, Michelson received the first of a long series of honorary degrees. This was a doctorate from Western Reserve University; it seems likely that Morley had a hand in bringing it about.

The rift between Michelson and his wife was superficially healing. He suggested taking her and the children to see his aging parents in California, telling the boys they would visit Murphy's Camp where they could explore the haunted ghost town, creep through the shaft of an abandoned gold mine, or drive to "Big Trees" for a picnic.

Samuel and Rosalie Michelson had left Virginia City, now in its decline, and moved to a comfortable house on Webster Street in San Francisco. The family fortunes had gone up and down according to Samuel's luck with his risky investments. Rosalie took this in her stride, finding deep satisfaction in the varied activities of her children. Pauline and Julie had found security as teachers. Miriam showed a genuine talent for writing and had been given assignments by the *San Francisco Chronicle.* She had inherited her father's love of a gamble but had better judgment or more luck. Bessie was not as brilliant as her sisters, but she had an appealing gentleness and beauty which won her the attention of several admirers. At this time, she was having a romance with Arthur McEwen, a rising young newspaperman. He was ". . . viking tall, and straight," Miriam said, and he wrote with the keenness of "acid etching steel."[5]

When Michelson arrived in San Francisco with his wife and children he was given a royal welcome. His sisters had a habit of all talking at once, and he had difficulty getting the gist of anything they said. The conversation was mostly about Charlie, who even when absent managed to steal the show. Five years earlier, when he was twelve, Charlie had run away from home, Pauline told Albert. She was instantly contradicted by Julie: Charlie had not run away. He had left school to join their brother Ben, who had been sent to work for a copper company in Arizona in the hope of restoring the family fortunes. Charlie had worked his way down to Lordsburg, New Mexico, and joined an ox team hauling supplies to the copper camp. The big Mexican boss had given him a goad to prod the weary beasts along, and he had walked nearly eighty miles before his legs gave out. Then the boss had taken pity on the small boy and hoisted him to the top of the lead wagon piled high with boxes, telling him to watch for Indians.

Geronimo and the Apaches were on the warpath. Charlie frequently saw their smoke signals and once or twice witnessed the sad processions of burros bringing in the bodies of prospectors who had been slaughtered in isolated camps.

Charlie had become a clerk for the Arizona Copper Company but was soon "advanced" to being in charge of the butcher shop. "There was no picking and choosing the cuts—the first customer got a chunk of the neck, the second customer got the next piece, and so on."

He lost his job because, he said, he consistently beat the proprietor at chess. "From then on I became a frontier tramp. I had a horse and a gun and I made my headquarters with an old prospector and friend. The country was full of game—deer in the hills, turkeys in the valleys, antelope on the plains; and when I needed money and did not care to fall back on my commercially minded brother [Ben], I had only to appear with my products of the chase to find a welcome market. The isolated prospectors working their claims had neither time nor opportunity to vary their diet of salt meat, beans and canned stuff." He did not loaf all the time, he said; he filled in wherever a job was vacated, sometimes as clerk, sometimes as bartender, and he was always available as a helper with cattle and mules. This idyllic life of adventure ended when his family finally rounded him up and shipped him back to Virginia City to enter high school.[6]

Charlie's natural gift for writing, revealed in letters to Arthur McEwen, won him after graduation a job for seven dollars a week on the *San Francisco Evening Post*. This was a good way for him to cut his teeth and Charlie made the most of it.

Albert, at thirty-four, might well have contrasted his own career of patient experiment with the excitements that seventeen-year-old Charlie had already savored. Different as they were, however, they both liked to work alone. They thrived in an era when a man could achieve his goal more or less by his own ingenuity. Michelson could never have developed his experiments with a team of five, fifty, or five hundred other physicists working on the "project." And Charlie's talent was just as much a one-man show. The Michelsons were a breed of individuals.

Michelson enjoyed seeing his relatives, but they exhausted him. He was never really happy away from his laboratory, and he found it a strain to make small talk when his mind was on his work.

After bringing his family back to Cleveland, he spent August and September contemplating his next undertaking. The basement laboratory was a few degrees cooler than the blazing heat outside. While everyone else was suffering and complaining, Michelson took the weather in his stride. In the late afternoon he used to wander over the meadow beside the lake in Wade Park to watch twilight approaching. He liked to shed his coat and lie on the grass under a tree. Sometimes he sketched the marsh with the ducks rooting about at the water's edge, but more often he just rested, turning over in his mind ways to raise the money for a second ether-drift test.

The Bache Fund had continued to supply him with financial backing, but the Case trustees were a constant source of irritation in their demands for elaborate accounting. Michelson was not in the habit of presenting orderly accounts. Eckstein Case, nephew of the founder and the school's treasurer, said: "Mike was a trifle liberal with other people's money. He would simply go ahead and buy whatever he wanted."[7] The worst of his difficulties came when he had to sort out whose money he had spent on what. Sometimes a piece of apparatus was billed to the school, sometimes paid for with Bache funds, and, from time to time, he simply bought what he needed himself in order to obviate the paper work and the lengthy explanations as to why such and such a tool was needed. This habit irritated Margaret to exasperation. Michelson maintained that he spent only his own salary on the much-needed equipment, but Margaret would find the household account inexplicably short upon occasions. She was frustrated by his refusal to discuss such matters. Any allusion to money would put her husband into one of his black moods, which might last for several days.

In the fall of 1886 fate struck a severe blow at the Case School and all its members, students and faculty alike. The first news of the disaster came at two-thirty in the morning of October 27, 1886.[8] A fire broke out in the tower of the main hall of the school. A few minutes later, a deafening explosion wakened the whole neighborhood. The frightened students in Adelbert College dormitory at Western Reserve, only a few hundred feet from the fire, sprang out of bed and dressed like lightning. Some stood spellbound in horror, but others with presence of mind and considerable courage dashed into the southeast corner of the flaming building and rescued some of Michelson's instruments, papers, and books.

As the fire engines arrived, a large crowd of people collected to watch the fire. A strong wind from the northeast aggravated the flames, carrying sparks and burning fragments toward Fairmount Street and igniting a barn. The fire engines had difficulty getting their hoses to the building because Euclid Avenue was undergoing repairs and the approach was blocked. Police and firemen strung up a cordon to keep everyone at a safe distance. Eisenmann, the architect, watched as fire caught the wooden lining under his handsome slate roof. The whole roof soon crashed downward with a deafening noise. Faculty members, hearing the crash, came up the hill in time to see the wooden joists, now blackened coals, crumble and fall to the ground. Jets of water from the hoses played over the steaming skeleton. It was long after daylight before the flames were brought under control. At eleven o'clock in the morning, the last fire engine left the charred wreck of the Case School.

No cause for the fire was ever discovered. Henry C. Walker, the caretaker, who was known to be trustworthy, told a story that cleared him of suspicion. While he was planting trees on the campus the afternoon before the disaster, he had checked the boilers. He found that the fire under them had burned out at four o'clock. That evening he had gone into the city and returned to the college on the last trolley around midnight. He went through the building to make his last rounds as usual and found everything in order. Sometime between midnight and 2 a.m., the fire had started.

News of the disaster reached Michelson some time before Dr. Staley called a meeting at Western Reserve. There he heard the grim details and the vast extent of the damage. Staley had lost all his personal papers, scientific works, and library in the fire. He had to report that the insurance on the building was totally inadequate—the loss amounted to $165,-000. The apparatus of the physics and chemistry laboratories had cost $30,000. The great library of scientific books given by the founder was completely destroyed.

The trustees of Adelbert College, Western Reserve, offered their dormitory and laboratories to the stricken faculty and student body of Case. "An ancient poet," Morley said in making the offer, "has declared that men, not walls, make a city. Your greatest power and force remains in your own strong corps of educators."[9] The faculty found some comfort in these words, and discussion turned to plans for rebuilding.

Michelson began reconstructing his instruments in Morley's laboratory. He worked patiently throughout the winter. The gloom was lightened by the arrival of a letter from Lord Rayleigh, suggesting that the time had come to repeat the ether-drift experiment. Rayleigh's wish was equal to a royal command, and Michelson knew that if Rayleigh took a positive stand on the importance of the experiment, money would be forthcoming.

Michelson's reply sums up his reasons for trying the test a second time.

Cleveland, March 6, 1887

My dear Lord Rayleigh,

I have never been fully satisfied with the results of my Potsdam experiment, even taking into account the correction which Lorentz points out.

All that may be properly concluded from it is that (supposing the ether were really stationary) the motion of

(123)

the earth thro' space cannot be very much greater than its velocity in its orbit.

Lorentz' correction is undoubtedly true. I had an indistinct recollection of mentioning it either to yourself or to Sir W. Thomson when you were in Baltimore.

It was first pointed out in a general way by M. A. Potier of Paris, who however was of the opinion that the correction would entirely annul any difference in the two paths; but I afterwards showed that the effect would be to make it one half the value I assigned, and this he accepted as correct. I have not yet seen Lorentz' paper and fear I could hardly make it out when it does appear.

I have repeatedly tried to interest my scientific friends in this experiment without avail, and the reason for my never publishing the correction was (I am ashamed to confess it) that I was discouraged at the slight attention the work received, and did not think it worth while.

Your letter has however once more fired my enthusiasm and it has decided me to begin the work at once.

If it should give a definite negative result then I think your very valuable suggestion concerning a possible influence of the vicinity of a rapidly moving body should be put to the test of experiment; but I too think the result here would be negative.

But is there not another alternative?

Suppose for example that the irregularity of the earth's surface be crudely represented by a figure like this:

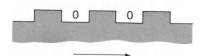

If the earth's surface were in motion in the direction of the arrow, would not the ether in the 0 0 [see diagram above] be carried with it?

This supposes, of course, contrary to Fresnel's hypothesis, that the ether does not penetrate the opaque portions, or if it does so penetrate, then it is held prisoner. Fizeau's experiment holds good for transparent bodies only, and I hardly think we have a right to extend the conclusions to opaque bodies.

If this be so and the ether for such slow motions be regarded as frictionless fluid—it must be carried with the earth in the depression.

Would this not be partly true, say in a room of this shape?

If this is all correct then it seems to me the only alternative would be to make the experiment at the summit of some considerable height, where the view is unobstructed at least in the direction of the earth's motion.

The Potsdam experiment was tried in a cellar, so that if there is any foundation for the above reasoning, there could be no possibility of obtaining a positive result.

I should be very glad to have your view on this point.

I shall adopt your suggestion concerning the use of tubes for the arms [of the interferometer] and for further improvements shall float the whole arrangement in mercury; and will increase the theoretical displacement by making the arms longer, and doubling or tripling the number of reflections so that the displacement would be at least half a fringe.

I shall look forward with great pleasure to your article on "Wave Theory" (hoping however, that you will not make it too difficult for me to follow).

I can hardly say yet whether I shall cross the pond next summer. There is a possibility of it, and should it come to pass I shall certainly do myself the honour of paying you a visit.

Present my kind regards to Lady Rayleigh and tell her how highly complimented I felt that she should remember me.

Hoping soon to be able to renew our pleasant association, and thanking you for your kind and encouraging letter,

> I am,
> Faithfully yours,
>
> Albert A. Michelson[10]

When Rayleigh's answer brought further encouragement, Michelson and Morley began work on the experiment that was to bring them lasting fame.

In April 1887, Morley wrote his father that he and Michelson had begun a new experiment, the purpose of which was "to see if light travels with the same velocity in all directions."[11] They also hoped to learn from the experiment the speed of the earth in orbit and in movement with the solar system; whether the ether was moving or stationary; and, most important to Michelson, some clear proof of the ether's actual existence, with which to confront the skeptics. The diagrams on page 127 represent two identical interferometers, one stationary, somewhere in outer space, and one in motion with the

(*Opposite*) Identical interferometers of the Michelson-Morley experiment, 1887

(*Upper*) Stationary: The ray of light *sa* is partly reflected in *ab* and partly transmitted in *ac*, returning from the mirrors *b* and *c* along *ba* and *ca*. These rays are reunited along *ad*, where they interfere.

(*Lower*) Moving: If the apparatus is moving with the speed of the earth in orbit in the direction *sc*, the ray *sa* is reflected along *ab* (not *ab*₁) and is returned along *ba*₁. The transmitted ray goes to *c* and

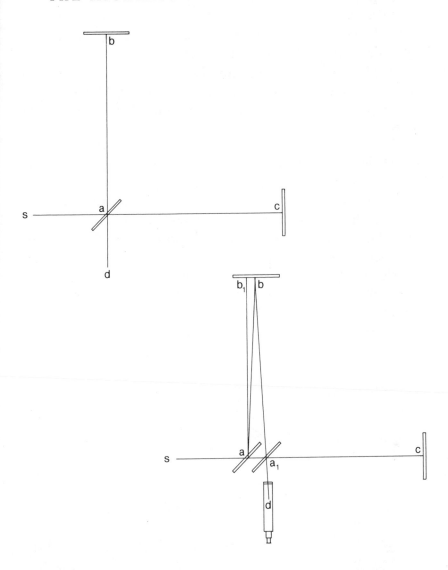

returns to a_1, where it coincides with the first ray along a_1d. The difference between aba_1 and aca_1 (a second-order effect) should have revealed the earth's speed. No such effect was observed, which showed that the speed of light is not affected by the motion of the apparatus through space.

earth. The problem was to find the difference in the paths of light traversing these two instruments.

Michelson and Morley were hopeful about their chances of measuring this difference in the light paths because of their success in repeating Fizeau's experiment of light in moving water.

Two changes improved the apparatus over the one used at Potsdam. Morley suggested floating the heavy sandstone slab bearing the optical parts on mercury. The stone, about 5 feet square, was mounted on a doughnut-shaped wooden block, which floated in a cast-iron trough containing the mercury. This method was economical and efficient, for the mercury-bearing removed practically all stresses and allowed the interferometer to glide smoothly around all points of the compass. Vibrations from outside disturbances, so troublesome in Berlin and even in Potsdam, were virtually eliminated.

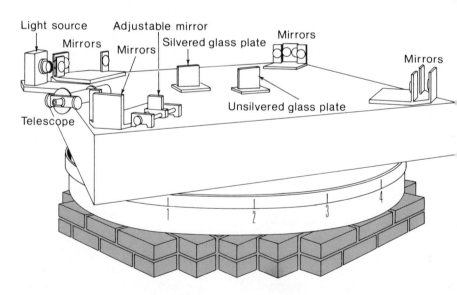

The Cleveland interferometer of 1887, mounted on a stone floating in mercury

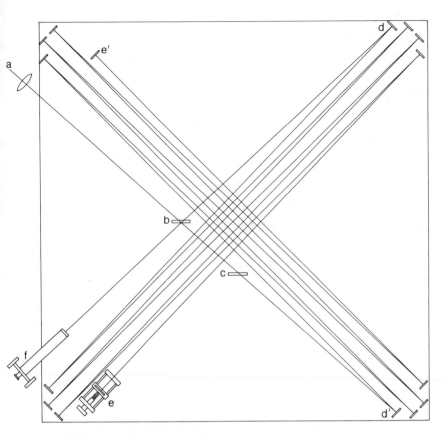

The paths of light in the 1887 interferometer

By using sixteen mirrors, instead of two as in the Potsdam experiment (see diagram, page 79), the light path was extended to 36 feet, thus increasing the sensitivity of the instrument tenfold. Light from *a* is split into two parts by the lightly silvered mirror at *b*. One ray is reflected to the plane mirror at *d* and is flashed back and forth between the four mirrors at *e* and at *d*. Retracing its path from *e* to *d*, it returns to *b* and is transmitted to *f*, the telescope. The second ray penetrates the mirror at *b*, is transmitted through *c* to *d'*, and is reflected between the mirrors at *d'* and those at *e'*, returning through *c* to *b*, where the interference may be examined as both rays enter the telescope at *f*.

(Diagrams on pages 127–129 adapted from Michelson and Morley, "On the Relative Motion of the Earth and the Luminiferous Ether," 1887)

With the new "interferential refractometer" Michelson and Morley were able to determine effects of the second order with an accuracy hitherto unobtainable. The second improvement lay in placing the mirrors so that the light was reflected over a path about ten times longer than that of the earlier experiment.[12]

While the stone, floating on its channel of mercury, turned steadily on its axis, one of them walked around it in a circle, keeping his eye on the moving eyepiece. The observer could not touch the instrument, nor could he for a moment lose sight of the interference fringes. It was tiring to watch these through the small aperture of the eyepiece, only about a quarter of an inch in diameter, and the physical, mental and nervous strain told particularly on Michelson. As Morley said later, '. . . patience is a possession without which no one is likely to begin observations of this kind."[13] The final readings were taken at noon, on July 8, 9, and 11 and near 6 p. m. on July 8, 9, and 12. They revealed no difference in the paths of light that could be interpreted as having been affected by the movement of the earth through the ether. Reluctantly, Michelson wrote to Rayleigh:

> The Experiments on relative motion of earth and ether have been completed and the result is decidedly negative. The expected deviation of the interference fringes from the zero should have been 0.40 of a fringe— the maximum displacement was 0.02 and the average much less than 0.01—and then not in the right place.
>
> As displacement is proportional to squares of the relative velocities it follows that if the ether does slip past [the earth] the relative velocity is less than one sixth of the earth's velocity.[14]

Michelson concluded, exactly as he had after the 1881 ether-drift test, that the ether surrounding the earth could not be at rest, as Fresnel had said it was, but must be whirling about, moving with the earth, so that it was not possib measure the speed of the earth against it.

The experiment had been eagerly watched, and as its impact struck the world of science, physicists reacted with astonishment and incredulity. However, reluctant as they were to accept the result, none of them thought of questioning either the experiment or the reliability of the verdict.

In the interim between the 1881 and 1887 ether-drift experiments, H. A. Lorentz had made a searching analysis of the whole problem. He worked out the mathematical transformations between the dimensions of a body at rest and one in motion. He explained the theory by comparing the space and time coordinates of a glass moving uniformly with the earth's motion with those of a glass at rest.[15] Space and time must readjust, much as they do everywhere on earth where men go by local time, derived from the time the sun reaches a given location, rather than by absolute stellar time as it is calculated at Greenwich, England. Lorentz pursued his transformations into the electromagnetic field and found that his equations showed complete invariance between events in the moving glass and the glass at rest. This theory seemed to eliminate completely any idea of an ether dragged into motion with the earth, a theory that Michelson clung to because it explained the negative result of his experiment. Lorentz's ether stood even more firmly at rest than had Fresnel's. However, when Michelson's experiment was repeated in 1887 with more accuracy and the same negative result, Lorentz's stationary-ether theory was shaken to an ominous degree. But he, in turn, could not accept the idea that the earth dragged the ether along. In 1892 he wrote to Lord Rayleigh:

> I am totally at a loss how to solve the contradiction and yet I believe that if Fresnel's wave theory is abandoned, we should have no adequate aberration theory at all. . . . Can there be some point in the theory of Mr. Michelson's experiment which has as yet been overseen [sic]?[16]

About 1892 George F. FitzGerald of Dublin visited Oliver Lodge in Liverpool to discuss the negative result of the Michelson-Morley experiment as well as the first-order effect of an ether-drift experiment that Lodge had made. FitzGerald said: "Well, the only way out of it that I can see is that the equality of paths must be inaccurate; the block of stone must be distorted, put out of shape by its motion . . . the stone would have to shorten in the direction of motion and swell out in the other two directions."[17]

Lodge reported the substance of this conversation in *Philosophical Transactions of the Royal Society of London* in 1893. A length of 8,000 miles (approximately the diameter of the earth), he wrote, would have to be shortened only 3 inches in order to account for the zero result of the experiment.

Lorentz came upon the same idea independently and embellished it with fervor. His hypothesis stated that every body which is moving at velocity v with respect to the ether contracts along the axis of motion by the factor

$$\sqrt{1-\beta^2} \;=\; \sqrt{1-v^2/C^2}\;[18]$$

This means that the earth is squeezed very slightly into an elliptical shape because of its motion in orbit; that a ruler is shortened if pointed in the direction of this motion; and consequently Michelson's interferometer underwent this same modification only on the leg that was pointed in the direction of the earth's motion, thus canceling any hope of measuring a positive effect.

For different reasons, Michelson and Lorentz both longed for a positive result for ether drift. Michelson's frustration came to some extent from the feeling that mathematicians were taking the question out of his hands into a realm beyond his comprehension whence they drew their own, somewhat preposterous conclusions. He wished the dogged little Dutchman would drop the matter and accept the fact that both of Michelson's ether-drift experiments had been miserable failures. The ether was out there, but at present his instruments were unable to detect its presence. Lorentz, however, was not in a mood to let go of such a lively issue. With bulldog determination he wrestled with it until his fertile imagination produced an astounding explanation, which others also endorsed —that "rigid matter" may not really be "rigid." By the turn of the century, physicists would be calling this hypothesis the "FitzGerald-Lorentz Contraction." The idea was so shocking that only mathematical physicists could read about it without recoiling from the implications. The contraction theory was one solution to the question, and by this ingenious explanation Lorentz had managed to keep his stationary ether intact.

Michelson's disappointment at the failure of the second ether-drift experiment was harder to bear than at that of his first attempt, which had left some hope of finding a positive result with a different method. One of Albert Einstein's biographers later explained this disappointment.

The famous Michelson-Morley experiment . . . proved conclusively that there are no different velocities of light! They are the same in all directions and their value is *c*, the speed of light, which strangely enough always remains true to itself, always constant, always unchangeable.
For the mechanist the result is catastrophic.[19]

Margaret, fearing another breakdown for her husband, urged Albert to go east with her and the children in August of 1887. There he could forget the whole problem and refresh himself at the seashore.

While he was in the East he attended a meeting of the American Association for the Advancement of Science and was elected vice president of the physics section in recognition of his original contributions.

On the Michelsons' return to Cleveland at the end of the summer they met with a shock. When they entered the house, Margaret saw at once that it had been robbed. She had left three servants there, all of whom had disappeared. A letter from Mary O'Dell, the chambermaid, blamed the robbery on the waitress and announced that she [Mary] had married the neighbor's coachman and gone to Chicago.

Margaret was shattered. Wedding presents and family heirlooms worth nearly a thousand dollars were missing—things she could never replace. The drawers of the chiffonier which had contained her monogrammed point de Venise lace underwear lay empty. Gone from her dressing table was the jewel box with its precious contents: earrings, brooches, a silver tiara with a diamond crescent, and a favorite glove buttoner of coral and gold which she had bought in Italy. With little opportunity to feel important in her husband's eyes, Margaret had substituted an outward show of opulence. The collection of pretty feminine furbelows on her travels abroad had become a consuming interest. Through the years she had lavished gifts upon her husband in a vain attempt to hold his interest. Michelson on his birthdays had received with cold politeness a sealskin cap, gold cufflinks, silver studs, and the alligator-tooth stickpin; these too were gone and she knew he would never miss them.

In a state of panic, Margaret called the police and began the difficult task of listing each of the stolen articles with its value. For two days the police questioned everyone who could throw any light on the robbery. They found that Mary O'Dell had a police record dating back several years. Her references, which Margaret had failed to check, were forged. She had been married four or five times, never bothering to get divorced, and she was registered under several false names.

On September 3, the thieving Mary and her latest bridegroom were discovered in Ravenna, Ohio, at the Etna Hotel where they were employed and there they were arrested. Margaret recovered most of her jewelry and underwear, but she was much shaken by the whole experience. Michelson refused to get excited about it. He made her go out to Ravenna alone to identify the thief and her possessions.

Nor was this the end of the Michelsons' troubles that autumn. No sooner had the business of Mary O'Dell been cleared up than Margaret hired a pretty, dark-haired, blue-eyed Irish girl who nearly succeeded in ruining Michelson's career at the Case School.

Ruth Whitfield, the maid, seems to have been a good-natured girl who would never have plotted to lay a trap. But evidently she confided to her sister-in-law, Emma Whitfield, that the Professor liked her very much indeed. Emma realized that the situation, combined with Mrs. Michelson's frequent absences from Cleveland, offered excellent opportunities for extortion.

Michelson and his wife were sitting in their drawing room one evening drinking after-dinner coffee when the butler announced that Ruth and another woman were in the kitchen asking to see Professor Michelson. Much to Margaret's astonishment, her husband shoved back his chair and went to the kitchen. The sound of angry, threatening voices made her follow him to the back door and there she heard him tell Ruth and Emma that he would pay them one hundred dollars if they would come to the laboratory on the following Monday morning.

Back in the living room Michelson told Margaret that Ruth and Emma were attempting to blackmail him. He immediately sought the advice of Professor Morley, who put him in touch with an attorney and volunteered to help him catch the blackmailers.

When Ruth and Emma arrived at the laboratory on Monday morning, Michelson was waiting for them with Morley and the attorney. When Ruth threatened to make trouble for the family unless she received a hundred dollars, two policemen, who had been listening in the hall, came in and put the two women under arrest on the charge of blackmail.[20]

Michelson heaved a sigh of relief. But his troubles were not over. That very evening, a constable came to the house with a warrant for his arrest and a sworn affidavit by Ruth Whitfield charging him with attempted seduction, assault, and battery, on given dates.

The scandal spread quickly over the campus, and the *Cleveland Leader* headlined it mercilessly on October 13, 1887:

MICHELSON ARRESTED AND CHARGED WITH ATTEMPTED SEDUCTION, ASSAULT AND BATTERY

Throughout the whole ugly episode Margaret kept her poise and behaved with dignity. In due course Michelson was completely exonerated by the court. Furthermore, President Staley and the board of trustees of Case School agreed to overlook the incident. Michelson was an important man in his field and he was also highly respected among the faculty.

After the disturbance subsided, Michelson resumed his work in Morley's laboratory. Reassembling the instruments rescued from the charred ruins of the Main Building, he began work on the analysis of "luminous emissions," or spectra, which he had studied in Bunsen's classes in Heidelberg. Michelson was looking for light of a "simple" nature represented by a single wavelength in the hope of finding an answer to one of the most important problems troubling the scientific world, that of finding an unalterable standard of length.

Michelson proposed to Morley his scheme for comparing the standard meter with the length of a light wave.[21] With Morley's help, Michelson undertook to look for a suitable element. On the wall he tacked a large chart of the Maxwell electromagnetic spectrum, or "gamut of radiant energy." At the time X rays, gamma rays, and violet rays, had not been discovered, and although Heinrich Hertz had generated "electric" or radio waves in 1887, this was still not commonly known. Michelson and Morley worked with a vapor lamp that burned zinc, sodium, mercury, cadmium, and other elements. Studying the visibility curves of these incandescent gases, they analyzed the structure of the spectral lines. In their search for the perfect wavelength they tested over a hundred lines. Many revealed too complex a pattern—that is, the burning element gave off light of several differing wavelengths. Their first choice was the sodium line. Charles S. Peirce had attempted to use the sodium line in his experiment with a diffraction grating,[22] a method that lacked the needed accuracy. Sodium gave off two pencils of light instead of one and was therefore called the sodium "doublet," but it served Michelson and Morley in their preliminary research. They designed an interferometer specifically suited to measuring the wavelengths of light given off by the heated vapor of these elements, and with it were able to measure one-tenth of a fringe's width with an order of accuracy of one part in two millions.[23]

In Paris, Dr. Benjamin A. Gould, a well-known astronomer and the American member of the International Committee of Weights and Measures, read in *The American Journal of Science* the paper on this work that Michelson and Morley had published. He was impressed with the accuracy of the new instrument and brought it to the attention of the committee.

The Bureau was searching for a constant unit of linear measure that would be unaffected by change in temperature or the passage of time, that would remain unaltered in all parts of the world, and that could never be destroyed. A prototype platinum meter bar, against which all other meter bars had to be checked, lay in a sealed vault in the Pavillon de Breteuil in Sèvres, near Paris. But not only was this bar, like all material objects, subject to destruction by war or natural calamities, it was subject to shrinkage and expansion with even the slight variations of temperature brought about by the body heat of any person standing near it. For the fine measurements needed by the new science it was altogether inadequate. The Bureau's director, J. René Benoît, through a friend in the United States Coast Survey, got in touch with Michelson and Morley by letter and suggested that they continue their analysis of the incandescent vapors until they found one from a homogeneous source to serve their purpose.[24] Michelson proposed to Gould that the sodium doublet might be used as a unit of measure, but investigations continued.

Work also continued on the "comparer," a specialized interferometer devised to compare a wavelength with the meter. Warner and Swasey, an industrial firm in Cleveland, built the instrument, and the optical parts were ground by John A. Brashear, the highly talented producer of lenses whom Michelson had met at Sir William Thomson's Baltimore lectures. He was fortunate in having this unusual man's interest and help. Brashear had started in life as a mill worker in Pittsburgh. In the hours after work he had made a lens and a telescope so as to observe the stars and found such joy and satisfaction in this avocation that he resigned from the mill to have time to improve his equipment and his ability. The astronomer and aeronautical pioneer Samuel Pierpont Langley interested him in aeronautics and encouraged him to continue his work with lenses and instruments. Soon Brashear was the most-sought-after man in his field, building telescopes for observatories in the United States, England, Canada, Ireland, Italy, and France. He now served on the board of directors of the Carnegie Institution, had become Acting Chancellor of the Western University of Pennsylvania, and counted among his friends leaders of industry such as Andrew Carnegie, Henry Clay Frick, Harry K. Thaw, George Westinghouse, Henry Phipps, and Charles M. Schwab.

Describing his work for Michelson in a letter to Edward Holden of the Lick Observatory, Brashear wrote:

> . . . we have completed two of the most difficult pieces of work ever undertaken by us. One was a set of 16 *plane* and parallel plates for Prof. Michelson for his research on the absolute value of a sodium wave length, and its transference to a steel bar in a freezing mixture, (i.e., multiples of the wave length) which is proposed as a new standard of measurement.

The limiting error allowed was .05 *sodium wave length* for every plate. . . . Hastings [who tested it] wrote us an unsolicited letter in which he said . . . that "it was the most perfect piece of optical work he had ever seen, and that nowhere else in the world could he have obtained it." . . . After Michelson tested them he used two adjectives—*"Exquisite"*—*"Superb"*—both underscored. So they must be good. . . .

It did take a vast amount of time to work and test them finally. You couldn't *look* at them [the fringes] without disturbing them. . . . [25]

The next meeting of the American Association for the Advancement of Science took place in Cleveland, beginning on August 15, 1888. The delegates were entertained with lawn fêtes and dinner parties. The Michelsons contributed to a fund which, among other things, provided fifteen carriages for the use of the visiting scientists. On one evening a special train took the delegates over the Lake Shore Railroad to the country estate of L. E. Holden, owner of the *Cleveland Plain Dealer*, where they dined.

On the morning of August 16 Michelson addressed the physicists as vice president of their group, Section B. The crowd attending his lecture overflowed the lecture room where he had planned to speak, and the lecture had to be moved to the general assembly hall. Michelson had announced the theme of his talk as "A Plea for Light Waves." He began with a tribute to the gigantic strides made in electricity during recent years, then mentioned some of the problems that light waves could solve and urged other scientists to work with interference fringes. It would soon be possible, he said, to use a light wave itself as a unit of measuring minute distances. It could be used to test the flatness of a plane or the volume of a cubic decimeter with an error of less than one part in a million.[26]

It is curious that he made no mention in this lecture of the ether-drift experiment. He may have felt a premonition that his experiment had put an end to the mechanical world with which he was familiar—this beautiful edifice, Sir James Jeans later called it, that, built on Newton's foundation, had stood for two hundred years, foursquare, complete, and unshakable. In any case, for Michelson in 1888 there was no cause for jubilation over the ether-drift experiment. He belonged to the earlier age of physicists who sought a definite answer to a definite problem. Some day, no doubt, an ether wind would still be discovered!

For the time being, Michelson had to content himself with the exquisite accuracy he had attained with the interferometer and the brilliant future that its application would open to astronomers. Two of these were in Michelson's audience, and in their minds his idea struck fire.

One was Edward Singleton Holden, an acquaintance of Michelson's from Annapolis days when they had worked at the Naval Observatory as Simon Newcomb's assistants. Through Newcomb, Holden had been appointed director of Lick Observatory in 1888 where he was making a name for himself with his beautiful photographs of the moon.

The other was George Ellery Hale, who was to be the founder of the Mount Wilson and Palomar observatories. Long afterward, Hale wrote:

> . . . I met him [Michelson] first at Cleveland in 1888 when in my student days I attended a meeting of the American Association for the Advancement of Science and listened with delight to his vice-presidential address before Section B. I had worked since boyhood in spectroscopy and was thus partially prepared to appreciate some of the limitless possibilities of the interferometer he described. Little did I realize, however, to what a point he would carry them in future years.[27]

Michelson and Morley made plans to carry out their work on the sodium doublet, but before these could be realized, their collaboration was ended by Michelson's departure from Case.

His reasons for leaving were manifold. Frustration dogged his life and work during the last years in Cleveland. Chiefly through lack of proper equipment, he was still greatly dependent on Morley's laboratory. The trustees had been unable or unwilling to appropriate adequate funds to replace the damage done by the fire of 1886. He grew restless and dissatisfied with his makeshift laboratory in temporary quarters. When a tempting offer came to him from G. Stanley Hall, the president of Clark University at Worcester, Massachusetts, he snapped it up.

Hall had been head of the psychology department at Johns Hopkins, where Michelson had met him during Thomson's lectures. In his younger days, Hall had studied in Germany. The stimulating atmosphere of the European university inspired him with the wish to bring this kind of culture to the United States. His ambition was to establish a college for graduate study only, where students could enjoy freedom from the cramped and stultifying routine then typical of American education.

With the backing of Jonas Clark, a millionaire furniture manufacturer, Clark University was founded along these lines. Hall had spent two glorious years culling a faculty of brilliant teachers, mostly scientists, from great universities in the United States and Europe. He promised them each a department to head, and, as an added lure, they were to be given time and space for original research in their chosen fields.

To Michelson's ears, this opportunity for a fresh start sounded almost too good to be true. He responded warmly to Hall's invitation and accepted the first Chair of Physics at Clark.

CHAPTER 7

Clark versus Hall

O N the chilly afternoon of October 2, 1889, Michelson attended the exercises marking the opening of Clark University. A glow of anticipation spread among the townspeople of Worcester who had gathered to watch the ceremony. On the dais, distinguished guests and trustees sat on either side of President Granville Stanley Hall and the founder, Jonas Clark. They were an impressive group: Senator George Frisbee Hoar, General Charles Devens, who was then attorney general of the United States and was to be a justice of the Massachusetts Supreme Court; John D. Washburn, member of Congress, later appointed minister to Switzerland; Stephen Salisbury, president of the American Antiquarian Society; the Reverend Dr. Edward Everett Hale, author of *The Man Without a Country*, who later became chaplain of the United States Senate.

A hush fell over the gathering as the president rose to

deliver the inaugural address. Hall had a gracious manner and the bearing of a New England aristocrat; among his ancestors he numbered John and Priscilla Alden and Elder William Brewster, who came to America on the *Mayflower*. He was a tall, well-built man of forty-five, who gave the impression of being thoroughly at home in the world. He delivered his speech in strong, rich tones accompanied by dramatic gestures, stressing the ideas to which he would hold throughout his years at Clark about the type of institution he wanted to build. The university must be of the highest and most advanced grade with special prominence given to original research. It was not to be a "graduate department," attended by so-called graduate students, in which most professors conducted undergraduate work, but a school for professors. Clark must eliminate college work, selecting rigorously the best students, seeking to train leaders only, educating professors, and advancing science by new discoveries.[1]

Hall ended his speech with unqualified praise for the founder who had donated a million dollars to the new university. Jonas Clark listened closely. He had a face that rarely changed expression. A native of Worcester County, Jonas had spent his childhood on his father's farm. At sixteen he had been apprenticed to a wheelwright and at twenty-one had gone into the manufacture of furniture and tinware. He soon began to accumulate a fortune by shipping miners' supplies and tools to California during the gold rush.

Clark was a frugal man. When his cargo of furniture was loaded at Boston, the crevices were filled with oats and barley and even the stoves were stuffed with bacon. Every cubic inch of space was utilized in order to make a profit on the costly charter of the clipper ship.

After Clark became rich, he and his wife made several trips to Europe, bringing home an ill-assorted collection of books, paintings, and statuary. They were described by people who knew them as a lonely, childless couple, wishing to enter the social life of Worcester and not knowing how to do so. Clark's shyness was particularly acute in the presence of the learned gentlemen on the dais. He had asked Washburn to read the speech which had been written for him.

Few people at the time realized the vast discrepancy between the aims of the president and those of the founder. Clark had little or no understanding of graduate study and remained suspicious of it. He had envisioned the university as a glorified high school, where the sons and daughters of the less fortunate citizens of Worcester could acquire knowledge and understanding of the culture and beauty which he and his wife had recently come to appreciate. Clark felt that he had gone more than halfway with the president. He had financed a two-year trip abroad, during which Hall had swung through all the capitals of Europe, studying European methods of teaching and hiring anyone he chose to head the various departments of the university. But Clark always secretly hoped that in time he could bring Hall around to the idea of teaching impoverished undergraduates.

Clark University began classes with a small, elite group of highly educated students, erudite enough to offer a real challenge to their instructors. Five subjects were to be taught: mathematics, physics, chemistry, biology, and psychology. Hall had selected the most gifted men he could find for the faculty. Among them were the mathematician, W. E. Story, who had been on the faculty of Johns Hopkins; Oskar Bolza, a German scholar and associate professor of mathematics; Michelson, in physics; Arthur Michael, professor of chemistry, a leader in his field; John Ulrich Nef, Michael's assistant. In the biology department were Charles O. Whitman of the biological laboratory at Woods Hole, a pioneer in zoology; F. P. Mall, in anatomy; W. N. Wheeler, fellow and assistant in zoology; Dr. George Baur, in paleontology; and Frank Lillie, a fellow in biology. In psychology, besides Hall himself, there was E. C. Sanford, a former pupil of Hall's at Johns Hopkins; in education, William H. Burnham; in neurology, H. H. Donaldson; as instructor in anthropology, Dr. Franz Boas, destined to become the leading American authority in his field; and in physiology, Warren P. Lombard.

The main building of the university left something to be desired. Clark had not consulted Hall or any of the professors regarding the design of the building. The structure that was to house the university was identical with the one erected for Clark's department store in downtown Worcester.

Michelson had his first disappointment when he realized that neither the funds for equipment of his laboratory nor the full-time mechanician Hall had promised him had materialized. He complained to Morley: "There is much to weary one —but that must be so in every new establishment—and I think within a year I'll be moderately comfortable."[2]

The prospect brightened when Frank L. O. Wadsworth came to Clark in the summer of 1889 as Michelson's assistant. Wadsworth had a degree in mechanical engineering from Ohio State University. He was twenty-two, full of ambition, and eminently qualified to help Michelson with the design and construction of instruments. They set about equipping the laboratory with stands and tables to support the delicate optical parts of the "comparer."

Michelson had brought with him from Cleveland the apparatus that he and Morley had devised. He missed Morley, because their association had been, by and large, a happy one, but he was also relieved to be working on his own again. During the first year of separation, he and Morley exchanged frequent letters. On December 3, 1889, Michelson wrote:

The papers came all right as also your welcome letter.
I can well understand how you must have felt about that thermometer—and hardly suppose you even *attempted* to find consolation in swearing. . . .
I am also sorry that I have to work alone at the "wave

lengths"—but if—as I hope when the time is ripe—there is a disposition to adopt the method either here or (more likely) in France—I shall of course advocate duplicate measures—in which case you will have your hands full.

I am not progressing very fast—cannot—in fact—for want of necessary laboratory facilities—which th[ough] not denied me are fearfully slow in materializing.

I have however sent Brashear plans (for estimates) for a modification of the "comparer" and hope to have it made for me by the University (The correspondence is carried on chiefly through the office—which B. probably finds extremely unsympathetic)

Hoping to hear from you soon and often and to have you stay with us in case you come East—and with kind regards to Mrs. Morley and remembrances to mutual friends. . . .[3]

And, again, on March 6, 1890:

Was very glad to receive your welcome letter and to rejoice in your successes and sympathize with your "misfortunes."

I've had a few of the last myself and know how it feels. One of the queerest of them was a mistake of Brashear's by which on the new refractometer he did everything beautifully but *put all the adjusting screws at the wrong end of the machine!*

I am working up the applications of interference methods to astronomical measurements and am confident of being able to *measure discs* with an accuracy of about one to two per cent where the telescope barely *shows* a disc.

Everybody works exasperatingly slowly here—but there is lots of time for research.

Hoping you are doing all you wish in your own work and expecting soon to hear from you again.[4]

When Morley decided to go to Worcester to see how the work on the comparer was coming along, his old friend seemed glad enough to see him. But when Morley looked over the setup and began making suggestions, Michelson told him pointblank that he intended to finish the experiment alone. This abrupt ending of the collaboration was a shock to Morley. He regarded Michelson highly both as a physicist and as a friend, and it hurt him to be summarily pushed aside from a work which had deeply interested him. But Michelson, fond as he was of his partner, had probably been wishing to extricate himself from the collaboration even before he left Cleveland.

There is no doubt that Michelson owed a debt to Morley over and above the real affection he felt for the man who had sustained him through the trials of the past several years. Morley had been his only friend through the period of his nervous breakdown, taking over the responsibility of completing the half-finished experiment of light in a moving medium. He had been a witness during the anguish of the blackmail threat and had placed his laboratory at Michelson's disposal when Main Hall burned. He had contributed the wisdom of his long experience, his superior knowledge of mathematics, and his faith in the importance of the ultimate outcome of their work, regardless of the negative result. It was only right that he should share the authorship.

On the other hand, Michelson had contributed the original idea of the ether-drift experiment, which had been made at a moment in the history of science when it proved decisive. He had invented the instrument that made it possible. He had raised the funds for the trial in Potsdam and the repetition in Cleveland. He had achieved the backing of Rayleigh and Thomson. He had also attracted the attention of Lorentz, who, inspired by the negative result, created the "Contraction Theory."

Michelson had matured since the beginning of his association with Morley and by this time he felt capable of going it alone, but he did not know how to extricate himself gracefully.

In situations of this kind, he showed a certain ruthlessness. Where his work was concerned, no relationship was considered. He could work better when he could take the full responsibility. In later years, however, he said, he could never tell exactly what he owed Morley.

Morley seems to have taken the disappointment philosophically, so that the friendship continued. Among their letters is one from Michelson in May 1891: "I am very glad to learn that you have received the money from the Smithsonian and it is of course pleasant to me to think that I may have assisted in the good work."[5]

Several weeks after the university opened in 1889, Michelson's wife and children arrived in Worcester. Margaret rented a splendid house, designed by the distinguished and fashionable architect Andrew Jackson Downing, who had laid out the grounds for the United States Capitol, the White House, and the Smithsonian Institution in Washington, D.C. The Michelsons' house, next door to President Hall's, was built of white clapboard in Victorian style. It had a steep gabled roof crowned with two handsome chimneys and a spire-topped lookout tower. Intricate fretwork under the gables dressed the house as if in lace for a party. Wide porches looked out over a carefully tended lawn, and a grove of tall chestnut trees framed the sparkling whiteness in cool green. Behind the house, a kitchen garden sloped down to a barn for the horse and carriage. Margaret felt more at home than she ever had in Cleveland. The faculty was composed of brilliant men, some of whom had attractive wives. Most of them had spent some time in Europe.

But the pattern that Michelson had established in Cleveland continued. Although he and Margaret maintained an outward façade of politeness, the gulf between them had widened, and Michelson spent most of the hours at home in his own suite of rooms. Margaret filled her life with social engagements and university activities. She entertained beautifully, but her own conversation dominated every gathering. She became aggressively talkative. This symptom had on Michelson the unfortunate effect of making him seek to avoid her on every possible occasion.

In her loneliness Margaret turned for comfort to her children. She played upon their sympathies to the point where they began to resent their father, and he, in turn, noticing their coldness, withdrew his affection. Describing her father at this period Elsa wrote: "My brothers and I saw very little of him. To us he seemed like a very important guest in the house. Wherever we lived, in my memory, he always had his own suite of rooms, but he was always with us at meals, unless some business of his interfered. My parents were unfailingly polite to each other, and we hardly realized that their relationship was not usual. To us our mother did not seem unhappy, though she must have suffered at the beginning of their drifting apart."[6]

Among themselves the children had a marvelous time. The Michelsons' back yard became the center of activity for faculty children. In the winter, young Albert sprayed the frozen walk down to the barn with water to make a slide. Sledding was excellent. In the summer, the swing was constantly in use, but the real attraction was the barn loft filled with Albert's pedigreed pigeons. There was a great deal of fluttering and excitement when he caught them in a net. He exhibited his prize fantails and tumblers in an agricultural show. Albert also kept bees, which he could handle skillfully without getting stung. Truman kept rabbits, which were less spectacular but which he dearly loved. He wrote a book about them, illustrated with his own woodcuts.

Elsa was a slender, beautiful girl with black hair that reached her waist. She was a great reader and lived in the world of books and imagination. Sometimes her mother had to drive her outside for fresh air and exercise. On weekdays she and her brothers rode to a private school in their pony cart.

Her playmates were President Hall's children, Bob and Julie. Julie was Elsa's age, a jolly, round-faced little girl with blond curls; her brother, a year or two older, was a gentle, imaginative boy somewhat overshadowed by his father's fire and verve. He admired Elsa extravagantly, but although she was very fond of Bob, she preferred Will Story, son of the head professor of mathematics, and gave him most of her attention.

Elsa's friends seldom saw her father, of whom they stood in awe. Albert and Truman gave them to understand that he was an inspired, aloof being, who must not be disturbed under any circumstances.

Michelson's powers of concentration, however, were such that he remained blissfully oblivious to the children's voices beneath his window as he sat at his desk preparing his weekly lecture on optics. In these lectures, he reviewed for his students the work which had been done in attempting to account for the phenomena of light propagation, reflection, and refraction. The course also included a series of lectures in theoretical optics, electricity, magnetism, and thermodynamics. Students with a fair knowledge of integral and differential calculus had no difficulty following the course. They showed good preparation in the blackboard recitations and quick comprehension of the derivations he developed in the classroom. Michelson used some of Henry Rowland's gratings in his demonstrations of the dark and bright lines in the spectrum. With these gratings he was able to identify the vaporized light of various elements according to the position of their spectral lines and to infer with almost absolute certainty the presence of a similar material in the light of the sun or any star which he examined.[7]

To illustrate this phenomenon, he set up an incandescent mercury lamp. Students would analyze the light with the grating, noting the distribution of bright and dark lines. When they discovered the same pattern in the spectrum of light from a star, they could be certain that mercury existed in that star.

In 1890, Arthur Gordon Webster, a New Englander with

a dash of Celtic blood, became docent (assistant) to Michelson in the physics department after four years of study in Europe, most of them spent in Helmholtz's class at the University of Berlin. In the anteroom outside Helmholtz's office where all prospective students were told to assemble, he had made friends with Michael Pupin, the inventor, and Joseph Ames, the Johns Hopkins physicist. "He had a beautiful baritone voice that rang like an organ," Pupin remembered, and he seemed to embody all the qualities that made Pupin, a Serbian, eager to become an American: ". . . heir to the noble traditions of New England and of Harvard. . . . It was through Webster that the full meaning of these traditions was first clearly revealed to me and for that I shall always be grateful to him."[8] At Harvard, Webster had been the foremost scholar in his class, not only in mathematics, his specialty, but as an all-around student. An excellent linguist, he was fluent and very well read in five modern languages and also had a thorough knowledge of the classics.

On the morning of May 15, 1890, the Michelsons were sitting around the breakfast table when they heard cries for help from President Hall's house next door. The Halls' maid came running across the lawn calling, "Dr. Michelson, Dr. Michelson!"

As he hurried back with her to the president's house, she explained that she had been unable to awaken Mrs. Hall and Julie, who were locked in the upstairs bedroom. She had pounded on the door and called them because their breakfast was cold on the table, but there was no answer. Dr. Hall was away on business. Michelson first tried breaking in the bedroom door, but as it was unusually solid, he could not open it. Bob, alone and bewildered, was much upset. Michelson fetched a ladder and climbed to the second-story window, which was tightly closed but not locked. As he raised it, he was appalled by heavy fumes.

On the bed, as if asleep, lay the lifeless bodies of Cornelia Hall and her pretty little daughter, Julie. The covers were not disarranged, and both of them appeared to be sleeping peacefully. Mrs. Hall was lying on her back, while Julie's face was half buried in the pillows. Michelson sent across the street for Dr. Adams, the family physician, who came at once. He gave each of them an injection to stimulate the heart. Together, he and Michelson carried Julie's body, still warm, over to the window and began administering artificial respiration, while a trained nurse, who had been sent from the Michelsons' house, and two more doctors worked over Mrs. Hall. But help had come too late. The victims had been asphyxiated by gas from an open jet.

Cornelia Hall had apparently pulled the cord of the gas burner to turn it off, and when it did not function, she pulled it again, turning it on. As the sparker did not light, the gas was left flowing. Young Bob was upstairs in his room, but Julie was sleeping in her mother's room because she had caught cold playing with soap bubbles, with which she had drenched her own bed.

Stanley Hall heard of the tragedy on his way home from the station. A coachman called out to his driver: "Tell that man his wife died last night." Upon arriving home, Hall was horrified to hear the news confirmed by his son.[9]

The Michelsons, along with the whole community, grieved over this tragic accident. Fortunately, the summer holidays were approaching and faculty members were leaving Worcester for various parts of the world. Boas went to the far Northwest and Alaska to make a study of the mores, language, and culture of the indigenous peoples. Dr. Baur went to the Galápagos Islands to study the curious fauna and flora of the area. The biology department under Whitman made the first study of the breeding habits and embryology of the American lobster. Dr. Nef was unhappily forced to spend the summer recovering from an explosion in the chemistry laboratory which left him temporarily blinded in one eye. Webster went to an electrical congress at Frankfurt, the meeting of the British Association for the Advancement of Science at Cardiff, Wales, and the opening of the Reichsanstalt (The Royal Institution) at Berlin. Hall was persuaded by friends to take a trip to Russia and Germany, on which Professor Bolza accompanied him. By autumn he was able to resume his duties at Clark.

CHAPTER 8

The Satellites of Jupiter

IN the fall of 1890 Michelson applied himself to what was for him an entirely new field—astrophysics. Astronomers at that time had pushed their stellar investigations close to the limit of their instruments. Poor seeing, or "boiling," inhibited further findings. Also, they had arrived at the limit of the telescope's resolving power—its ability to separate two objects at a great distance and make them visibly distinct one from the other—even with the aid of the spectroscope. Michelson discovered that the interferometer could be adapted so as to measure the diameters of very small and distant sources of light such as planetoids and satellites. Hitherto these had shown up only as points of light in the largest telescopes it was possible to construct.

To demonstrate the resolving power of the instrument, Michelson simulated in his laboratory a night sky with two tiny stars in it so close together as to be indistinguishable to the naked eye. These artificial stars were minute pinholes in a sheet of platinum with a bright light shining behind them. Two slits catching the light from these "stars" could be moved toward or away from each other by turning a screw. As Michelson gradually separated the slits that indicated the size of the star, the fringes grew less and less distinct. When the fringes disappeared entirely he could calculate the diameter of the "star," or the distance between artificial double stars, from the separation of the slits. The clarity of the fringes was the essential point.

If a sodium flame is used, it is quite easy to see the interference bands, even when the difference in path is several thousandths of a light wave. But in white light he had to get the two distances which the beams travel correct to 1/50,000 of an inch, and this he frequently did.

In its first form the interferometer had surpassed the microscope for measuring minute displacements. Now, the stellar interferometer was to transcend the telescope in measuring extremely small angles. It would begin to function where the telescope left off.[1] The gains were almost half again as accurate as those obtained with the microscope or the telescope.[2] From then on, Michelson's work was to center around the interferometer. Combining the mirrors and lenses in many different patterns, he could attack a variety of problems. He had an uncanny talent for making this equipment work. No one disputed its effectiveness, but when others attempted to use it they met with difficulties. It was said in later years that a Michelson interferometer was a marvelous instrument— when operated by a Michelson. He himself considered it his greatest contribution to science.

He was now ready to try out, on a celestial source, the method he had been testing with pinholes in a sheet of platinum, and to Edward C. Pickering, Director of the Harvard Observatory, he wrote:

July 6, 1890

I would like very much to spend a few hours at the great telescope—partly for amusement and partly for information—and would like to know if these summer evenings are too precious to be wasted in such an indefinite manner. If you can assure me that I will not be interfering with more important work, it would give me much pleasure to make you a visit at such a time as will best suit your convenience.

I have also a little matter to talk over which is to be publishedintheJuly *Phil. Mag.* [*Philosophical Magazine*] which will interest you, on the possibility of measuring star discs, etc., by interference method. (I read an abstract at the last meeting of the N.A. [National Academy] and was sorry to miss you there.[3]

This letter is typical of Michelson's low-keyed way of discussing his work, and it illustrated the manner in which scientists usually talk to each other. He showed a lifelong adherence to understatement.

A week later, when he had Pickering's consent, he wrote again:

July 14, 1890

If the day is clear and nothing unforeseen should happen I hope to start for Cambridge next Wednesday afternoon.

If that day should fail I hope it will not inconvenience you if I should select any of the following days of this week.[4]

That day, and many others, did fail as far as Michelson's sidereal measuring at Harvard was concerned; nevertheless, he planned to send his apparatus to Cambridge. There were more delays, however, and he waited a long time to hear from Pickering that at last the apparatus had been mounted on the telescope.

There must be something provocative about the satellites of Jupiter, for they have often been the focal point of a crucial discovery. Galileo, with the whole of the heavens to scan, focused his telescope on those satellites. Römer, by watching those same little moons disappear in eclipse behind their planet, concluded that light had a finite, measurable speed. The prosaic explanation is that they are well placed for observations, just what Michelson needed to test his instrument.

He spent the summer at Harvard Observatory, experimenting with the combination of telescope and interferometer. His young friend George Hale was assisting Pickering at the observatory. It was here that Michelson, the physicist, and Hale, the astronomer, began to see the possibilities of applying the methods of physics to the problems of astronomy. This union was cemented five years later in Hale's founding of *The Astrophysical Journal.*

During the first year at Clark, the atmosphere had been stimulating and the university had received wide acclaim. "Clark was a marvelous place," one student said, "and the work accomplished under its brilliant faculty was of a high order."[5]

But when the faculty returned from their summer vacations, there began to be signs of trouble and discord. The brief period of perfection enjoyed by the knights of Hall's Round Table was already in decline.

One source of irritation to Michelson was Clark's intrusion into the affairs of the physics department. The founder took it upon himself to order equipment for the laboratory and to give instructions to the men in Michelson's department without consulting him. The first time this happened, Michelson went straight to Hall and told him in no uncertain terms that if he wanted to keep a first-class physicist he would have to treat him as such.

In addition, the paper work was exhausting. Michelson had to write out a requisition for every nut and screw, stating its use. He urged the president to allow the professors the authority to order such small items on their own, pointing out that this was the plan followed in a number of other institutions. Hall was sympathetic, but he had a habit of agreeing with the person to whom he was talking, thus evading discomfort for the time being.

Professor Michael of the chemistry department complained of interference in his work and was summarily dismissed. There was no attempt to correct the injuries done him, no proper hearing of his case. This injustice caused other valuable men to leave the university.

President Hall remonstrated with Jonas Clark, but it was a ticklish thing to try to change the habits of the founder. It became increasingly difficult to persuade Clark to continue to support the highly specialized type of work to which Hall was dedicated. Sometimes the situation had its humorous aspects. Clark would drive out from Worcester in his carriage and, under the influence of Hall's charm and extraordinary powers of persuasion, agree to spend a sum of money on a particular program dear to Hall's heart. After Clark left, there would ensue a frantic scramble to put the idea into action before the founder changed his mind. Throughout these trials Hall maintained his lofty ideals, the courage of his deep convictions, and the staying power of Job.

It was, however, a losing battle. Clark became more and more evasive, failing to show up at board meetings, refusing to see the trustees, and finally withdrawing his financial support altogether. Hall was beside himself. The crisis meant dismissal of some men and drastic salary cuts for the others. He dared not tell anyone of the real shortage of money for fear that the whole scheme would blow up and he would have to face recriminations from the men who had trusted him. He preferred to describe the shortage as temporary, and even to himself he seemed unable to admit defeat. When dismissals took place, he claimed that the man had proved unsatisfactory, and when a man's salary was cut, a punishment was implied. These measures were practiced first among the laboratory assistants, instructors, and docents. The professors he gave to understand that, with a little patience, they would again receive their salaries. All would be well, perhaps, when Mr. Clark returned from Europe. Hall was extremely optimistic and managed to preserve his illusions long after the average man would have given up.

There was, of course, the possibility that Clark would die and leave his fortune outright to the university. But Jonas Clark had other plans for his fortune. By the end of the second winter, he felt that Hall had pushed him too far, and he made up his mind to retaliate. Calling in a lawyer, he wrote a codicil to his will, not excluding Clark University but stipulating that the president must be someone other than G. Stanley Hall if the university was to get his money.

Michelson found his only relief from this struggle in the prospect of getting away from Worcester in the spring. His work at Harvard Observatory during the summer of 1889 culminated in his paper "On the Application of Interference to Astronomical Measurements," which was published in *The London, Edinburgh, and Dublin Philosophical Magazine* of July 1890. It makes more skillful use of mathematics than any other paper he ever wrote.

Michelson had confidence in the feasibility of measuring the diameter of one of Jupiter's satellites but poor atmospheric conditions at Harvard and the procrastinations of Professor Pickering had spoiled the chances of getting accurate results. Michelson began to put out feelers in another direction.

He wrote to Edward Holden of Lick Observatory, enclosing two papers, one as yet unpublished, and asked if he might be allowed to try the experiment at Mount Hamilton, California. He received an enthusiastic reply and made plans to spend July of 1891 at Lick. He asked Holden to send him the exact dimensions of the 12-inch refracting telescope so that his apparatus could be mounted on top of it. The interferometer weighed 20 pounds, and it was necessary to compensate for this weight at the other end of the telescope. As a postscript he wrote:

> I should appreciate an offer from the Stanford [University] if it should come from them without solicitation, and I think it might be mutually advantageous and agreeable—but besides having an unconquerable aversion to asking for things I believe I should be in a better position to make my own terms if I waited for the other side to make an opening. If you think differently, please let me know.[6]

Michelson was not the kind of absent-minded scientist who ignores the world and its dealings. He knew how to apply his gaming sense and his knowledge of human nature to press his advantage at the strategic moment. This time, however, although Holden presented his name to the board of regents at Stanford, no offer followed.

Holden was particularly interested in having Michelson measure the satellites of Jupiter with his new method because four men, using the largest telescopes in the world, had obtained widely varying figures for their sizes. These actual micrometric measurements showed the satellites as having an angular diameter of approximately one second of arc, which would be easily measurable with the interferometer.

Michelson anticipated with pleasure working in the cool, clear air of the California mountains where he had spent his childhood. As soon as he heard that his apparatus had arrived at Lick Observatory, he took a train, alone, for San Francisco, arriving there toward the end of June 1891. Atmospheric conditions on Mount Hamilton made trouble, so that out of the three weeks Michelson spent there only four nights were clear enough for observations. But one of these was almost perfect and on that one night most of the measurements were made. The results were satisfying. Even a 6-inch glass, Michelson found, could obtain measurements which were as accurate as those obtained by the largest telescopes known.

Michelson's underlying idea with this experiment was not only to measure the diameters of satellites and planets, although these were interesting sidelights. His real ambition was to measure the diameter of a star. The nearest of these is so far away that it takes light several years to reach the earth.

While Michelson was working on Mount Hamilton, he was lucky enough to find Dr. Holden in a genial and friendly mood. This was not always the case. He had been warned by Brashear and Mendenhall that Holden was sometimes very difficult. If a disagreement arose between him and his staff, he sometimes refused to communicate with them. Mendenhall, during a visit on the mountain, had been asked to carry messages back and forth between the enemy camps.

Michelson, however, found the astronomer most entertaining. Holden had a wide range of interests, as any protegé of Newcomb's was bound to have. In collaboration with Newcomb, he was already at work on a book about the Mogul emperors of Hindustan and later he wrote a book on Sir William Herschel and one on Galileo. Like Newcomb, Holden had been educated by the military, graduating from West Point in 1870.

Holden was responsible for the founding of the Astronomical Society of the Pacific, and in August 1891 Michelson, at his request, read a paper on the measurement of the diameter of the satellites of Jupiter before the society.

Before leaving San Francisco, Michelson paid a surprise

visit to his parents, who had not seen him for five years. They hastened to tell him the family news. Bessie had married Arthur McEwen in 1883. Their life was stormy, unpredictable, but never dull. All Albert's brothers and sisters except Ben seemed to be caught up in the world of journalism. Charlie was working for Hearst on the *San Francisco Examiner.* He had a ringside seat at every San Francisco happening. He wrote about murders on the waterfront, opium dens in Chinatown, scandals involving the politicians, and feuding among the tycoons of the West.

Charlie had been brought up on stories of the accomplishments of his serious-minded brother, but he would never admit to being in awe of anything. "This nonsense about light and the ether, Al, why do you mess around with it?" asked Charlie. "I just enjoy it," came the cool answer.

When the summer was over, Michelson returned to Worcester. He found in his pile of mail a letter from Commodore William M. Folger, a gunnery officer in the Bureau of Ordnance. Because Michelson had patented a design for a range finder,[7] he was asked to report on a range finder designed by his old Naval Academy friend, Bradley Fiske. Fiske's range finder was in use aboard three U.S. Navy ships and had been tested on a French man-of-war. After studying the report, Michelson began to suspect that a far more accurate instrument could be designed. Folger encouraged him to build a model, which he proceeded to do.[8]

The instrument consisted of a tube with a rotating lens like an eye at either end. When these "eyes" were brought into focus on a target at sea, the distance was easily reckoned, and guns could be trained on the target with great accuracy. When the model was ready, he took it to Annapolis and tested it from the deck of a small launch on the Severn River. Michelson's range finder had several distinct advantages over Fiske's. It needed no electrical outlet, it was readily transportable, and the operator could hold it in one hand while his other hand focused the prisms on the target.

However, using the range finder on board a vessel in a heavy sea was far more difficult. Michelson found it impossible to hold the instrument steady long enough to observe the images in the field and to bring the rays parallel. The short, quick motion of the launch was more difficult to deal with than the slower motion of a larger vessel. Any movement presented a problem.

Michelson agreed to make certain changes. He would reduce the weight from 8 pounds to 4 so that the observer could more easily balance it in his hands. The mirrors and lenses were to be enclosed in a tube, and the apertures were to be made watertight.

Returning to Worcester, Michelson made arrangements to patent his "telemeter," as he called it. Brashear was given instructions for building the new model. While this was being done, Michelson's attention was drawn to more pressing problems.

His classes went along as usual, but the discontent among the faculty had begun again. A crisis threatened the school with total disintegration. Mall and Lombard were the first to suggest that the only hope of saving the university lay in speaking their minds with frankness. They conferred with Donaldson and Whitman and decided to demand a meeting of the president with the heads of all departments in order to state their views and find out what rights they had.[9]

The movement gathered momentum during the winter when Michelson and Boas joined the rebels, and on the evening of January 14, 1892, they held a secret meeting at Donaldson's house. Each man stated the injustices he had endured. Great pains were taken to stress positive views as to how the institution could be saved, and it was urged that no one should join in the movement who did not do so in the best interests of Clark University.

Boas, Whitman, and Donaldson all complained that the salaries of their helpers had been curtailed, and Michelson was particularly angry over the treatment of his laboratory helper, whom Hall had dismissed without consulting him.

Another sore point was the ordering of books. Hall took this task upon himself, and although he was capable of doing it for his own department of psychology, it was presumptuous of him to prescribe for the needs of other departments. Although Nef, Sanford, and Bolza had been appointed to the library committee, they had never been consulted or asked to order a single book.

The professors further complained that they were governed by a set of unpublished rules, manufactured according to Hall's whims. No one wanted the unpleasant task of presenting President Hall with an ultimatum, but Michelson was given the assignment. He was to make three requests:

1st   All the rules must be published.
2nd The faculty members must be permitted to call a meeting, when two or more so desired.
3rd   Each member must be allowed to introduce whatever subjects he chose for mutual discussion.

In the event that Hall suggested an intention to resign as president, Michelson was to express regret and the hope that another solution might be found.

Michelson spent two hours alone with the president in which he presented these requests as tactfully as possible. Hall behaved like a martyr about to be thrown to the lions.

Realizing that he could never convince Hall of the justice of the requests, Michelson gave up trying. But he did ask that some means of direct communication be established between the faculty and the trustees. Hall did not intend to let that happen.

Michelson persuaded him to call a faculty meeting, which everyone attended. President Hall, with disarming humility asked for a frank and open discussion of all the troubles and promised to receive what was told him without resentment.

When Michelson started to speak Hall interrupted: "Are you speaking for yourself or in behalf of all the others?"

"I believe I am speaking for all of us, Dr. Hall, but I hope that anyone present will correct me, if necessary."

Michelson then brought up the same points which he had presented privately, asking whether the president would call a meeting if two or more members of the faculty requested it.

"I cannot see the slightest objection. Have I ever failed to do so?" Hall's attitude was one of surprise that such unnecessary questions should be asked.

Michelson inquired if the faculty would be allowed to bring up subjects for discussion at these meetings. Hall indicated bewilderment: "I am completely in the dark and I demand a statement of grievances from each individual."

Finally, Donaldson, urged by the president, said, "The fact is, Dr. Hall, we have no confidence in you on account of your two-sided statements." All except Story and Sanford agreed with Donaldson's accusation, citing broken promises and unjustifiable interference. Michelson told the president that this multitude of petty grievances was the cause of the discontent.

"Do you want to see the president of this University humiliated?" Hall asked.

The meeting broke up without any real progress. Outside in the corridor Donaldson and Story nearly came to blows. That evening Story left a card at Michelson's door with a request for a private meeting. Michelson brought him a copy of the propositions. Story's attitude showed that the president was making a counterattack.

When the faculty next met with the president, Hall questioned their right to bring up a subject for discussion but declared, "I am at your service, gentlemen of the committee, or however I may call you."

Michelson objected, "We are not a committee but a faculty." This Hall denied. He insisted that no action could be taken because this was not a regular faculty meeting. Michelson began to lose patience with Hall's hair-splitting. He called for a vote on the propositions, and these were duly passed. The president then said, "In view of your action, I can meet you as gentlemen but not as a faculty," whereupon Whitman rose and said, "Sir, I, for one, shall withdraw." On this note the meeting terminated.

In the following days both Michelson and Whitman talked to the president alone, trying to make him see reason. They encountered the same evasive, stubborn attitude. Donaldson then called an evening meeting to which he invited Dr. Hall. Hall refused to come. Donaldson, Michelson, Whitman, Nef, Mall, Lombard, Bolza, Boas, and Baur were present. All agreed that their efforts to save the university had been brought to nothing because Hall had refused to meet them officially or to hear their complaints. He had placed them in the role of conspirators.

Michelson said, "I can see no other course open but to resign, and this I shall do." Each of the others expressed the same intention. They drew up a document:

Jan. 21st, 1892

To President G. Stanley Hall,
Sir:–

The undersigned Officers of Instruction request the President to transmit to the Board of Trustees of Clark University, the following communication:–

Owing to the lack of confidence in the President of Clark University, the undersigned Officers of Instruction hereby tender their resignations, to take effect Sept. 1st, 1892.

Albert A. Michelson   Prof. of Physics.
C. O. Whitman . . .   "   " Zoology.
Henry H. Donaldson   Asst. Prof. of Neurology.
Warren P. Lombard   " " " Physiology.

John Ulric Nef	. . .	Asst. Prof. of Organic Chemistry.
Franklin P. Mall	. .	Adjunct. Prof. of Anatomy
Oscar Bolza	. . . .	Associate Professor of Mathematics.
G. Baur	. . . . . .	Docent in Comp. Osteology and Paleontology.
Franz Boas	. . . .	Docent in Anthropology.

The following morning, Michelson gave this communication to the clerk of the university. The key figures in the rebellion then waited anxiously for the reaction of the trustees.

When Edward Cowles, chairman of the board, received this startling document, he called a meeting of the trustees for Saturday, January 30. The trustees found themselves in a very difficult situation. They were dealing with a keg of dynamite. To begin with, the founder seemed to have left them in the lurch. His original endowment had been supplemented by $50,000 the second year, but his gifts thereafter had dropped to $12,000, and everyone feared that he might even disinherit the university entirely. The professors, in the trustees' view, all resembled prima donnas, each wanting to play the leading role. Even Hall, who had selected them, could not get on with them. They concerned themselves only with abstract science. The peculiar activities carried on in the name of education had alarmed the townspeople of Worcester. Boas had measured the heads of several hundred townsfolk to compare them with the heads of savage tribes of the Northwest. Donaldson was running electric currents through the dead brain of Laura Bridgeman, a criminal who had been electrocuted, and the biologists were examining a human embryo twenty-seven days old. Vivisection of animals had received some extremely hostile publicity. No one understood what the physicists were doing, but it was certainly not useful training to enable young men to earn a living.

Echoes of these rumors had been troubling the trustees for some time, but the immediate problem was the rebellion of the faculty against the president. Cowles was an authority on mental disease and later became the founder of the first laboratory in the world for the vital study of conflicts of the mind. His sympathy lay with Hall, a psychologist closely related to his own field, who had undergone deep tragedy and was now faced with an insoluble situation. He was able to convince the other trustees of the urgent necessity of giving Hall an unqualified endorsement. If Hall's authority were undermined, he would be useless in the position of president. A letter of confidence was therefore delivered to Hall, but at the same time he was privately urged to bring the rebels back into camp if this could be done without losing face.

The trustees had given Hall full power to act upon the tendered resignations in any way he deemed advisable. Once this position was established, Hall began his last attempt to reconcile the professors and save his university. His eloquence was such that Michelson and Whitman reconsidered their decisions. The rest followed their example. A truce was declared and the document of mass resignation was destroyed.

How long this peaceful interval would have lasted if Hall and the professors had been left alone to work out their destiny with the founder is purely guesswork, for into the fragile structure of their unstable relationship swept a human hurricane in the shape of William Rainey Harper. With John D. Rockefeller behind him, Harper was scouting for talent to staff the new University of Chicago. He had received a doctorate in philosophy from Yale at the age of eighteen, and at thirty-two he became the first president of the University of Chicago. A short stocky man with a jovial appearance, he had a broad nose, a plump face, and dancing eyes that sparkled with enthusiasm and energy, even through the heavy lenses of his glasses. When rumors reached him of the discontent at Clark, he lost no time in getting to Worcester. Whitman invited Michelson and the other heads of departments to his house, and here Harper met and engaged, in one morning, the great majority of Clark's scientists. He promised them new laboratories in beautiful surroundings, fitted with every possible convenience, the best equipment, books, laboratory assistants and helpers. Chicago was a big city with fine libraries, medical schools, and many advantages that were lacking in Worcester. Of the sixteen scientists at Clark, all but four accepted Harper's offer.

Notably absent from the list of dissenters is the name of Arthur Gordon Webster. He was not of professorial rank and would not have been included in a meeting of the heads of departments. Whether he declared his loyalty and refused to leave, or whether he was not given the opportunity, the records do not reveal.

The end came when Harper walked into Hall's office and broke the news that he had engaged most of the faculty for Chicago. He had the impudence to conclude with an offer to Hall of the chair of psychology at double his present salary. At this, the tall New Englander rose to his full height, shaking with indignation, and invited his guest to leave the office immediately. Harper, shrinking under the force of Hall's bitterness, left the room. It was not long before Hall was besieged by reporters, and the newspapers broke the story. The attitude of the Worcester papers and the Boston *Globe* angered Michelson. On May 6, 1892, an open letter appeared in the *Worcester Gazette:*

> In view of the misleading statements circulating through the press to the effect that men are deserting Clark University from mercenary motives, it may be of some interest to University circles to learn that according to the testimony of all the gentlemen concerned, this is a mistake which does them great injustice. It is, let us hope, unnecessary to go further into details than to state that Dr. Lombard, the head of the physiological department,

has resigned while his plans for the future are as yet wholly undetermined. One important resignation from the mathematical department, that of Dr. Bolza, occurred under somewhat similar circumstances. It is well known here that Drs. Boas, Donaldson and others announced their intention to leave quite independently of inducements or opportunities offered elsewhere.

It is due to Mr. Clark as well as to the able staff now leaving the University to say that neither financial difficulties here nor pecuniary inducements offered by·President Harper have prompted and decided this wholesale exodus from a University whose lofty ideals have had from the beginning the enthusiastic and self-sacrificing devotion of every member of the faculty.

C. O. Whitman
A. A. Michelson

Michelson's arrangement with Harper was a loose one, for no salary had been mentioned between them. Harper had been considering Henry Rowland, in some respects more suitable than Michelson, but he chose the younger, less eminent man.

In the ensuing months, there were still more resignations. Hall, like a defeated general, gathered up the few who were loyal to him. Only two men of full professorial rank remained. After his first explosion with Harper, Hall bore the calamity silently and with grace. "We closed up the ranks as best we could," he wrote in his autobiography, "and settled down in a spirit of exceptional harmony and close fellowship"[10] to make the best of the depleted staff and limited activities.

Albert A. Michelson, about 1928

Commemorative plaque at Michelson's birthplace in Strzelno, Poland

Murphy's Camp, California, in 1852 (KENNETH M. CASTRO)

Rosalie Michelson, Albert's mother, at about fifty (from a pencil sketch)

Albert and his sister Julie, about 1862

Albert, as a First Classman at the U.S. Naval Academy, making a self-portrait
(COURTESY U.S. NAVAL ACADEMY MUSEUM)

"Double Diamond" Michelson—
the insignia indicates the
cadet-officer rank of First Captain
(COURTESY U.S. NAVAL ACADEMY
MUSEUM)

BELOW LEFT. Simon Newcomb,
the distinguished astronomer
who befriended young Michelson
(NATIONAL ACADEMY OF SCIENCES,
Biographical Memoirs, VOL. XVII)

Margaret Heminway Michelson,
Albert's first wife

Michelson in 1887, at the time of the
Michelson-Morley experiment
(COURTESY CLARK UNIVERSITY ARCHIVES)

Edward W. Morley, professor of chemistry at Western Reserve University,
partner in the experiment
(LIBRARY OF CONGRESS COLLECTIONS)

The interferential refractometer of the Michelson-Morley experiment (COURTESY
HALE OBSERVATORIES)

Granville Stanley Hall, first president of Clark University (COURTESY CLARK UNIVERSITY ARCHIVES)

Jonas Clark, Worcester, Massachusetts, businessman who founded the university (COURTESY CLARK UNIVERSITY ARCHIVES)

George Ellery Hale as a young man

The Etruscan seal of which Ogden Rood gave Michelson a replica (THE METROPOLITAN MUSEUM OF ART, GIFT OF JOHN TAYLOR JOHNSTON, 1881)

The Michelson house in Worcester (COURTESY CLARK UNIVERSITY ARCHIVES)

A donkey at Sèvres, France, sketched by Michelson in his own copy of his paper "La Valeur du mètre en longueurs d'ondes lumineuses"

Watercolor of the Seine, painted by Michelson in 1892

F. L. O. Wadsworth, Michelson's assistant at Clark and again at Chicago (COURTESY CLARK UNIVERSITY ARCHIVES)

S. W. Stratton, assistant at Chicago, who became director of the National Bureau of Standards (COURTESY NATIONAL BUREAU OF STANDARDS)

Laboratory assistant Fred Pearson, with the harmonic analyzer designed by Michelson and Stratton (PRESS ILLUSTRATING SERVICE)

Henry A. Rowland with his ruling engine (PORTRAIT BY THOMAS EAKINS, ADDISON GALLERY OF AMERICAN ART, PHILLIPS ACADEMY, ANDOVER, MASS.)

Lord Rayleigh and Lord Kelvin in the laboratory at Rayleigh's estate, Terling, in 1900

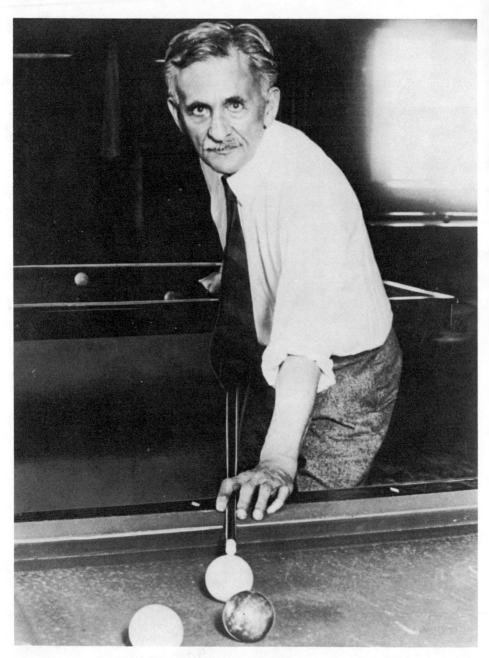

Billiards champion at the Quadrangle Club, Chicago (ACME)

Edna Stanton Michelson, with Domino

Michelson relaxing; at left, his oldest daughter, Madeleine; center, Dody, the youngest

Dody and her father at Desbarats, Ontario, Canada, where the family spent the summers

Beatrice, the second daughter

Ryerson Laboratory at the University of Chicago

Lullaby for Madeleine, composed by her father (ACME)

A sample of Michelson's laboratory notes (dated October 3, 1899)

Took careful observation of Zeeman effect with green Hg with following Result:— Vibr. parallel field.
open.

E ?   abc de

That is, the satellites' middle line of the Zeeman triplet is doubled — whereas the chief line is tripled. The distance between components de is (roughly) the same as ac (too small in drawing). Could not observe well in perp. dir. on account of overlapping.

Tried to resolve chief line but without success. It is readily seen however that width is about twice that of satellite, and roughly one tenth E. Distance from satellite was 0.7 E (or 0.6 E ?)

4 P.M.

Reexamined Hg. g. with 25 El. 30 cm. (III) Echelon and found it appeared as a unsym. double with dist. bet. comps. apx. 1/10 E. but a prism showed the supposed companion was the yellow line.

The Nobel medal; left, obverse; right, reverse

Albert A. Michelson; portrait by Bosco Craig, about 1910

The stellar interferometer mounted on top of the 100-inch telescope at Mount Wilson Observatory (COURTESY HALE OBSERVATORIES)

The ether-drift experiment at Clearing, Illinois. Left to right: Charles Stein, Tom O'Donnell, Fred Pearson, Dr. Henry Gale, Joe Purdy, unknown man

Michelson with his "she devil," the ruling engine at Ryerson Laboratory

The vacuum-tube experiment on the Irvine Ranch near Santa Ana, California, 1931 (ACME)

The assembly of scientists at the Solvay Congress in 1921; left to right, front row: A. A. Michelson, P. Weiss, M. Brillouin, E. Solvay, H. A. Lorentz, E. Rutherford, R. A. Millikan, Madame Curie; second row: M. Knudsen, J. Perrin, P. Langevin, O. W. Richardson, J. Larmor, H. Kamerlingh Onnes, P. Zeeman, M. deBroglie; third row: W. L. Bragg, E. van Aubel, W. J. de Haas, E. Herzen, C. G. Barkla, P. Ehrenfest, M. Siegbahn, J. E. Verschaffelt, L. Brillouin

Plaque on the pier where the rotating mirror was mounted in the 1924 velocity of light experiment at Mount Wilson (COURTESY HALE OBSERVATORIES)

Michelson congratulating Arthur Holly Compton on receiving the Nobel Prize, 1927

Michelson with Robert A. Millikan in Pasadena (COURTESY HALE OBSERVATORIES)

CHAPTER 9

Convocation in Chicago

W HEN Chicago University opened its doors in the fall of 1892, Michelson was not there to celebrate the occasion with his colleagues. Instead, he was dining in a Paris restaurant, drinking a pleasant, full-bodied French wine.

An invitation from the International Bureau of Weights and Measures had materialized at a time when he was delighted to extricate himself from the turmoil at Clark. It resulted from his discovery that the spectral lines of an incandescent cadmium vapor, more suitable than sodium, might be used as an unvarying unit of measure.

In January 1892, President Hall had received a letter from Benjamin A. Gould, the American representative at the last meeting of the Bureau, with whom Michelson had corresponded some years earlier. Gould asked that Michelson be released from his duties to come to Sèvres. There he was to measure the meter in terms of cadmium light waves in an attempt to establish a nonmaterial international unit.

January 17, 1892

Dear President Hall,

. . . The proposed investigation is a magnificent one; audacious, yet already proved by Professor Michelson to be feasible. The honor inuring to our country by the selection of an American Professor to carry it out, and an American artist for constructing an apparatus requiring such surpassing delicacy, is one which I am confident you will appreciate as highly as I do. . . .

It is my conviction that the assent of Clark University will not only redound to its high honor, and be gratefully recognized throughout the civilized world, but will constitute an unending title to remembrance, and full appreciation in the history of science. It seems to me a just source of pride that our country should be called on to take the chief part, both scientific and technical, in such an undertaking, and I will not deny that I am considerably elated by it.[1]

Hall granted permission as a matter of course, and the trustees contributed Michelson's time and salary to the undertaking for six months. The indispensable Wadsworth was to go along.

Michelson had few regrets at leaving Worcester. However, his anger at Hall had abated. He remembered times when Hall had shown real cooperation and understanding for the needs of the physical laboratory. Not long before, in order to improve the facilities at Clark and to inform himself on the nature and methods of research being carried out in British and European universities, Michelson had wished to send Wadsworth on a tour of inspection. The cost of such a trip, $500, was apparently more than Hall could justify to the trustees. He had suggested that he and Michelson share the expenses and they had agreed to put up $250 apiece of their own money.[2] The trip, however, never materialized.

When Michelson accepted the position in Chicago, he arranged to take Wadsworth with him after they had finished their work in Paris. But just at this time Wadsworth received an offer from the Smithsonian Institution in Washington to work on the pioneering design and construction of Samuel P. Langley's new flying machine, then called the aerodrome. The lure of this opportunity proved irresistible to Wadsworth. It would not interfere with the work in Sèvres, he told Michelson. In fact, the Smithsonian agreed to defray his expenses on the voyage over and back as well as to pay his salary during the six weeks he would be assisting Michelson. The meter measurement would not be set back. But this was small consolation to Michelson for the permanent loss of his valuable assistant. He was thoroughly annoyed by this turn of events and left Worcester without even saying good-by to his friends. Arthur Webster reported to his wife that Michelson had gone off "mad as a hornet."[3]

The Michelsons sailed on the steamer *Bourgoyne* for Le Havre on July 9, 1892. Wadsworth would follow in August. Dr. Benoît, the head of the International Bureau, had offered to meet Michelson at the dock and had suggested that Michelson stand near his luggage and boxes, which should be clearly marked with his name. Michelson replied that he would certainly do this but that he thought Benoît would recognize him immediately by the difficulties he would encounter explaining the purpose of the interferometer to the customs officials.[4]

Michelson went directly to Sèvres to start work, and Margaret took the children to London. There they waited a long time, for Michelson had neglected to inform the Bureau that he was bringing his family and therefore no accommodations had been arranged for them.

When he finally sent for them, he installed them in Paris while he continued his work at a comfortable distance. Margaret and the children were growing accustomed to these arrangements. She took a suite of rooms in the Hotel Scribe and entered the boys in a good French school. They boarded during the week and returned to her on weekends. On their first day of school, Albert and Truman reported triumphantly they had "licked a count, a marquis and another 'swell' " whose title they could not recall. Elsa was proud of her brothers. They were not quarrelsome boys and never picked a fight, but when someone provoked them, they knew how to defend themselves. Michelson had seen to it that they were taught to box at an early age.

Elsa was taken to a day school in a horse-drawn bus. The first week of classes was lost upon her because, as she said, "Everyone spoke French!" But after a while she settled down to her studies and the school made quite a pet of her. When the teacher asked her what her father did for a living, she replied, "He makes experiments."[5]

The Pavillon de Breteuil, where Michelson was carrying out his work, stands at the entrance to the Parc de Saint-Cloud. It was built in the seventeenth century for Louis XIV's brother, the duke of Orléans.

The main Château de Saint-Cloud, about which much French history has revolved, was destroyed in 1870 during the Franco-Prussian War. The little Pavillon escaped with only superficial damage and in 1875, it was presented by the French government to the newly formed International Bureau of Weights and Measures.

Until the metric system was officially adopted after the French Revolution, each separate department of France had

had its own standards and methods of weighing and measuring produce. People were as reluctant then as they are today to change from familiar ways, and the old weights continued to be used, with a little added here and something else subtracted there. In 1840, a law was finally passed outlawing all measuring units except those of the metric system.[6]

At the Paris Exposition in 1867, a Committee on Weights, Measures, and Moneys invited industrialists and scientists from many countries to participate in choosing a standard of linear measurement. They unanimously selected the meter, based on a fraction of the earth's circumference. This was not a very reliable standard, because the earth's circumference changes with every earthquake. But the committee was satisfied with a meter equal to one ten-millionth of that fourth of the earth's meridian at the Pavillon de Breteuil, and, the new International Bureau of Weights and Measures moved into its home at Saint-Cloud.

A metal bar was constructed of an alloy containing platinum, iridium, and palladium. On this bar, ×-shaped in cross section, the lines marking the limits of the "perfect" meter were ruled. The bar itself was kept in a sealed vault where temperature changes could be held to a minimum. Copies of the meter were distributed to each member nation, and from time to time these were checked for accuracy against the original.

Although these precautions seemed more than adequate for the research of the 1870s, scientists soon feared the original meter might be destroyed by a bomb if war broke out. Temperature fluctuations were another source of concern; even the body heat of a technician making the necessary comparisons raised the room temperature by several tenths of a degree. In 1892, the Bureau turned to Michelson, hoping that the work he had done in measuring the wavelength of various gases would produce a standard of length that would remain forever constant and could not be destroyed.

Upon his arrival, Michelson was warmly greeted by Benoît, who had arranged that a room be prepared according to Michelson's specifications. Michelson had asked that it should be provided with dark curtains or shutters, an incandescent overhead lamp, two Bunsen burners, a small glass-blower's table with foot bellows attached, and a mercury lamp in good working order. In addition, he needed two tables against the walls, a chest of drawers, a sink with running water, and three sets of storage batteries with proper connections for charging and discharging.

The instruments came, without being delayed by the customs, through Paris to Sèvres, but when Michelson unpacked them, he found that in spite of meticulous care in crating, the comparer had been smashed to pieces in the rougher-than-usual voyage. His patience in the face of this severe loss won him the admiration of everyone at the Bureau. There was nothing to do but begin again. Wadsworth proved his ability in this crisis by reconstructing the comparer with superior optical parts supplied by French glass makers.

The six weeks during which the comparer was being rebuilt passed rather pleasantly for Michelson. Long walks in the park under the shade of the giant chestnuts and sketching the Paris bridges along the Seine rested his mind. Among the pages of his own copy of the paper he wrote at this time he inserted a pen-and-ink sketch of a donkey grazing near the Pavillon, along with several interminable long-division problems, written out by hand, determining the length of the various light waves from cadmium.

To establish the new standard of length, Michelson had to count how many red cadmium wavelengths there were in the international prototype meter. His method was characteristically simple. Lining up his interferometer so as to mark off a space equal to a small portion of the meter bar as an etalon, or section, he slowly extended the mirror at the end of one arm of the interferometer by the length of this etalon. As he did this, light and dark fringes slid by the eyepiece, which he counted as they passed. It was a tedious task, but the comparer achieved a precision of about one part in a hundred million. Multiplying the fringes in the measured etalon by the number of etalons in the meter gave him the figure for the entire meter: 1,553,163.5.[7]

Laser light has since improved this measurement to a precision of about one part in a million millions. This is possible because laser light is far purer than the cadmium light or any other available to Michelson in 1892. But although the fringes are now counted by electronic methods, the technique is essentially the one he demonstrated at the time.[8]

This measurement had taken Michelson much longer than he had anticipated, and he realized, toward the middle of October, that he would not be able to complete his half-finished design of the range finder on schedule. The instrument was not satisfactory in its present state and under the circumstances he had no heart to return to Worcester to complete it. He explained to Commander Folger in a letter to the Bureau of Ordnance:

Owing to a number of unforeseen circumstances among which I may mention my severing connections with Clark University, I have been unable to give the attention necessary to perfect the telemeter and I shall not be, until my return to America the date of which is very uncertain.[9]

Further work on the range finder was to wait for many years.

Michelson took time off from his work at the Pavillon de Breteuil to attend the 1892 meeting of the British Association for the Advancement of Science in Edinburgh. Sir Richard Glazebrook, the physicist and optician, introduced Michelson to the British Association and in only twenty words gave a clear account of Michelson's investigations. Helmholtz and Thomson reported to the absent Rayleigh that it was a splendid meeting, the best they had ever attended, and Michelson wrote to Harper at Chicago that his own paper had been very well received.

For Michelson's work on the meter he was made a member of the Société Française de Physique, and there were several farewell dinner parties given in his honor. Margaret and the children had left Paris when school closed, and soon he too sailed for the United States.

Michelson reported immediately to Chicago, but Margaret lingered with her parents in the East. Wishing to maintain a foothold there, she bought a house on the seashore at Wainscott, Long Island. Edgewater, as she called it, stood on a neck of land looking out across Georgica Pond to the ocean, from which it was divided by a narrow strip of beach. The house stood alone on the shore, visible from quite a distance across the fairway of the golf links. The approaches to Edgewater lay through broad, flat potato fields, dusty at harvest time. Tall, graceful elms shaded the roadway, giving way to scrub pine near the dunes by the sea. Here Margaret swam with her sons in the towering surf, while Elsa watched from the shade of her parasol.

When Michelson arrived in Chicago, the Columbian Exposition was in full swing all around the area that would become the University of Chicago. Little Egypt, the belly dancer, was grinding her way to fame to a catchy hula rhythm that stuck in Michelson's mind. He was sometimes overheard whistling it as he dressed in the morning. Up and down the midway between Jackson and Washington parks stood the villages brought from Ireland, Germany, Old Vienna, Japan, China, and the South Seas. Elsa and her brothers, now in their teens, arrived in early fall. They spent the days before school opened in running from one exhibit to the other. In the Moorish Palace, the chamber of horrors held a particular fascination for them. At night the giant Ferris wheel, 250 feet in diameter, was turning profitably in a blaze of electricity which illumined the pseudoclassical splendor of the "Great White City."

Outside the gates, Chicago was generating its own energy. Skyscrapers were rising in the "Loop" downtown. The "Chicago construction" was thought by some to be a terrible evil, while others said it was not incompatible with a certain stately beauty. Trade dominated the city. Meat packers and grain dealers were piling up fortunes. To windward from the stockyards prairie breezes blew smoke and odors across the city. Thousands of Negroes made their way north to Chicago while immigrants from Europe also poured into the slums. Graft and crime obtained a stranglehold on the city government, and along South Clark and State streets vice flourished unrestrained.

Successful businessmen, philanthropists, and planners were working hard, however, to improve the physical and cultural aspects of Chicago. With clever engineering and some political maneuvering, the polluted waters of the sluggish Chicago River were reversed to empty into a drainage canal to the Illinois River and thence down the Mississippi. The Illinois Central Railroad was eventually electrified, and a park was laid out on the newly filled land along the whole south shore of the city's lake front.

Some of these far-sighted men became trustees of Chicago University. Marshall Field gave ten acres of land on the Midway, and Martin Ryerson, chairman of the board of trustees, donated $200,000 for the physics laboratory where Michelson was to spend most of the next forty years of his life.

The university, as originally conceived, was to be ". . . an institution wholly under Baptist control as a chartered right, loyal to Christ and his church, employing none but Christians in any department of instruction; . . . seeking to bring every student into surrender to Jesus Christ as Lord."[10] But this fundamentalist sentiment was greatly watered down when John D. Rockefeller urged Harper and the trustees to raise funds comparable to his own donation from Chicago businessmen, regardless of their religion. Harper departed radically from the Baptist concept when he hired the scientists from Clark, and Michelson in particular. These men were not constricted by any church dogma.

The quadrangles, designed by Henry Ives Cobb, were still mostly in the blueprint stage when Michelson began his courses. The "campus" was piled high with stones, and the foundations of the buildings were great staring holes in the ground. Workmen were everywhere, operating derricks and driving teams of powerful horses. The students, passing a goose farm on their way to class, picked their way through piles of earth, brick, iron girders, and lumber.

A four-story brick building on the corner of Fifty-fifth Street and University Avenue housed the entire department of science—physics, chemistry, biology, and geology. The kitchen of a dingy apartment in this building became Michelson's temporary laboratory. He shared it with Jacques Loeb, the biologist who first produced artificial insemination. Loeb, who was experimenting with the nervous reaction of reptiles, kept his frogs in the bathtub, while Michelson was mixing alkali and acid in the kitchen sink into a chemical preparation for the silver backing to his mirrors.[11]

Among the 120 men and women of the first faculty there was a feeling of excitement that enabled them to rise above the temporary inconveniences. Nine were former college presidents. Besides the scientists who had come with Michelson from Clark, Harper had engaged a brilliant group of men in the liberal arts. Harry Pratt Judson, later Harper's successor as president, headed the department of history and assisted Harper in organization of the various departments. From Cornell came J. Lawrence Laughlin, head professor of political economy, and William MacClintock, in English. George S. Goodspeed headed comparative religion and ancient history, and Starr W. Cutting, the German department.

President Harper had his eye on acquiring Kenwood Observatory in the mansion of William Hale, who had equipped it for his son George Ellery Hale, Michelson's friend. Young Hale had invented a remarkable instrument called the spectroheliograph, with which he had photographed and studied the surface and the corona of the sun.

In July of 1892, Michelson had heard George Ellery Hale address the American Association for the Advancement of Science in Rochester, New York, and had been profoundly impressed with the capabilities of this new invention. In the audience he found Edward Morley and many others who championed Hale's new and more efficient method of solar research. Some of the old-guard astronomers, Simon Newcomb among them, reacted with skepticism. But Michelson was so impressed with Hale's brilliance that he immediately wrote Harper, wholeheartedly recommending the young astronomer and pointing out the importance of the new field of astrophysics: ". . . there are very few competitors, [and] results of great importance are likely to be obtained."[12] But Harper, saying he wanted a pure astronomer, did not make an offer, though he did attempt to annex the observatory. Hale held back until Harper finally invited him to join the faculty as associate professor of astrophysics and director of the Kenwood Astrophysical Observatory.

Michelson had heard of this in Paris and promptly wrote to Hale congratulating him: "I think the University is also to be congratulated on its acquisition and I also congratulate myself on the prospect of having a colleague who is so enthusiastic an investigator as yourself."[13] It was this enthusiasm that endeared Hale to his friends and later made him able to wring vast sums of money out of millionaires for the building of three great observatories. When his face lit up with the hope of accomplishing some feat, people came forward to help him.

Hale kept Michelson informed about the progress in Chicago: "I visited the University grounds last Saturday and found great activity there. They are at work on eight buildings already, and by the time you get back, you will see some marked changes. . . ."[14]

Students came pouring into Chicago from every part of the United States and from many European countries as well. Many were turned away because they could not pass the entrance examinations. No one was allowed to enter on the strength of his high school record alone, as students were in many other colleges. In the first year, 742 students were accepted. Alonzo Stagg, one of the most colorful figures on the campus, became head of physical education. Football practice began the day the university opened.

Michelson and his family moved into a house at 125 East 51st Street, in a row of identical brick houses on Chicago's south side. Margaret could hardly tell which house belonged to her. She found Chicago no improvement over Cleveland or Worcester.

As Ryerson Laboratory neared completion, Michelson and Harper made elaborate plans for the presentation and opening of the new building. Its gray stone façade was in the English Gothic style of architecture which prevailed throughout the university campus.

At the Seventh Convocation of the university, which Michelson addressed on July 1, 1894, he outlined for a gathering of distinguished men, "some of the objects and methods of Physical Science." On the following day occurred the dedication of Ryerson, to which Michelson had invited many of his friends in the limelight of physics. T. C. Mendenhall had gladly agreed to make the dedication address, but a railroad strike prevented him from coming to Chicago. President Grover Cleveland called out federal troops to suppress the disturbance and the labor leader Eugene Debs was jailed, but the strike continued until August 7. Several members of the faculty were in sympathy with the strikers, but Michelson supported the President, feeling that authority should be maintained.

On the day of the dedication, the procession formed in a courtyard near the Walker Museum. It was headed by President Harper and Albert Michelson. Next came Martin Ryerson, the donor, who walked alone, followed by the university chaplain, the trustees, official guests, members of the university senate and council, the faculty, the alumni, and the graduate students. The college orchestra, playing "Meisl's March," accompanied the procession across the campus to Ryerson.

Michelson opened the cermonies by reading the speech that Mendenhall had written. The subject was "The Evolution and Influence of Experimental Physics," and Mendenhall fairly gloated over this triumph of science.

Twenty-five years ago this building might have been dedicated to Literature, or to Art; it might have been opened as a Museum of Natural History, embracing a curious collection of specimens illustrating the freaks of Nature and the mistakes of man; it might have contained ill shaped, badly ventilated and poorly lighted halls for lectures on Logic or Philosophy, or for recitations in Latin, Greek or Mathematics, or what is indeed highly probable, it might have included a whole University in itself, not omitting colleges of law, medicine and theology. Whatever it might have been a quarter of a century ago, it could not have been what it is today, for it can be truthfully said that in the whole world there existed at that time only a germ, the growth and development of which has created a powerful, indeed a revolutionary influence upon systems of education, and of which the Ryerson Physical Laboratory is without doubt, today, the most complete and perfect product.[15]

Michelson then introduced Professor Henry Crew, the astronomer of Northwestern University, who conducted a panel discussion on the various methods of teaching physics. Professor Hiram Benjamin Loomis, also of Northwestern, said he was of the opinion that physics should begin in the kindergarten because a child is naturally a close observer: the simple facts would then be clear mathematically.

Michelson stated his view that since much of the work in physics required the use of graphical curves, it was important that students should have a course in the graphical representation of curves by means of their equations. Students should have an early course in descriptive geometry and freehand drawing and an opportunity to gain skill in mechanical manipulation in a workshop. Michelson believed that mathematics as an aid to the comprehension of physics and an instrument of physical research was highly overestimated. "What is important from the purely Physical standpoint? How many really important advances (discoveries or inventions) owe their existence to mathematics?" he asked. Granting that mathematics was useful in systematizing and in testing theories, he suggested separating the physics department into mathematical, theoretical, and experimental physics.

Mathematical physics should be taught as a branch of mathematics, theoretical physics either with the aid of only the simplest mathematical processes, including the elementary differential and integral calculus, or with higher mathematics used specifically as an aid to the understanding of the physical conceptions involved, "never as illustrating the beautiful power of the mathematical analysis." There existed a place for "more or less intricate *computation*" in connection with precision instruments and for methods and results of experiments, Michelson admitted. But experimental physics could otherwise stand on its own legs.[16]

That evening Michelson gave a dinner for some fifty visiting physicists. Robert A. Millikan, who met him for the first time on this occasion, wrote later: ". . . he was rallied for setting up too high a standard of pulchritude for physicists, for with his jet black hair, his fine hazel eyes, his red tie and his elegance of both speech and bearing, he made an unusually striking figure."[17]

Millikan had left his studies in Berlin in order to work under Michelson. He was to be closely associated with the older physicist for many years: as pupil, as assistant, as Michelson's director during the First World War, and as the friend of his old age in California.

I attended Michelson's first lecture with a group of six or seven graduate students who were there for the work of the summer quarter. . . . He was himself the graduate department, giving the only graduate course. The impression that was made upon me by that course and by his presentation of the "visibility curves" which enabled one by the aid of skillful observing and more skillful analysis to read for the first time the fine structure of spectral lines far beyond the power of any instrument to reveal it directly to the eye was memorable. . . . Elegance of observational technique, elegance of analysis, elegance of presentation—these were, I think, the impressions made on all of us younger men who had a chance to see Michelson's experimental work and hear him present it.[18]

Ever since his arrival in Chicago Michelson had been searching for a paid mechanician, not one of those bright young men studying for a fellowship, but, as he had written to Rowland from Clark in 1889, ". . . a man handy with his fingers and a good observer, who will do just what he is told and who is not too ambitious."[19]

Such a man was not easy to find. But eventually Michelson became friends with two brothers from Sweden who had been trained in the precision optical shop of the Frenchman Octave L. Petididier, at 5423 Lake Avenue, Chicago. Michelson spent a good deal of time in the company of Petididier, discussing the design of his instruments. Petididier was a man of genial disposition, and Michelson found him very pleasant to talk to. They enjoyed a nip of whiskey together on special occasions. The Swedish brothers, Fred and Julius Pearson, worked almost entirely on apparatus designed by Michelson in Petididier's shop until the aging Frenchman retired. Then Michelson hired them both, and his troubles were over. The Pearsons were paragons as craftsmen and instrument makers. Of the two, Fred worked more closely with Michelson. He was involved with every experiment for the next thirty years. His devotion lasted after the "chief's" death, when he worked with Dr. Francis Pease to finish Michelson's final experiment.

On November 2, 1894, Michelson attended a meeting called by George Ellery Hale to create a new journal devoted to spectroscopy and astronomical physics. The meeting, held at the Fifth Avenue Hotel in New York, was the kind of informal gathering of influential men that was typical of this period in American science. Henry Rowland and E. C. Pickering were leaders of the group. The solar physicist Charles Augustus Young, professor of astronomy at the College of New Jersey (later Princeton University), Charles Sheldon Hastings, professor of physics at Sheffield Scientific School in New Haven, and James E. Keeler, director of the Allegheny Observatory near Pittsburgh, made up the editorial board. They chose as a title for the periodical "The Astrophysical Journal." The field it covered was new at that time, and the universities were skeptical. Raising money was not easy, but Hale's enthusiasm and determination brought the journal into existence and awakened physicists to the role they could play in astronomy.[20] The University of Chicago contributed its wintry trio of astronomers—Hale, Gale, and Frost—to the board of editors.[21]

About this time Michelson received a letter that led to a long and warm friendship. It was from Ogden Rood, professor of physics at Columbia College. To some investigators, an experiment is only the means by which they attain a definite result. But to Rood, an ingenious method was in itself worthwhile. He had a passion for the beauty of a delicate experiment and rejoiced in a challenge to push the sensibility of an instrument to its limits. Better than anyone else, Rood understood what Michelson had done in Paris. He wrote:

My Dear Professor Michelson:

Today I began the examination of my last three months mail, and found at the top of the heap your magnificent work on the determination of the meter in terms of wave-lengths of light, a stupendous monument of genius and delicate scientific work, the like of which the world has hardly seen before. Every American will be proud of you, and the people on the other side will begin to open their eyes, and think more of the Republic over the waters. Gibbs and Gould had talked to me a good deal about the affair, but today for the first time I saw the publication. . . . [22]

Coming from a man like Rood, these compliments delighted Michelson. The two men had much in common. They shared a fondness for music and painting, as well as a fascination for the mysteries underlying natural phenomena.

During his student years in Munich, Rood had studied painting, achieving a fair skill. Later he became a member of the American Water Colour Society. His book, *Modern Chromatics*, published in 1879, embodied many of his contributions to the physics of color. He was able to explain in simple terms that when yellow and blue light from the spectrum are mixed, the result is white, whereas if these colors are mixed in pigment, absorption of light produces green. Preferring conservative techniques, he was not overjoyed to find his work referred to as "The Impressionists' Bible" by the group of painters in Paris who called themselves the Pointillists, one of whom was Georges Seurat. Their method of broken color was based on Rood's theory concerning the physics of color sensation.

Ogden Rood was striking in appearance and manner and a popular member of the Century Club. He had a wide range of interests, with particular concern for classical cultures. Reproducing the insignia on ancient coins was a hobby of his. At one of their meetings, Rood presented Michelson with a replica of an Etruscan seal, which depicted in delicate relief the image of a man pierced through the breast by a bolt of lightning. Rood said that the figure represented a man who was struck down by the gods with a thunderbolt as a punishment for having gained too much wisdom, thus incurring their jealousy. Michelson was in danger of a similar fate, Rood warned him, because he was prying into the holy secrets of light. Michelson was much amused by the implication of the legend, and he wore the trinket as a watch fob the rest of his life.

During the years from 1895 to 1897, as Michelson's fame grew, honors poured in from many countries. A beautifully engraved medal from the University of Paris arrived in 1895. He was made a member of the Royal Astronomical Society in 1896, of the Cambridge Philosophical Society and the Société Hollandaise des Sciences in 1897; in that same year he replaced Gould as member for the United States of the International Bureau on Weights and Measures in Paris.

At this time Michelson was occupying himself with further analysis of spectral radiations and the effect on these rays of temperature changes, pressures, and magnetism. But his work was constantly interrupted by quarrels between his two teaching assistants. Before Michelson arrived, S. W. Stratton, a young man of thirty-four with a B.S. degree, had been engaged to teach the undergraduates, equip the physical laboratory, and organize the department. For more than a year, he was senior in the department and it was perhaps inevitable that he should feel some regrets at giving up his authority to work under orders, even if they came from a highly respected physicist. If Michelson had been content to work closely with Stratton alone, things might have gone more smoothly. But he moved heaven and earth to retrieve Wadsworth from Langley, whose airplane and ideas of manned flight had aroused overwhelming ridicule from all sides and had lost government support.

With tact, flattery, and probably hints at a raise in salary, Michelson achieved his purpose. With Wadsworth's arrival, however, trouble began. Wadsworth, five years younger than Stratton, held the same position, assistant professor, at the same salary. Having been associated with Michelson at Clark and in Paris, he naturally expected to have the inside track.

Wadsworth had devised a plan for driving a revolving mirror in synchronism with a tuning fork, an idea which might prove useful in future measurements of the speed of light, which were never far from Michelson's thoughts. Stratton, on the other hand, was also doing excellent work and relieved Michelson of much tiresome administrative detail. Although both men had their assets, valuable time was lost listening to the grievances of one or the other. Unable to resolve their quarrels, Michelson appealed to Harper:

. . . Stratton has acted in a very manly and generous fashion.

I have since had a serious talk with Wadsworth and regret to say that notwithstanding every effort on my part to straighten the matter out I fear I have failed in this respect. I have his assurance however that he will do what he can to avoid any open rupture.

The chief difficulty seems to be that Wadsworth thinks Stratton has tried to exercise authority—and no assurance of mine or Stratton's appears to have any effect.

If you wish it we can have a talk over the matter and then—if you judge it expedient–you might talk with Wadsworth yourself.

The whole attitude of Wadsworth's mind is so sensitive and so suspicious that it is a matter of great delicacy to approach him.

Nothing pertaining to the Department has given me so much anxiety and nothing would give me more satisfaction than to see it happily settled.[23]

Wadsworth apparently had too much ambition for Michelson's taste, so that when it came to a showdown, he was the one who left Ryerson, for a job at Yerkes Observatory, while Stratton, for better or worse, remained.

Early in 1896, Michelson received from Wilhelm Conrad Röntgen, professor of physics at Würzburg, Germany, a small pamphlet describing his discovery of a curious new kind of radiation which could penetrate many opaque substances. Röntgen suggested these rays might be longitudinal waves in the ether; whatever they were, he described how to produce them and, because their nature was unknown, he called them "X rays."

The *Sunday Times Herald* in Chicago published pictures, photographed by the new process, of the bone of a hand and of a bullet lodged in the flesh of an ankle. Never before had a scientific discovery received such sensational publicity. Michelson, like most authorities on light, was besieged by reporters to make a statement regarding X rays and their future. He replied cautiously to the questions put to him:

I have not the slightest doubt that his discovery has been truthfully set forth and is an important one in the scientific world. But at present I confess I do not see just how any important scientific or even practical application can be made of it.

The principal scientific interest just now should be to find out what this new agent is. We know that it is not light. It has some resemblance to light and to Kathode [cathode] rays; but the fact that it is not stopped by opaque substances shows it is not light and the fact that it is not deflected by a magnet shows it is not Kathode rays.

It does not seem to me likely, from what we know of it at present, that this discovery would be of any practical use in locating minerals in the earth. However, as I said before, it is a little too early to prophesy what wonderful things its development may bring forth.[24]

In the 1890s unseen radiation was not recognized as light. Michelson was understandably cautious. Thomas A. Edison, however, went overboard in his enthusiasm for the possibilities of X rays. He said the new invention might soon photograph a man's thoughts inside his brain. He suggested humorously that henceforth a safeblower would carry his camera along on his expeditions to determine whether or not the contents were worthy of the risk; that a mining prospector would have no further doubt as to where gold lies; that the South African diamond fields would hold no more secrets; and pearls would be seen inside their oysters. Edison gave the reporters a field day.

This and other such plays to the gallery by Edison thoroughly prejudiced Michelson against him. As an inventor, he was undeniably a genius, but he did not fit Michelson's idea of a scientist.

Although the newer physics, radioactivity, electronics, and quantum theory lay outside his immediate field of interest, Michelson put aside his accustomed activities to try to explain the new phenomenon of X rays. Two papers, "The Theory of X-Rays" and "The Source of X-Rays," appeared in 1896, the latter also signed by Stratton.[25] It is evident that Michelson had been persuaded to express himself on a matter which he did not really understand. Few did.

In his yearly departmental report of 1897, Michelson wrote to President Harper:

The science of spectroscopy has accomplished a number of remarkable feats within the past decade, and there appears every reason to expect that an improvement in the essential element, the "grating," will be followed by a corresponding unfolding of hitherto hidden secrets of nature's laboratory.[26]

Michelson undertook the building of an engine for ruling gratings rather lightheartedly, thinking that it would take him only five or six months. He hoped to improve on Rowland's gratings, which were hard to come by. But during thirty years of trial and error, struggling with the "she-devil" in the basement of Ryerson, he was never to be completely satisfied with his results.

The engine consisted mainly of a "carriage," floated in mercury so that only one-tenth of its weight rested on the ways. On this carriage lay a slab of speculum or glass to be ruled by a diamond. Between strokes of the diamond the carriage was driven forward by a large worm screw, the most vital part of the engine. The temperature in the sealed chamber where the engine labored night and day was thermostatically controlled, but the sensitivity and delicacy of the instrument were such that it was almost impossible to check and supervise it without destroying the grating.

The diamond, which traced a furrow several miles long on the hard surface of the grating, had to be selected and mounted with great care. After weeks and sometimes months of preparation, the diamond point would give way and further time had to be spent trying out another. If the diamond broke while the ruling was in progress, the grating itself had to be thrown out and work started all over again on a new one.

The most difficult part of the engine to prepare was the screw which moved the grating forward after each stroke of the diamond. Any flaw in the screw, nut, or carriage, or in the moving parts controlling the diamond, showed up at once in the grating. To perfect the screw required years of patient grinding and testing, and the longer the screw, the more difficult the task. Later Michelson used his interferometer to test the screw for accuracy. He admitted he had spent ten years working on a screw to rule a 15-inch grating. Rowland spent about two years on his 6-inch grating. The actual ruling of a large grating took only eight or ten days; what took so long was the tedious preparation and the necessity of starting over again.[27]

"I have given up my trip abroad on account of the perversity of the screw of my ruling engine,"[28] Michelson wrote to R. S. Woodward of the Carnegie Institution, the organization which financed his research on the ruling engine over a number of years.

Ruling engines have had a curious way of dominating their makers. A man who was by nature gregarious and trusting of his fellows became secretive after spending much time in the company of such a machine. One fellow who ruled gratings for Lord Rayleigh in the 1870s never revealed his method. H. J. Grayson, an Australian who improved the technique of ruling, made his wife promise to burn all relevant papers immediately after his death. Even Henry Rowland refused to publish any complete paper on his invention. Michelson said that his difficulties would have been diminished if his predecessors in the field had been more communicative.

The only man to whom Michelson ever lent his ruling engine was Arthur Holly Compton, who came to the physics department at Chicago in 1923. This was a mark of his affection for and confidence in his young friend. On one occasion, however, Compton brought P. A. Ross from Stanford into Michelson's office. Ross wanted to build a ruling engine himself and was eager for suggestions on how to begin. Michelson took in the situation with growing animosity. Turning to Compton, he said, "Ross wants to borrow my engine. I see no reason why he should have it, do you?"[29]

Such was the fascination of Michelson's "monster" that the men who worked on it developed peculiar neuroses about the temperamental machine. Julius Pearson talked about it in his sleep night after night. Oscar Lange, another mechanic, flew into a rage if anyone came near it. One day when Michelson went down to the basement to check his machine, Lange grabbed a wrench, threatened to strike him if he took a step nearer the engine, and drove him back upstairs. Fortunately Michelson was able to retain his sense of humor.

> One comes to regard the machine as having a personality —I had almost said a feminine personality—requiring humoring, coaxing, cajoling—even threatening! But finally one realizes that the personality is that of an alert and skillful player in an intricate but fascinating game—who will take immediate advantage of the mistakes of his opponent, who "springs" the most disconcerting surprises, who never leaves any result to chance—but who nevertheless plays fair—in strict accordance with the rules of the game. These rules he knows and makes no allowance if you do not. When *you* learn them and play accordingly, the game progresses as it should.[30]

CHAPTER 10

The Lowell Lectures

A S interest in astronomy increased, Harper began looking for a donor to provide the University of Chicago with a vast observatory. Looking over the local crop of newly wealthy men, he selected Charles T. Yerkes, owner of the Chicago Street Railway. This millionaire had recently spent some time in a Philadelphia jail on charges of embezzlement and was therefore eager to reinstate himself in the public's good graces. Hale composed for Harper a letter calculated to appeal to the tycoon's vanity. The telescope was to be the greatest in the world. Its light-gathering power would be 35,-000 times greater than that of the human eye; through it one could theoretically see a 25-cent piece at a distance of 300 miles. In resolving power and efficiency it would dwarf the powers of the famous 36-inch telescope at Lick Observatory on Mount Hamilton in California, at that time the best in the world. Yerkes Observatory would become the Mecca of thousands of science-loving pilgrims, and its donor would be forever remembered for his munificence.

Yerkes surfaced like a trout for this bait and before long had agreed to endow the observatory. Certain pious members of the board of trustees took an unenthusiastic view of this "tainted money," but Harper, undeterred, proceeded with the plans. A stately, classical building, designed by Henry Ives Cobb in the form of a Greek cross, rose on the shores of Lake Geneva at Williams Bay, Wisconsin. The giant dome covered a refracting telescope weighing 16 tons. Michelson was interested in every detail of the new observatory, where he planned to spend much of his time.

A pair of 42-inch optical disks, made by Maintois of Paris, had been ground into lenses at the workshop of Alvan G. Clark in Cambridge, Massachusetts. These great lenses had been finished, at a cost of $66,000, with the perfection that had made Clark and his sons justly famous. They were the last work of the great maker of optical instruments, who did not live to see his masterpiece installed or to attend the dedication ceremony on October 21, 1897.

Eight hundred dignitaries from Chicago, as well as noted scientists and astronomers from all over the world, were taken to Williams Bay in special trains. Simon Newcomb, now retired from the Nautical Almanac office, was the star of the occasion. As the designer of Lick Observatory he had frequently been consulted in the problems of Yerkes.

Energy and enthusiasm radiated from the astronomer. Although he was on crutches as a result of an accident, he had lost little of his former elegance. His dignified appearance and easy delivery made him a popular speaker.

For several days preceding the ceremony, there was a demonstration of the instruments, to which the scientists had been invited. After examining a sun spot through the telescope, Newcomb pronounced the instrument to be far and away the best in the world. Hale and Michelson were busy entertaining their guests and hoping as usual for clear night skies. F. L. O. Wadsworth, Michelson's former assistant, who was now an associate professor on the staff at Yerkes, demonstrated the application of interference methods to astronomical measurements. Pickering of Harvard gave an illustrated lecture on variable stars and clusters.

When the formal day of celebration arrived the entire faculty of Chicago University marched into the rotunda leading the way for the two "lions" of the occasion, President Harper and Charles T. Yerkes. Yerkes was installed in a throne garlanded with "laurels" (actually sumac and red oak leaves), from which he made a jovial speech: "Everything is in excellent condition. I am satisfied with the entire plant. . . . The management, too, could not be improved upon," he declared, slapping Professor Hale on the back.[1]

Newsmen tittered and Martin Ryerson feared that the proceedings might get out of order. Harper, stepping forward, cordially thanked the man "who made possible the erection of this temple of science." The occasion was restored to its proper dignity.

On the following day, back in Chicago, Michelson scheduled a tour through Ryerson Physical Laboratory for the visiting scientists. He and Stratton, now promoted to associate professor, demonstrated a new invention of theirs called the harmonic analyzer. This machine was a development of Michelson's calculations on the analysis of light given off by the burning of various gases. "There is a close connection between the distribution of light in any source and the visibility curve which can be obtained with the use of that source," he explained. He was now occupied with the reverse of this discovery—"determining the nature of the source from observation of the visibility curve."[2] The harmonic analyzer was a mechanical calculator devised to facilitate this task. The interference fringes were represented by simple harmonic curves. The machine was capable of analyzing eighty such harmonic

THE MASTER OF LIGHT

elements, and it could also give the formula for any curve that was fed into it. Michelson demonstrated this talent of the instrument by sketching the wife of one of the scientists. From her forehead, down over her chin to her neck, his pen skillfully followed the line of her profile. The result was an excellent likeness that was then reduced to factors and fed into the machine, which returned the corresponding mathematical formula of her curves. The demonstration enchanted the women guests and they at least considered the visit to Ryerson the high point of the week's excursions.

During the 1890s, Oliver Lodge, passionate devotee of the ether theory, had constructed an "aether machine to determine aethereal viscosity." The machine used two steel disks, each a yard in diameter, joined together with a space between them. These he mounted on a perpendicular axis and spun them around first in clockwise, then in counterclockwise direction as fast as they would go without flying to pieces. Between the disks he flashed a beam of light divided by a half-silvered mirror such as Michelson had used in the ether-drift experiments. The two beams were then projected in opposing directions and reunited at the observer's eyepiece. If the motion of the air or the ether had any effect on the velocity of light, it should have been seen at this point.

Lodge recorded his findings:

At first I saw plenty of shift. In the first experiment the bands sailed across the field as the disks got up speed until the crosswire had traversed a band and a half. The conditions were such that had the ether whirled at the full speed of the disks I should have seen a shift of three bands. It looked very much as if the light was helped along at half the speed of the moving matter, just as it is inside water.

On stopping the disks the bands returned to their old position. On starting them again in the opposite direction, the bands ought to have shifted the other way too, if the effect were genuine; but they did not; they went the same way as before. The shift was therefore wholly spurious. . . . [3]

Still Lodge remained steadfast in his conviction that if light (and therefore light waves) exist there must be an ether. He was perhaps the foremost scientific proponent for retaining the luminiferous ether:

. . . it is absurd to imagine one piece of matter acting mechanically on another at a distance, whether that distance be large or small, without some intervening mechanism or connecting link. . . .

There is no real heat in the ether, nor any sound. Nothing but one simple type of propagation by waves goes on in free space, and that with a definite unchangeable velocity which is known as the velocity of light. . . . It is the one definite measurement which has been made concerning the ether of space, and of itself is sufficient to show that space empty of matter is endowed with finite and measurable physical properties.

It is absolutely transparent and undispersive. In other words it quenches no light but transmits it undiminished in total intensity, though diluted by spreading, to and from the greatest distances in astronomy. [4]

Lodge's experiment appeared to prove that the velocity of light is not affected by the motion of adjacent matter, [5] a conclusion that pointed in the opposite direction from Michelson's thinking.

This contradiction renewed interest in the problem, and Michelson was urged by Lodge and others to repeat the Michelson-Morley experiment. Michelson agreed. In his own mind, a disturbing doubt had always persisted that the negative result might have been due to the ether's having been "trapped" in the basement laboratory in Cleveland and that for this reason his delicate instrument had appeared insensitve to its flow. In 1897, therefore, he set up an interferometer that traversed the entire north wall of Ryerson Hall, so that the vertical arm pierced the ceiling, and the other arm pointed eastward. Light traveled a path about 200 feet long, shooting up to 50 feet above the ground. Temperature changes plagued Michelson as usual, making it necessary to cover the entire path of light with a wooden box.

The observations showed no appreciable difference between this test and the one laid flat at gound level. The displacement of the fringes, if any, was less than one-twentieth of a fringe, Michelson said. This could mean that the earth's influence upon the ether might be extended to distances of the order of the earth's diameter, a view which Joseph Larmor later expressed.[6] The earth in its motion might carry the ether along so that the movement at its surface would extend out into space to the farthest regions which man might explore. Had Michelson lived to see the astronauts fly to the moon, he would no doubt have urged that an interferometer be taken along to test his theory in outer space.

When pushed to draw some definite conclusions from his results, Michelson said the choice lay among three alternatives:

1. The earth passes through the ether (or rather allows the ether to pass through its entire mass) without appreciable influence.
2. The length of all bodies is altered (equally?) by their motion through the ether.
3. The earth in its motion drags with it the ether even at distances of many thousand kilometers from its surface.[7]

These appear to be the views taken respectively by Stokes, Lorentz, and Larmor. These men were particularly responsible for bringing the Michelson-Morley experiment into the limelight of science because of the problems regarding the ether which its negative result raised. Larmor, who had just been made a fellow of the Royal Society, was lecturing in mathematics at Cambridge University at this time. His famous work *Aether and Matter*, in which he dwelt at length on the crucial experiment, was published in 1900.

Before that, however, the detailed account in Lorentz's treatise, the "Versuch" of 1895,[8] first widely publicized the Michelson-Morley experiment. Albert Einstein stated that he first read of the ether-drift text for a second-order effect in Lorentz's work. "He had . . . been conscious of Michelson's result before 1905 partly through his reading of the papers of Lorentz and more because he had simply assumed this result of Michelson to be true."[9] In 1907, Einstein made reference to the Michelson-Morley experiment three times in the introduction to his article "On the Principle of Relativity and Similar Conclusions," which was published in the *Jahrbuch der Radioactivität.*

Lorentz tells of the "very lively discussions" held on this subject at meetings of the German Society of Natural Sciences in Düsseldorf in 1898, which were attended by Max Planck, Wilhelm Wien, Paul Drude, and many other German physicists. They discussed the question of first-order effects in particular, and some of them proposed devices by which this effect might be observed. None of these experiments materialized. The assumption that first-order effects could not reveal an ether drift became generally accepted. But it was far more difficult to explain why tests of second-order effect gave a negative result. The Michelson-Morley experiment was the first such test ever made,[10] and Lorentz, Larmor, the French mathematician Jules Henri Poincaré, and others were much puzzled to explain it.

William Thomson (who was now Lord Kelvin, Baron of Largs, having been given a peerage by Queen Victoria in 1892), in a lecture at the Royal Institution on April 27, 1900, described the experiment as one of the two clouds on the horizon of physics "obscuring the beauty and clarity of the dynamical theory which asserts heat and light to be modes of motion."[11] The second cloud was the discrepancy in the measurements of radiant energy that soon led to Planck's formulation of the quantum theory. Lord Rayleigh agreed that the negative result was a real disappointment.

The majority of physicists accepted Lorentz's contraction theory wholeheartedly, but Michelson was never happy with any of the explanations. The Lorentz hypothesis seemed artificial to him because, for one thing, it implied that the contractions were independent of the elastic properties of material of which the instrument was made. Like a tennis ball when it is struck, the instrument might contract momentarily and then return to its normal proportions. He wrote: "Such a conclusion seems so improbable that one is inclined to return to the hypothesis of Fresnel and try to reconcile in some other way the 'negative results' . . ."[12]

One facet of the ether theory that did appeal particularly to Michelson was the "vortex." This theory offered an explanation for atoms in a continuous ether. Originally a Greek concept, it found devotees in Descartes, Kelvin, and Helmholtz.

Helmholtz's indestructible vortices, once established in a frictionless medium, must theoretically go on forever. Michelson would illustrate the theory by smoke rings, either blowing them with his favorite cigar if he were at home, or manufacturing them at his laboratory in a box filled with smoke which had a circular aperture at one end and a rubber bulb at the other. The friction against the side of the opening as the puff of smoke emerged produced a rotary motion that resulted in rings or vortices. If a smaller ring was blown through the center of a larger ring (and Michelson was quite adept at this trick, which he had learned from Kelvin), at the moment of contact the larger ring seemed to expand while the smaller one contracted, allowing the smaller one to slide through the orifice,

after which both rings resumed their original size and continued "as if nothing had happened." He could also produce
the vortex effect with a drop of ink in a glass of water.

Two smoke rings were frequently seen to bound obliquely
from each other, shaking violently from the effects of the
shock, very much as if two large india-rubber rings struck each
other in the air. The elasticity of each smoke ring seemed as
perfect as that of a solid india-rubber ring of the same shape.

The problem remained unresolved. Michelson later expressed his position:

> Suppose that an ether strain corresponds to an electric
> charge, an ether displacement to the electric current,
> these ether vortices to the atoms—if we continue these
> suppositions, we arrive at what may be one of the grand-
> est generalizations of modern science—of which we are
> tempted to say that it ought to be true even if it is not—
> namely, that all the phenomena of the physical universe
> are only different manifestations of the various modes of
> motion of one all-pervading substance—the ether.[13]

Long before the outbreak of the Spanish American War in
1898, Michelson was back in uniform, commanding the First
Ship's crew of the Illinois Naval Militia. No quandary about the
morality of the cause perturbed his thoughts. If any nation had
the gall to question United States policy, he was for fighting.

Stratton, who had taken a course of "military" as an undergraduate, became an excellent drillmaster, assisting Michelson
in the organization of a Volunteer Naval Militia at Chicago.
Some 400 men comprised the battalion, which underwent
training for the operation of a warship. Most of them saw
action, but the "splendid little war" of the summer of 1898
ended before either Michelson or Stratton had a taste of it.

After the war, Stratton, who had demonstrated his ability
to command men, kept up his naval connections and spent

much of his time in Washington. Michelson returned to his laboratory.

Shortly after New Year's Day of 1899, Michelson received from the Lowell Institute of Boston a flattering invitation to deliver a series of twelve lectures on light. The Lowell Lectures had great prestige. Many famous scientists had preceded Michelson—among them Benjamin Silliman, Louis Agassiz, Aza Gray, Joseph Lovering, Charles S. Peirce, John Tyndall, Joseph Whitney, Simon Newcomb, Samuel Langley, Benjamin Gould, and George Howard Darwin. To prevent interruption, the doors were closed at the beginning of the lecture and not opened again until the end. One reputable Bostonian was so incensed to find he was excluded because of a moment's delay that he kicked his way through an entrance and was taken to jail.

The preparation for these lectures presented something of a problem to Michelson. He was used to speaking of his work to students of physics or other physicists. Although his audience in Boston was highly intelligent, he still could not make his speech too technical.

However, at the first lecture he stepped onto the podium radiating confidence in himself and pride in his subject. His appearance was youthful and his voice pleasant to hear. He moved with the grace of an athlete and, thanks to his training at Annapolis, carried himself with the bearing of an admiral. But he introduced his formidable subject on a note of tenderness, devotion, and humility.

> ... To few is it given to combine the talent of investigation with the happy faculty of making the subject of their work interesting to others. I do not claim to be one of these fortunate few; and if I am not as successful as I could wish in this respect, I can only beg your indulgence for myself, but not for the subject I have chosen. This, to my mind, is one of the most fascinating, not only of the departments

of science, but of human knowledge. If a poet could at the same time be a physicist, he might convey to others the pleasure, the satisfaction, almost the reverence, which the subject inspires. The aesthetic side of the subject is, I confess, by no means the least attractive to me. Especially is its fascination felt in the branch which deals with light, and I hope the day may be near when a Ruskin will be found equal to the description of the beauties of coloring, the exquisite graduations of light and shade, and the intricate wonders of symmetrical forms and combinations of forms which are encountered at every turn. . . .

These beauties of form and color, so constantly recurring in the varied phenomena of refraction, diffraction, and interference, are, however, only incidentals; and, though a never-failing source of aesthetic delight, must be resolutely ignored if we would perceive the still higher beauties which appeal to the mind, not directly through the senses, but through the reasoning faculty; for what can surpass in beauty the wonderful adaptation of Nature's means to her ends, and the never-failing rule of law and order which governs even the most apparently irregular and complicated of her manifestations? These laws, it is the object of the scientific investigator to discover and apply. In such successful investigation consists at once his keenest delight as well as his highest reward.[14]

He went on to discuss the wave theory of light, comparing it with a sound vibration. He showed how one light wave moving half a length ahead of another can neutralize it, how light added to light may produce darkness. He demonstrated the various uses of the interferometer and the many marvelous possibilities being opened to astronomers with this new instrument. When he finished, the audience responded warmly. Many of his friends pressed forward to congratulate him and to examine the interferometer.

As the course of lectures drew to a close, he wrote to President Harper:

. . . I am already feeling a little regret that the time has been so short.

My stay in Boston has been in every way delightful and I think the reputation of Bostonians for lack of cordiality is pure libel.[15]

The Lowell Lectures formed the basis for Michelson's first book, *Light Waves and Their Uses*, edited by his good friend Henry Crew and published in 1903.

In June 1899, Michelson went to England to receive an honorary degree from Cambridge University. He had a cordial invitation to spend June Week with H. F. Newall, secretary of the Cambridge Philosophical Society, and his wife at Madingly Rise, on the outskirts of Cambridge.

Professor Newall had visited Michelson in his laboratory at Clark University. Newall, who was working in spectroscopy, saw the trend of Michelson's investigations, and was able to appreciate him as an artist.

It was to Michelson a pure aesthetic delight to develop the study of the marvellously beautiful phenomena of physical optics . . . and Michelson had a supreme intellectual power of fashioning his weapons to the best advantage for each region to be explored. One feels almost tempted to interchange the personality and the characteristics of the man and the subject of his choice, and to sympathize with the delight and satisfaction that Light itself must have felt in finding a man so worthy of being entrusted with the control of its powers to penetrate into the mysteries of Matter.[16]

On the day of graduation, before a brilliant assemblage of scientists and Cambridge dons resplendent in their flowing robes of red and purple, the Duke of Devonshire as Chancellor of Cambridge bestowed the degree of Doctor of Science upon Michelson, describing him as one of the most brilliant investigators in the domain of light and radiation.

Returning to London, Michelson conferred with Frank Twyman, at the British instrument makers who were grinding the plates for his spectroscope. He named this instrument the echelon, from the naval term for ships going into battle in *échelle* (ladder) formation. It was built of a series of plates of optical glass of identical thickness laid one on top of the other, and was designed to solve the problem of separating the spectral lines without having the light grow fainter. When light was projected through the echelon, none was dissipated, yet the resolving power was seven and a half times higher than that in an ordinary spectroscopic grating. This spectroscope became a powerful tool, particularly effective in showing the influence of magnetism on light, which Pieter Zeeman had discovered in 1896. With the new instrument, Michelson was able to show that all spectral lines are tripled when the radiations emanate in a magnetic field.[17]

Twyman had read Michelson's 1898 paper on the echelon spectroscope[18] and it had excited his interest to such an extent that, upon joining the firm of Adam Hilger, Ltd., he persuaded Otto Hilger to let him build one and found a wealthy customer to finance the work. Michelson attended a lecture on the echelon grating given by Twyman before the Royal Society. No doubt he enjoyed the warm praise accorded him.

Michelson spent the weekend of June 9 with Lord Rayleigh at Terling Place, Chelmsford, in Essex, where the British physicist had turned the stables of his mansion into a laboratory. He found the jovial scientist romping on the lawn with his grandchildren, as a reward to them for paying strict attention to their lesson on the basic principles of mathematics.

The visit was a success from every point of view. Rayleigh had gathered a stimulating group of people with varied interests. These included Helmholtz and his wife and Sir Richard

Tetley Glazebrook, director of the National Physical Laboratory, an authority on physical optics and the author of searching papers on the problem of the ether. Sir Richard, who had introduced Michelson at the 1882 meeting of the British Association, was thoroughly familiar with his experiments. There were several other interesting guests, among them Lady Evelyn Rayleigh's brother, Lord Balfour, soon to become Prime Minister of England.[19]

The announcement of the Paris Exposition of 1900, which was to emphasize science and engineering, moved President Harper to urge Michelson to exhibit his instruments in the fair. Michelson was against the idea from the start. He probably felt it was beneath his dignity as well as risky for the instruments: he remembered all too well the comparer smashed in transit to Paris. But Harper prevailed, and Stratton was sent over with the harmonic analyzer on which he had collaborated. In May, Robert Millikan was dispatched to aid in unpacking, repairing, and setting up the interferometer and the echelon spectroscope. The effort paid off. Michelson was awarded the Grand Prize of the Exposition Universelle Internationale in the University of Chicago exhibit group 1, class 3, Higher Education, Scientific Institutions. Harper was delighted. He felt it was the best possible publicity for the university and he wrote Michelson to congratulate him.

Stratton's next move ended his collaboration with Michelson, not without some bitterness on the part of the elder partner. The National Bureau of Standards in Washington, before it became a government bureau in 1902, was called the Office of Weights and Measures in the Coast and Geodetic Survey. With the growing demands from science, engineering, industry, and commerce for more and more accurate standards of reference, Congress took steps to expand the agency into a bureau. A director would have to be appointed, and Michelson's measurement of the meter in terms of a light wave qualified him as a candidate for the position. When he learned of this possibility, Michelson thought it could do no harm to let President Harper hear that other organizations were eager to lure him away. He was convinced that the needs of the department of physics were being neglected in favor of Harper's own specialties, religious and classical studies. Sometime around 1899, Michelson confided to Stratton that he would welcome an offer to head the new bureau. When Stratton volunteered to go to Washington to lay the groundwork, Michelson was delighted. Stratton knew his way around the various government agencies and he had a talent with people.

Edward Morley actually had been offered the appointment as director by Dr. Henry S. Pritchett, head of the Coast and Geodetic Survey, but had declined. Mendenhall had described to him the trials of government service. Morley might discover that he was subordinate to one who was himself a subordinate. He would be reminded to be at his desk by 9 a.m., with half an hour for lunch, and would have to leave by 4 p.m. Official life, Mendenhall warned, was insincere and hollow.

No word came to Michelson from his assistant for an unwarranted length of time, and he had begun to wonder what Stratton was up to. It was a considerable shock when the newspapers announced that S. W. Stratton had been appointed director of the National Bureau of Standards. This was a blow to Michelson's vanity and he was furious.

In what seems like a conciliatory gesture, Stratton recommended his former superior for membership on the Visiting Committee of the Bureau of Standards. A letter from Pritchett advised Stratton on the move: "I think it wise to ask Michelson also as a member . . . because of his reputation and standing; no doubt we shall be able to keep him in good order."[20] Pritchett must have been an optimist! The invitation was sent to Michelson on June 6, 1901, but there is no record of an answer.

Stratton's move, however, in the long run was a good thing for everybody concerned. In organizing the bureau, he showed excellent executive powers, a talent Michelson lacked.

The stresses of the position forced Stratton to give up his research in pure science, a step Michelson could never have justified for himself. Nevertheless, seventeen years passed before he forgave Stratton, and even then it took a world war to bring about a reconciliation.

In the spring of 1899 Michelson was sorry to hear from Arthur Gordon Webster that Henry Rowland was ill with diabetes, for which at that time no cure existed. Knowing that he had not long to live, Rowland had enlisted Webster's help in organizing the American Physical Society. He wished to establish the search for knowledge in the field of physics as a professional cause. Webster took the initiative in rounding up some of the best minds in the country for a preliminary meeting at Fayerweather Hall, Columbia University. Present were Rowland, president; Michelson, vice-president; and, as members of the council, J. S. Ames, H. S. Carhart, William Hallock, Charles S. Hastings, W. F. Magie, Ernest Merritt, Edward L. Nichols, Charles S. Peirce, Michael Pupin, and Arthur Gordon Webster. A year later, at their first general open meeting, Rowland delivered a speech that became the creed of professional physicists of his era.

. . . We meet here in the interest of *a science above all sciences* which deals with the foundation of the Universe, with the constitution of matter from which everything in the Universe is made and with the ether of space by which alone the various portions of matter forming the Universe affect each other. . . .

. . . We form a small and unique body of men, a new variety of the human race as one of our greatest scientists calls it, whose views of what constitutes the greatest achievement in life are very different from those around us. In this respect we form an aristocracy, not of wealth, not of pedigree, but of intellect and of ideals, holding him in the highest respect who adds the most to our knowledge or who strives after it as the highest good. . . .

Above all, let us cultivate the idea of the dignity of our pursuit so that this feeling may sustain us in the midst of a world which gives its highest praise, not to the investigation in the pure etherial physics which our society is formed to cultivate, but to the one who uses it for satisfying the physical rather than the intellectual needs of mankind. . . .

How stands our country, then, in this respect? My answer must still be now as it was fifteen years ago, that much of the intellect of the country is still wasted in the pursuit of so-called practical science. . . . But your presence here gives evidence that such a condition is not to last forever. . . .

What is matter; what is gravitation; what is ether and the radiation through it; what is electricity and magnetism; how are these connected together and what is their relation to heat? These are the greater problems of the universe. . . .

Nature is inexorable. . . . Our only course, then, is to act according to the chances of our knowing the right laws. If we act correctly, right; if we act incorrectly, we suffer. If we are ignorant we die. . . . Let us go forward, then, with confidence in the dignity of our pursuit. Let us hold our heads high with a pure conscience while we seek the truth, and may the American Physical Society do its share now and in generations yet to come in trying to unravel the great problem of the constitution and laws of the Universe.[21]

The American Physical Society patterned its meetings after those of the French and British societies, at which papers were read and new ideas discussed. The *Bulletin*, containing abstracts of these papers, was published quarterly. The only new name added to the roster during the first year was that of Henry Crew of Northwestern, probably at Michelson's suggestion.

During the following year, the members of the society were deeply grieved by Rowland's death. Michelson was immediately elected president, and he led the physicists to dedicate themselves to the ideals that Rowland had set down. Webster was made vice-president, and later followed Michelson as president.

The wounds inflicted upon Clark University by the departure of most of its faculty members had healed to the extent that President Hall invited many of them to Worcester in 1899 for the tenth anniversary of its founding. Hall was justifiably proud of having survived the hegira, and Michelson was pleased to find that graduate education was moving forward along the lines that Hall had envisaged. At Webster's house, he spent a pleasant evening discussing with Émile Picard of the Institute de France the Fourier series and J. Willard Gibbs's new work on the electromagnetic theory. Webster had become an authority on the latter subject. His book, *The Theory of Electricity and Magnetism*, had received wide acclaim. Crew called it the most clear and elegant exposition of the electromagnetic theory ever set forth in any language.

Webster and Dayton C. Miller, who were close friends, were among the first Americans to take a serious interest in developing the field of acoustics. Webster's presence at the early meetings of the Physical Society always promised a lively discussion. His stentorian tones had a compelling effect. On one occasion when Miller was demonstrating a delicate recording instrument he had developed—the phono-deik, a forerunner of the oscilloscope—Webster looked at it and bellowed at close range, "What on earth is that?" Geared to its master's gentle voice, the machine was literally shattered and silenced by this sudden explosion of sound so close to its "ear." It was heard no more that day.[22]

CHAPTER 11

Departure from Symmetry

THE separation and subsequent divorce of Albert and
Margaret Michelson burst like a small bombshell
upon the quiet respectability of the Chicago academic community. There was a good deal of gossip, but no one
knew much about the Michelsons' private life and the basis for
a good scandal was lacking. One day early in 1897 Michelson
left home, taking all his belongings, and moved into a hotel.
Margaret agreed to start divorce proceedings with the understanding that he would pay her $10,000 toward the support of
the children and, later, tuition at Harvard for both boys.[1]

He underwent some painful and humiliating moments in
the courtroom on January 6, 1898, when his three children,
carefully schooled by their mother, testified to his acts of cru-

elty in their home. He made up his mind never to see them again. In parting, he said, "Just remember that you have never heard my side."[2] Margaret was given complete custody of the children and disappeared with them overnight. Michelson heard later that they had gone "home" to live with the Heminways in New Rochelle.

The loneliness that settled down upon him then had, in a sense, always existed. It was never easy for him to share any part of his life with another human being. He was cold to the people who were so unfortunate as to love him. Affection had a cloying effect upon him and sooner or later he shook himself free of it.

Yet his very aloofness seemed to attract people, who were forever trying to "get at" him. During the period of the divorce Michelson kept to himself until the day he met Edna Stanton. Ironically, he was attracted to her by the same qualities that had appealed to him in Margaret when he first knew her. Edna and Margaret were both intelligent women with gentle manners and a certain beauty. Each had a family of some social standing and the prospect of inheriting enough money to lift from his shoulders the burden of supporting a family.

Edna Stanton had come to the University of Chicago in 1895, a serious, young idealist. During her student years, she fell in with a group of literary wits, some of whom shaped this period of emerging American thought. Among her friends were Robert Herrick, the novelist and poet, and Robert Morse Lovett, a pacifist writer, both philosophical rebels who had fled from the trammels of Harvard to the freer air of the Midwest. Edna enjoyed these literary Bostonians and admired the cutting power of their words. It was in their company that she honed a rather fine edge on her own phrases, which she was later to use with startling effect on her husband, her friends, and her children.

At the Poetry Club she made the acquaintance of Harriet

Monroe, founder and editor of *Poetry: A Magazine of Verse*, Donald Culross Peattie, Edgar Lee Masters, Robert Frost, Carl Sandburg, and Vachel Lindsay. Edna considered herself emancipated from the conventions of the era. She was the antithesis of the typical college belle. She smoked cigarettes in public, and she admired the radical economist Thorstein Veblen, whose phrase "conspicuous consumption" she quoted to castigate the "bourgeoisie." Her sympathies were with Eugene Debs and the railroad employees striking for a living wage. She believed in absolute candor and despised women who resorted to flirting and deception. A woman in love should say so fearlessly. Nevertheless, she was piqued to find some of the men whose minds she most admired falling in love with "silly" women. *Cap and Gown* published her verses about a classmate:

ONE OF THEM

Under meekly parted curls
Note her sweet pure breadth of brow,
Note her smiling eyes, allow
She's the prettiest of girls.

And this winsome little elf
Tends a shrine within her heart
Worships there with love and art
Her one goddess—her fair self.

In a more serious vein she wrote:

LIFE

Let others mourn for death
And sing their tearful dirges
To wild sea surges
With sobbing breath.

My tears shall flow for life,
Life that outlives its love
And its faith from above
In bitter strife.

Edna saw Albert Michelson for the first time at an "at home" party given by a Chicago hostess, Mrs. William L'Engle, though she knew him by reputation.

"There's the physicist Michelson, who's divorcing his wife!" said her roommate, Ethel Keene. The divorce was still a subject of disapproval in the eminently conservative Baptist community.

"He doesn't look like a rake, Ethel," Edna said. Nevertheless, she noticed the exhilaration in the faces of the ladies with whom he was talking. Mrs. L'Engle, taking his arm, extracted him from the group.

"I want you to meet Miss Stanton," she said. "She's a student at the university, but not in physics, I'm sure."

"I understand you discourage education for women, Mr. Michelson," said Edna, giving him her hand.

"If they were all as pretty as you, Miss Stanton, I'd be happy to teach them."

"'Be good, sweet maid.' Isn't that your theory?" asked Edna. "That's what my parents think."

Although he was almost twenty years her senior, Michelson was piqued at being classed with her parents. He noticed an impertinent ring in her voice that was rather refreshing in contrast to the deference people usually showed him and the saccharine compliments they paid. Studying her sensitive face and appraising her pretty figure, he decided that the haughty manner might conceal a very charming woman.

"May I drive you back to your dormitory when you leave here, Miss Stanton?" asked Michelson, with characteristic directness and simplicity.

She accepted, blushing at her own eagerness.

A little ripple went through the room as Edna thanked Mrs. L'Engle and left on Michelson's arm.

"She's not even half his age, I believe, and she only met him a moment ago. I've half a mind to call her mother," said one of the ladies. But by this time Michelson and Edna were settling themselves in the back of a carriage. He tucked the robe around her and the coachman started his horse down Prairie Avenue.

Edna enjoyed the feeling of being with an "experienced" man. There would never be a clumsy gesture, she thought, remembering one of her younger beaus who had quite lost his head the other evening. She had an aversion to being pounced upon. On the other hand, she thought, any man who would ask permission to kiss her didn't know the first thing about a woman and deserved a turndown. As she studied Michelson's handsome profile she wondered if any woman had ever been able to resist him.

Born in 1871, in Bristol, England, "under the flag," Edna grew up in the various cities where her father, Edgar Stanton, served as American consul. With his appointment in 1876 as Consul General to Russia, St. Petersburg became her home for twelve years. Her German mother, Helene Ernst Stanton, had a taste for the festive activities of the glittering and sumptuous Russian Court under Nicholas II. A series of teas, balls, operas, sleigh rides, and house parties made lively by the scandals and intrigues of the Court prevented Helene from spending much time with her serious-minded little daughter.

In 1888, Edgar Stanton was forced to resign his appointment when President Benjamin Harrison swept Cleveland's appointees out of office. Helene became hysterical and fainted when her husband told her of his decision to join his father's firm in Chicago. Stanton and Company were wholesale dealers in fine wines and foods, and to Helene, being "in trade" was a definite comedown from the consular service. She was also genuinely frightened of being scalped by Indians. Her protests were futile, however, and the packing began.

The Stantons bought a comfortable house in Lake Forest, a fashionable suburb of Chicago, and Edna was entered in Miss Kirkland's School for Young Ladies. After several years she felt she had exhausted the educational possibilities of that seminary and announced to her parents that she wished to enter the new University of Chicago. There was some opposition to her plan, but she gained their reluctant permission to commute some sixty miles a day by train and trolley car. When she proved that her intention to take a degree was serious, she was finally allowed to live in the college dormitory and take part in university life.

Edna's Continental education and her ability to study enabled her to stand near the top of her class, and to graduate in three years' time instead of the usual four. Shortly after her meeting with Michelson, she maneuvered her way into an advanced physics class for which she should have had two years' preparation and some knowledge of mathematics. These subjects were far removed from her previous interests, which were in botany, biology, history, and English. The move was obvious to her classmates Ethel Keene and Harriet Rew, who encouraged her romance with the physicist in spite of her parents' opposition.

The Stantons could no longer dictate to Edna, but in the weeks that followed her meeting with Michelson they did not encourage her to invite him to Lake Forest, and they managed tacitly to signify their disapproval of what they considered an unsuitable match. Edna ceased to confide in her parents. She made up her mind that she would marry Albert Michelson even if it meant that she would never see them again.

Helene had been disappointed to see her daughter put so much emphasis on education and give so little thought to acquiring the graces that would turn her into a likely wife for one of the eligible sons of the Chicago meat packers, who by 1899 had at least one generation of polish at Yale or Harvard. But the Stantons, like most parents in such a situation, were slowly brought into line. Michelson went to Lake Forest to call on them. During the visit Edna thought she saw signs of a thaw. Before long they agreed to her engagement, and the date of December 23, 1899, was set for the wedding. Because of Michelson's divorce, no one outside the immediate family was invited. Edna's parents served as witnesses at the simple ceremony that took place in their house. The wedding had been carefully scheduled to allow a week at Christmastime before Michelson resumed his classes.

Michelson was stimulated and refreshed by the warmth of his young wife's passion, but he was not moved by an equally spontaneous love. Any tendency he might have had toward such unguarded feelings had been killed by his former marriage and his fear of trusting anyone but himself. The painful lesson began for Edna when she became aware of the overwhelming eagerness with which Michelson returned from their honeymoon to his work. She consoled herself temporarily with pleasant little parties and gatherings at which she was introduced to the university faculty. In choosing their friends, the Michelsons felt no obligation to cultivate the high and mighty, and they soon singled out the more lively members of the faculty.

Edna became pregnant in December of 1901. The following summer Michelson took a house on the seashore at Annisquam, Massachusetts. They spent much of their time sailing along the shores of Cape Ann in their small catboat, the *Amaryllis*. Although he seldom raced, Michelson observed all the rules he had been taught at the Naval Academy regarding the furling of sails, careful coiling of halyards and sheets, and scrubbing the deck, and he made a point of using the correct term for every nautical operation.

From time to time, physicists came down from Boston to visit Michelson. After they had talked shop for a number of hours he sometimes took his guests sailing. Not all of them knew how to handle a boat, and one chap from Germany, whose name is not recorded, seemed a little timid but nevertheless expressed his wish to go along. "Have you ever sailed before?" Michelson asked him. "Ach, nein," replied the professor, "but I heff de teory." They managed to avoid capsizing but Michelson was glad he did not have to depend on calculating wind velocity, thrust, and pressure while the boat was heeling over with a sudden puff of wind.

Edna enjoyed the aesthetic side of sailing more than the mechanics. She was always caught completely unaware when the order was given to come about and took some time to move her pillows up to windward of the centerboard. Michelson had to resign himself to the fact that she would never make a very able crew. Her only duty aboard the boat was to read the soundings from a chart. In a hasty departure one day Edna found that she had brought along a streetcar map of Boston instead of a chart. She dared not admit her carelessness, and she had only a vague notion of the depth of a fathom from Shakespeare—"Full fathom five . . ." she muttered. Clutching the map and watching the shoreline for clues, she invented plausible soundings in the channel, as well as names for the lighthouses and buoys. Disaster came inexorably when the *Amaryllis* drove up on a shoal where her centerboard and rudder were wedged fast in the mud. Michelson let fly some mouth-filling curses as he released the main sheet and snatched the map from Edna's hands. She was shaking with laughter.

"I don't think it's very funny," he said, as the sail flapped around his head. He had to go over the side to examine the damage and push the boat free of the shoal. It was quite a while before he took her sailing again.

At the seashore, Michelson became interested in analyzing the natural form of a snail shell. He noticed that curiously divergent forms of life, both animal and vegetable, resemble one another, and that these forms occur also in protozoa, crystals, and liquids. Delighted with the beauty of these shapes he took time off from struggling with mathematical work on the theory of a reciprocal relation in diffraction to enjoy a little recreation in comparing them. His thoughts on the subject were later crystallized in a paper published in 1906.

> In designing for the sake of decoration, symmetrical forms are everywhere manifest, and the perception of their mutual relations is indispensable to the student of art. Occasionally, however, there is in decoration a deliberate departure from symmetry, and such a variation may greatly enhance the beauty and effectiveness of the design. We tire of too great uniformity even of agreeable kinds, and the element of variety is as important in art as an occasional discord is in music—its purpose being to heighten the effect of the succeeding harmony.[3]

Edna's first daughter was born in their Annisquam house on August 31, 1902. She was named Madeleine, more for the sake of euphony with Michelson than for any family reason. She had enormous black eyes and a pale, oval face. Even as a little girl, she developed a deeply romantic disposition. Edna would have liked a son, but Michelson was delighted with his daughter. He composed a lullaby and played it to her on the violin.

Two more babies followed in the next few years, which were perhaps the happiest for Edna. Beatrice, the second child, was plump and roly-poly; a "bacchante baby," her father called her. Her laughter rippled up and down the scale as she reveled in the pure enjoyment of her senses.

The third baby, born in Chicago, was Edna's last try for a boy. On the day of her birth, Michelson returned from his laboratory as soon as he heard that the pains had started. During the long hours of waiting, Edna suggested he take Madeleine and Beatrice, aged four and two, to the Quadrangle Club for luncheon. Anna, the club waitress who served Michelson his daily luncheon, welcomed the little girls and brought a highchair for Beatrice. They sat at the table quiet and wide-eyed with the wonder of the occasion. Michelson told his daughters that there would be a surprise waiting for them at home. When they returned, Madeleine noticed the strange smell of anesthesia coming from her mother's bedroom. She was worried, until the trained nurse came out to show her the baby, its small, red face still angry at the outrage of birth. Michelson passed hurriedly by the wailing child to his wife's bedroom and assured her that another girl was just what he wanted.

Dorothy (her name was immediately shortened to Dody), according to her sisters, had one outstanding characteristic from birth—stubbornness. She would stiffen every muscle in her wiry legs to prevent the nurse from pinning on her diapers. This exercise strengthened her legs to such a degree that she was able to run around at a very early age and managed frequently not only to escape from the poor woman but to deliver vigorous kicks when she was caught. At four, Dody distressed her father by wrestling with the neighborhood children. More than once he returned from his classes to find her at the bottom of a heap of small boys. Recognizing an arm or a leg he would lay hold of it to extract her from the human pyramid. A severe talk followed, in which he informed her that she was not a boy and had no right to behave like one. She hung her head, sullen and rebellious. He told Edna that something radical would have to be done if she had any hope of making their little ruffian into a lady.

Michelson sometimes took one or another of his daughters to Ryerson on a Saturday morning. On one of these expeditions, when Dody was five, she was the lucky one. They walked past the gray gothic towers of the university and turned into the laboratory. Michelson pushed open the heavy arched door and Dody stood blinking in the dark, cool hallway, adjusting her eyes to the change from the sunlight, and sniffing the special scientific smell of the laboratory. Students glanced shyly at them as they passed in the corridor. They saw a gentle and good-humored father smiling at his little girl, quite different from the formidable professor who grilled them at the Friday morning recitations.

Fred Pearson's placid face lighted up when he greeted the two. "Dody has come along to supervise our work this morning, Fred," Michelson said. They led her down a stairway to the basement, where she was allowed to peek at the "she devil" ruling engine for thirty seconds through a window in the insulated wall. "How has the prima donna been behaving?" Michelson asked. He and Fred fell into a discussion about "Rowland ghosts"—false spectral lines caused by periodic errors in the screw or a wobble in the carriage. Dody grew restless after a while, feeling she had lost her father's attention. "Show me something interesting, Pahdie," she begged. Near the ruling engine stood a delicate balance. "How would you like to weigh a single hair of your head?" Michelson asked. He pulled one out and laid it on the scale, which staggered under the impact, so sensitive was it.

They moved on past some heavy instruments floating in mercury. As a parting present for her to take home, Michelson filled a small vial from the little spigot on the tank where the cold, heavy liquid was stored. Dody was in raptures.

Leaving the laboratory, they went upstairs to his office. A scratching at the window attracted their attention. It was Michelson's pet squirrel. From the lefthand top drawer of his desk, he took out a box of pine nuts that his brother Ben had sent from California and, opening the window, gingerly offered a few to the squirrel. Soon the little animal was inside, snooping into the drawers and cubbyholes of the desk looking for more. Michelson was so fond of this squirrel that he left the window open even when he went abroad. Quite a bit of damage was done to the desk, but he wouldn't have it otherwise.

The Michelsons had acquired a house on the corner of Fifty-eighth Street and Kimbark Avenue on a generous, oblong section of land only a short walk from the university. Kimbark was a quiet street, shaded by elms and maples. Many of the houses along it belonged to other university professors. The Michelson house was surrounded by a tall hedge of lilac bushes. In the spring, the heavy lavender blossoms weighed the branches almost to the ground.

Edna furnished the living room with oriental rugs, brocaded curtains in rich, warm colors, comfortable, well-upholstered chairs, and a sofa opposite the fireplace. The three inner walls were completely lined with bookshelves, scientific books on one side, classics in the middle, and modern novels on the third wall. The walls were hung with several of Michelson's watercolors and over the mantel was a painting of the school of his favorite artist, Corot.

Two broad steps led down from the living room into a glassed-in veranda, occupied largely by a pool table. This was also the music room, where Michelson played Mozart violin sonatas. As Edna's taste in music was somewhat more popular, Michelson bought her a "player" piano. Pumping vigorously, she played her favorite arias from *Fra Diavolo* and *Pagliacci*.

When the two younger daughters were about eight and ten years old, Michelson began to give each of them a half-hour violin lesson every morning before leaving for the laboratory. Pacing up and down as he counted out the beat, he drilled them with patience on their scales. It was a great moment when they reached the point of playing a real piece. "Nellie Bly" was the first one.

Michelson taught them to approach the violin with nicety. It had to be held up proudly, never allowed to droop. After he had listened to their squeaks and scratches, he would say, "Here, let me play it for you," The tone he drew forth was full and round and above all sharply in tune. The notes of "Nellie Bly" would dance under his skillful fingers. It was a happy way to start a day.

DEPARTURE FROM SYMMETRY

When the children returned from school they usually found their mother comfortably installed on the chaise longue in her bedroom, wearing a high-collared white blouse with a gold cameo brooch at her throat. Her soft brown hair rose from the temples in a pompadour. She had a full face, a small up-turned nose with arching nostrils, deep brown expressive eyes, and a large generous mouth. Her daughters admired her extravagantly.

The bedroom was hung with linen curtains of a peacock motif that blended with the dark violet carpet. Besides the chaise longue, an oversized brass bed, and a rolltop desk, the room contained a fireplace with artificial gas-burning logs, the latest innovation.

Michelson's room had an entirely different character. It was austere, with no knickknacks of any description. The white iron bed had very little "give" to it, and the only other pieces of furniture were a large writing table and a highboy on which lay a pair of military brushes and sometimes a plug of chewing tobacco.

Michelson was subject to nightmares. One dream, from which he would awaken in a cold sweat of fear, recurred all through his life. He was back in the Navy in charge of a training ship manned by the midshipmen who stood waiting for him to give them orders. There they would wait while he endeavored to recall the proper names of certain halyards and sails which utterly escaped him. Minutes went by, during which the men would begin to laugh and then to jeer in derision. Acute humiliation would wake him at this point, and he would have a struggle with his conscious mind to banish the terrifying vision. In another dream, he was riding a motorcycle up a steep incline. At the brink, the motor would fail him and the heavy vehicle would roll backward down the hill. Like Sisyphus with his stone, Michelson could never bring it all the way to the top.

In spite of his restless nights and his frequent insomnia, he always woke in the morning with fresh energy and a healthy appetite. Breakfast was his favorite meal.

Michelson occasionally went bicycling, wearing a sweater, "plus fours," and a sports cap, but his favorite form of exercise was still a good, evenly matched tennis game. After work, as long as the fair weather lasted, he went to the Quadrangle Club. This was a yellow clapboard building on the corner of Fifty-eighth Street and Ellis Avenue with a porch of tall white columns in front and behind it several tennis courts where faculty members played for relaxation. There Michelson was able to pick up a game with any one of a dozen excellent players, among whom were George Hale; Forest Ray Moulton, also an astronomer; Preston Keyes; Henry Gale, then a young star on the football team; and sometimes Alonzo Stagg, the famous coach. Michelson could beat most of his opponents by his excellent control of the ball, good placement, and clever anticipation of his opponent's next move. "Bully for you!" he would call when someone made a telling shot.

In bad weather, Michelson transferred his interest to three-cushion billiards. His knowledge of physics gave him an unfair advantage, his opponents complained. He soon became the club's champion.

In March 1902, Michelson was asked by President D. C. Gilman of the Carnegie Institution of Washington to act as an advisor to the Executive Committee of the Institution. At one of their early meetings a most ambitious plan for building a physical research laboratory was discussed. The geologists were to occupy two-thirds of the building, but Michelson raised no objection as long as a physicist was top dog.

In April 1902 Michelson wrote about the proposed building to the chairman of the advisory committee on physics, R. S. Woodward:

> . . . while . . . the scheme [Carl] Barus proposes may look very large to us—I have enough confidence in the prog-

ress of science to think that if such an opportunity is neglected our committee will be justly held responsible for
not looking ahead say twenty or thirty years.[4]

The Carnegie Institution financed Michelson's ruling engine for fifteen or twenty years. He had his ups and downs with
it (or it with him.) He was asked in December to fill out a
standard application for the grant, to which he replied, "During the twenty-five years of my scientific career I have never
had any difficulty in securing funds for my researches *without
conditions.* If these are still called for, I hereby withdraw my
application."[5]

Secretary C. D. Walcott graciously complied, sending
$1500. Three months later he asked Michelson to fill in the
form for the sake "of administrative orthodoxy," adding "you
are at liberty to make such emendations in the regulations as
you may desire."[6] Michelson struck out the offending "conditions" in the form.

On another occasion when Michelson asked for $5,000, he
received no reply for many months. On April 7, 1905, he sent
one sentence to the president: "I hereby withdraw my application for assistance from the Carnegie Institution." Ten years
would elapse before friendly relations were resumed.

Michelson's prestige from a lifetime of careful work was so
great that the results of his experiments were seldom called
into question. But in 1902, this had indeed occurred when
Dayton C. Miller, who had succeeded Michelson as professor
of physics at Case, repeated the Michelson-Morley experiment
in the hope of finding an error.

"Doubting Dayton," an expert in acoustics and in the
science of musical sound, made a remarkable collection of
flutes which he bequeathed to the Library of Congress. Like
Huyghens, Thomas Young, and many others, he was led by his
interest in sound waves to look upon light waves as an analo-
gous phenomenon. He had come to Cleveland in 1890 and

soon became as eager as Michelson to restore the supremacy of the undulatory theory and to establish experimental proof of the medium in which light waves were supposed to move.

Some time after his arrival in Cleveland, Miller moved into the boarding house where the Morleys lived. They were kind to the young man, and Miller soon filled the place that Michelson's departure had left empty in Morley's affection as well as in scientific collaboration. He learned from the older scientist every detail of the 1886–1887 experiments on ether drift. Pieces of the equipment were still lying about in Morley's laboratory when Morley and Miller together undertook to repeat the Michelson-Morley experiment with the specific purpose of testing the FitzGerald-Lorentz contraction theory. They hoped that "If this modification depends on the resilience or other physical properties of the solid materials, it might be detected by experiment."[7]

They built an interferometer much larger than Michelson's, its 430-centimeter arms made of white pine. The result was an infinitesimal positive effect, so small that it could only be said to prove that the pine base was affected by the contraction by about the same amount as the base made of sandstone. It was enough, however, to fire Miller with new hope and persuade the aging Morley to try again.

In July of 1904 Michelson received an urgent letter from George Hale, who was trying to organize a world scientific meeting in September in connection with the International Electrical Congress at the St. Louis World's Fair.

> I sincerely hope you will find it possible to be present . . . since it now promises to be a very important one . . . Poincaré is to bring over the views of the French physicists on the question of standard wave-lengths. The Royal Society and the Royal Astronomical Society have already appointed Committees and will also send delegates. . . . This will be a great opportunity to deal with the

question of standard wave-lengths, and you, above all men, ought to be present to take part in the discussion. Will you not for this reason make a special effort to come to St. Louis?[8]

Michelson replied that he would try to come but that he felt reluctant to advocate the use of his own standards. September was an inconvenient time, too. Hale had offered to change the date and place of the meeting to suit him, so important was it, he felt, that Michelson should appear.[9] This was flattering but Michelson thought it unwise to try to change the time or place on his account. On September 19 he wrote to Hale that he was exhausted by continued sleeplessness and would not be able to attend the meeting. Hale made the report for him.

The meeting proved to be all that Hale had anticipated and more. It was on this occasion that Henri Poincaré, the great French master of pure analytical mathematics who of all Einstein's contemporaries came closest to anticipating him in respect to the Special Theory of Relativity,[10] expressed the doubts which the negative result of the Michelson-Morley experiment had created in the minds of many physicists. He compared the present dilemma to the crisis brought on by Copernicus in 1543, when he proclaimed that the sun, not the earth, was the center of the solar system. Poincaré asked the assembled physicists:

Are we about to enter now upon the eve of a second crisis? These principles on which we have built all, are they about to crumble away in their turn? . . . Alas . . . such are the indubitable results of the experiments of Michelson. . . .

From all these results, if they are confirmed, would arise an entirely new mechanics which would be, above all, characterised by this fact, that no velocity could surpass that of light. . . .

Michelson has shown us, I have told you, that the

physical procedures are powerless to put in evidence absolute motion. . . .[11]

If wishing could have done it, the negative result would have been reversed. Dayton Miller did not stop at wishing. In 1904 and 1905 he and Morley made another valiant attempt with an interferometer made entirely of steel. The wooden arms had to be abandoned because of warping. They used the original cast-iron trough that Michelson and Morley had built and they sent to the master optician Petididier in Chicago for optical parts. He supplied them with a beam-splitter, a compensator, and sixteen plane mirrors. The new instrument closely resembled the classical interferometer but had a much longer light path.

In a darkened room Morley and Miller followed the moving apparatus in its rotation. A run of thirty turns was the usual stint, in which the observer walked half a mile, keeping his eye on the moving eyepiece, without interruption, for half an hour. In spite of all their care and efforts, they were unable to detect any significant displacement of the fringes, and they announced that the results of 1887 were ostensibly correct. In 1906, Morley retired from the research, leaving Miller alone with his doubts.

Michelson heard of all this activity with interest but was not exactly surprised at the outcome. His thoughts at this time were turning to Mount Wilson in California, where Hale, who had left Chicago in 1904, was planning to build an observatory with the backing of Andrew Carnegie. Stories of great plans on the mountain filtered back to Chicago as the giant scheme took form. Michelson envied Hale with all his heart. Soon after his departure he had written to him with nostalgia:

> Sorry to have you leave us and will miss you more than you can imagine. I realize however how much better you will be fixed for the splendid program you have outlined for yourself and so heartily congratulate you on the prospect.

The feeling is just a shade tinged with regret that I am not in like good fortune—tho I have but little to complain of here—except that the surroundings are not as congenial and esthetic as I should like. . . .[12]

On January 10, 1906, President Harper died. Educators all over the United States mourned his loss and flags flew at half-mast in many of the colleges. Michelson wondered if his successor would have the ability and the foresight to keep the university up to the high standards of the founder.

He and Hale had made a multitude of plans which had to be put aside when Hale left Chicago. Michelson sometimes thought of pulling up stakes altogether and heading for the clear mountain air of the Far West. Hale urged him to come, but the time was not yet ripe.

CHAPTER 12

The $Nobel$ $Prize$

T HE Nobel Prize has been called the highest honor that the world can offer for intellectual attainment. That it has accomplished this aim and maintained its prestige is due not only to the extraordinary gift of Alfred Nobel, but also to the men who shouldered the great responsibility of awarding the prizes.

Nobel made provision for the awards in a will in Paris, which he wrote without a lawyer, in 1895, about a year before he died. When the time came to execute the will, a number of difficulties arose, and five years passed before the will was finally approved. Four Nobel institutions were established. One of these, the Swedish Royal Academy of Science, was ready in 1901 to make the first award in physics. Twelve nominees were under consideration, among them the American astrophysicist W. W. Campbell of Lick Observatory. However, Nobel's instructions excluded astronomers, even those whose work was chiefly concerned with physics, and the Swedes still hold to this interpretation. The first physicist to receive the prize was W. C. Röntgen of Germany, for his discovery of X rays, from which the medical profession was already benefiting.

H. A. Lorentz and Pieter Zeeman shared the prize in 1902 for the discovery and explanation of the "Zeeman Effect"—a splitting of spectral lines in a magnetic field. The next year Pierre and Marie Curie, in conjunction with Antoine Henri Becquerel, were honored for the discovery of radium and radioactivity. In 1904 the prize went to Lord Rayleigh for his discovery of a new element, argon. Philipp Lenard won it in 1905; he had caused cathode rays to pass from the interior of a vacuum tube through a thin metal window into the air, where they produced luminosity. J. J. Thomson, the 1906 laureate, was honored for his discovery of "electrons" and his work on the conduction of electricity through gases.

It was customary for the Nobel Committee to consult experts in the field of the award. In physics they sought the opinion of past recipients and wrote to the professors of physics in well-known universities for their recommendations. William Pickering of Harvard, brother of the observatory director E. C. Pickering, received one of these inquiries, and in November 1903 he wrote the following letter:

My dear Michelson,

I have been asked by the Nobel Committee to name a candidate for the Nobel Prize in Physics. In view of your great work in determining the Velocity of Light and your varied applications of the interference of light, I wish to present to the Nobel Committee a statement of your work. Although Nobel specified "prizes to those persons who shall have contributed most materially to benefit mankind during the year immediately preceding," earlier work is also considered by the Committee. Copies of the published investigations must be transmitted to the Committee. Will you therefore send me a statement of your principal investigations with copies of publications that I may transmit them. If for any reason you cannot send me these during the next few days, will you let me know when I may expect them?[1]

Other recommendations in Michelson's favor accumulated over the next few years and finally, in 1907, he was summoned to Sweden.

Leaving Edna and the children at home he crossed the Atlantic late in November. On his way to Stockholm, he stopped in London to receive another great honor, the Copley Medal, highest award of the Royal Society. This was the one that he cherished above all others, for he believed that Rayleigh and Kelvin were the men who had backed him. It meant a great deal to him to stand high in their estimation as a physicist's physicist.

Edward Morley was honored separately with the Darry Medal at the anniversary meeting of the Royal Society which they both attended, but no mention was made of their joint work on the ether drift.

The Nobel Committee makes a practice of swearing recipients to secrecy, warning them to deny all rumors until the prizes are announced. Michelson found this increasingly difficult as the time drew near. At the banquet in London, Sir William Crookes asked him point-blank if he were receiving the award. Michelson replied that this was the first indication he had had of it. In order to avoid more embarrassment, he wired Stockholm to ask if he could admit knowing about the award, since apparently word had got around. He was told that he could not and that nothing was certain until the official announcement was made. This came on November 29.

On the ninth of December, Michelson boarded a small

steamer for Esbjerg, Denmark, on the first leg of his trip from England to Stockholm. In the deck chair next to his, he noticed a man with very sunburned features, small, dark, glittering eyes behind glasses, a receding hairline, and a black moustache. The stranger and his wife were discussing accommodations at the Grand Hotel in Stockholm and whether there would be time to have his clothes pressed before the Nobel ceremony took place. Michelson introduced himself and found that he was talking to Rudyard Kipling, who was on his way to receive the Nobel Prize for Literature. They fell into a conversation which ended rather abruptly when Kipling made some unflattering remarks regarding Americans and the United States. Smarting with indignation, the former naval officer rose and had his deck chair moved away from Kipling's.

From Denmark, Michelson proceeded across the narrow channel to Sweden. Arriving in Stockholm, he was shocked to find all flags flying at half-mast and the city plunged into deepest mourning. Beloved old King Oscar was dead. A pall fell over the whole nation, and the customary festivities of the Nobel Prizes were canceled. Normally the king himself awarded the prizes, at an elaborate ceremony in the Stockholm Concert Hall, but in this case the awards were to be made in the Hall of the Royal Academy.

Michelson went to the Hotel Continental where he was introduced to the recipient of the chemistry prize, Eduard Buchner of Bavaria, chosen because of his important discoveries in the processes of fermentation. Professor Buchner had had a very rough crossing on the Baltic, from Sassnitz to Trelleborg. His ship had put into port during a storm and after unloading most of the passengers, Buchner among them, the vessel was literally torn from the dock with Buchner's valet, in whose care he had put all the instruments and documents he had intended to use at his Nobel lecture, still on board. The Stockholm train departed before the unfortunate valet was able to disembark so that Buchner was forced to "come as he was." He managed to laugh off his dilemma and Michelson took a liking to him because of his good nature in the face of this trying situation.

The fourth laureate for 1907 was the French physician Alphonse Laveran, who received the award for physiology and medicine. He arrived from Malmö with the Kiplings, who had stopped overnight in Copenhagen. Laveran was a disciple of Louis Pasteur. He was credited with creating a new branch of medicine, protozoology, in which protozoa are designated as causing disease.

On Tuesday afternoon, December 10, at four o'clock, the four recipients and the savants of the Swedish Academy gathered in the assembly hall of the Royal Academy of Science. On the wall behind the desk hung a bronze relief of Alfred Nobel, encircled by a green wreath, the only decoration marking the occasion. Members of the press were immediately attracted to Kipling, whose lively manner of chatting with everyone, unawed by the serious occasion, made him the center of attention. He was the youngest of the prize winners. While he listened to the conversation of the Swedish scientists, his glittering eyes took in everything that happened around him. He smiled continuously, sometimes discreetly in response to a compliment, sometimes quite openly, in boyish exuberance.

Laveran could instantly be recognized as a Frenchman by the vivacity of his Gallic gestures. He had a sparse gray beard, an energetic face, and thinning gray hair; in his lapel he wore the red ribbon of the Légion d'Honneur. His small, slender figure contrasted sharply with the three stately Swedes, Chancellor Wachtmeister, Royal Historian Montelius, and Professor Medein.

"Professor Michelson has an appearance which at a distance somewhat resembles Kipling, because of his black moustache and prominent chin," one reporter wrote; ". . . his manner, however, is quite different; cautious, reserved, almost shy. In his strong features one can trace the energies of the big men of the American West."[2]

The ceremony itself took only half an hour. Count Wachtmeister addressed the laureates and a small audience.

We had hoped that our beloved King would have been able to distribute the prizes. But alas, this was not to be. King Oscar is no more. We cannot, therefore, celebrate the Nobel Prize ceremony, and the distribution of prizes will take place in all simplicity. His majesty, King Gustave, has authorized me to award the prizes for science and literature. Gentlemen, I ask the presidents of the institutions designated by M. Nobel to make known the results of their examinations.[3]

Michelson sat patiently through a long eulogy of Kipling, who was pronounced "the greatest genius in the realm of narrative literature which England has produced in our times." His poem "Recessional" was read to the gathering, after which he received his prize.

Then Count Mörner, president of the Royal Academy, addressing Michelson, stated that the Academy was awarding him the prize in recognition of his original methods for ensuring exactness in measurements, for his investigations in spectroscopy, and for his achievement in obtaining a nonmaterial standard of length. Again there was no mention of the ether-drift experiment, although Einstein's Special Theory of Relativity, which explained the negative result, had been published two years earlier.

Count Mörner then handed Michelson a beautifully decorated diploma enclosed in an elegant leather cover, the large gold medel engraved with a likeness of Alfred Nobel, and a check for 139,000 Swedish crowns (about $40,000).

The next two days passed very pleasantly in the company of the Swedish scientists who arranged unofficially to wine and dine the laureates with true Swedish hospitality. After one dinner Dr. Buchner told Michelson that he had been under the impression that the American could speak no German. "That is true," Michelson answered. "Then how is it that you regaled us all evening in German, speaking as fluently as if it were your mother tongue?" Michelson swore he remembered not a word. He regretted that his knowledge of the language had vanished with the delightful bouquet and the relaxing effect of the many varieties of wine that his host had pressed upon him.[4]

It was necessary to remain sober on December 12, for on that day he delivered his address to the Royal Academy. For his Nobel lecture, "Recent Advances in Spectroscopy," he compared the first prism with which Newton separated the colors of sunlight to the diffraction grating which he demonstrated.

> . . . As an example of progress made in this direction, I have the honour of exhibiting a grating having a ruled surface nine inches by four and one half inches (220×110 mm). This has one hundred and ten thousand lines and is nearly perfect in the second order; so that its resolving power is theoretically 220000 and this is very nearly realized in actual experiments.[5]

He discussed the various opportunities that were opened up to the observer of interference of light waves and ended his talk with a description of the echelon spectroscope and a demonstration of the interferometer. Everyone wanted a look at the grating, and Michelson had to guard against fingerprints or any contact which might injure its fragile surface.

Professor K. B. Hasselberg, one of the physicists on the committee who had assembled the dossier on Michelson, told him confidentially that when the actual vote was taken, there had not been a single dissenting voice. Hasselberg was particularly pleased by the choice because he was himself much interested in spectroscopy and he admired the beauty and fine precision in Michelson's work. Shortly after the decision was made he had written to Hale:

> As soon as I had read my paper the president only asked: "Does the Academy award the physical prize to Prof. M

on the grounds now explained?" Whereupon was heard only a vigorous *Yes* and thus the question was settled. I am also of the opinion, that this choice was a very good one and I will go further and say, that it is the *best* of all which have been made up to this date. Our earlier laureates Röntgen, Lorentz, Zeeman, Becquerel, Curie, Rayleigh, Lenard and J. J. Thomson are indeed men of eminent scientific merits, but for my part I must consider the work of Michelson as more fundamental and also by far more delicate.[6]

Reporters gathered around asking Michelson for his impressions of Sweden and the prize.

When I first heard that the celebration had to be cancelled I became very downhearted. But now that the awards have been made, I feel that it was a beautiful expression of heartfelt, Swedish friendship which I have heard about in America and of which I have had proof from my two laboratory assistants, the brothers Pearson, who by their faithfulness have contributed so much to my fortunate discoveries. When I come home with the Nobel money they shall certainly not be forgotten.

From the highest in your society down to the working man, they all seem to be unusually gifted and well educated, even the street urchins are quiet, decent and courteous. Here money is not Almighty God. You Swedes give yourselves time to improve your knowledge of art, literature and ethics. Here one does not find the pitiless rush of Chicago, here is a delightful country and a delightful people. I will be back for sure next summer to enjoy the weird light of the midnight sun.[7]

Among the members of the audience who came up to examine the grating and to congratulate Michelson was a young man who presented himself shyly. "You don't know me," he said as Michelson studied him with uncertainty. "I am your son."

Ten years had passed since they had last seen each other at the painful hearing in the divorce court. After the meeting was over and the dignitaries had been properly greeted, Michelson extricated himself from the scientists to have a quiet talk with young Albert. He was now twenty-nine, had graduated from Harvard in 1901, and had begun his career as American consular agent at Charleroi, Belgium. He had come to Stockholm from Turin, Italy, his second post, having read of his father's arrival. He had a handsome face and modest bearing. All the bitterness of the past seemed to disappear and friendship sprang up between them. Before parting, Michelson asked Albert to keep in touch with him by letter and offered to visit him on a future trip to Europe if the occasion arose.

While Michelson, at the crest of his career, was receiving the generous acclaim of his fellow physicists, another long and successful life devoted to science was drawing to a close. Lord Kelvin of Largs lay dying at Netherall, his home in Scotland. On December 18, 1907, death came peacefully to the great British physicist who had befriended Michelson in Baltimore and championed his research for more than twenty years.

Glowing tributes filled the newspapers along with accounts of the great contributions Kelvin had made to the dynamical theory of heat and the fundamental principle of the conservation of energy. His mariner's compass was one of the finest inventions of his time, and he had been knighted in 1866 for his pivotal role in the laying of the Atlantic cable.[8] Kelvin was buried in Westminster Abbey with all honor and ceremony, near the graves of Newton and William Herschel. With his death, the ether concept lost one of its staunchest supporters, leaving Michelson with a feeling of loneliness in the new world of electrons and quanta.

In Chicago Michelson's Nobel Prize was hailed in banner

headlines as a triumph for the city, for the young university, and for the nation as a whole. On the night of his return, a banquet was given in his honor by the university. Martin Ryerson presided and George Vincent was toastmaster, officiating with an 1893 Sauterne that flowed throughout the speeches. Henry Crew spoke on "Michelson's Researches"; Hale discussed "Light as a Means of Research." From then on, the evening took a more frivolous turn. Edward Leamington Nichols, president of the American Association for the Advancement of Science, chose to satirize "That Useless Science, Optics." After Paul Shorey's eulogy on the "Brotherhood of Creative Scholars" and a speech by R. S. Woodward of the Carnegie Foundation, Michelson ended the evening with a flippant little speech, "It is Blessed to Receive as Well as to Give."

On the voyage home Michelson had taken care never to let anyone but himself handle the case containing the grating. He had plans for its use in the next phase of his research and was anxious to get it safely back to his laboratory. Not long after the returning hero, overjoyed with success, had restored it to Fred Pearson's care, the historic grating was smashed into a hundred splinters. Fred could never understand how it slipped out of his grasp and shattered on the stone floor. He was horrified as he stooped to pick up one small fragment, worth saving if only for a memento. Michelson's grief over the accident was keen, but he knew it would have been senseless to reproach Pearson for carelessness. Instead, he quietly gave orders to start the ruling engine on a fresh slab of speculum so that they could begin again on the tedious process of replacement. Months of work were required, but Michelson maintained a stoical attitude throughout.

Edna had a different reaction. "You know who is responsible for it, Albert? It's that vicious little Etruscan god Dr. Rood gave you, demanding his sacrifice. He is filled with cunning and malice and he waited until you were really happy before he struck. Let's hope he has done enough damage to assuage his jealousy." She was looking apprehensively at the seal hanging on Michelson's watch chain.

Edna was pleased to hear of the reconciliation between her husband and young Albert. She also made an effort to heal the rift with the younger son. Franz Boas at Clark had excited Truman's boyhood interest in anthropology and later Truman had specialized in the subject, taking his Ph.D. at Harvard and studying for two more years at Leipzig and Bonn. In 1910 he joined the Bureau of American Ethnology in Washington. Later on he made yearly expeditions to the Algonquian tribes to experiment with an interesting new technique for reducing the Arapaho and Cheyenne languages to "normal Algonquian" by the application of phonetic shifts.

During the 1920s Edna persuaded Truman to visit the family in Chicago on his return from a summer spent among the Cheyennes in Wyoming. She and Michelson enjoyed hearing of the young man's adventures. He had been entertained all summer by a warlike tribe. The chief had taken a fancy to him and wished to express his friendship by making a farewell gift. As Truman was getting ready to leave, he found himself surrounded by a group of fierce-looking braves in war paint and battle dress. Beside the chief stood his daughter, whom he offered to Truman as a wife. The situation was a delicate one: the honor was overwhelming and refusal dangerous. Edna thought it was a pity that he hadn't brought back the little squaw, but somehow he had managed to escape without her, luckily for his wife, Catherine Harrison Michelson, whom he had married in 1903.

Elsa never saw her father after the divorce, nor did she write to him. She lived with her mother and her stepfather, Robert Barnes Sheppard, in the Bahamas most of the year and at Edgewater in the summers. Margaret found Sheppard far more manageable than Michelson and he suited her way of life to perfection. He was an amateur architect, had acted in amateur theatricals, was thoroughly personable, good company, very presentable, and had inherited an income of his own. He was a thoughtful host at her parties and he never interrupted her when she was launched on a subject. But as she grew older, her friends noticed that her thoughts turned frequently to memories of her first marriage. Michelson's name often entered the conversation, and she let it be known that the years of their marriage were the ones in which his original work was done. Edna was merely reaping the harvest now that he had become a Nobel Prize winner.

On his part Michelson was seemingly successful at putting Margaret completely out of his thoughts. (She had never dominated them to any extent during the later years of their marriage.) He never inquired about her.

Upon resuming his classes after his return from Sweden, Michelson became aware of a girl in one of them. As a rule his students were male. As Edna had implied in their first conversation, he had never been much impressed with female students. They tended to radiate an earnest air which his generation did not associate with feminine charm, or they became hysterical during the Friday recitation and burst into tears. But Margarite O'Laughlin Crowe was an exception. Their friendship began when he caught her toasting marshmallows over her Bunsen burner in the laboratory. In his most severe tone he told her that the penalty was a fine of two golden-brown marshmallows which she must bring to his office at teatime. After the ice was broken she grew bolder. On St. Valentine's Day, Michelson walked into Ryerson to find his name plaque decorated with hearts and cupids. Margarite Crowe had arranged a party. Fred and Julius Pearson had helped her trim the somber hall with red and white twisted streamers. Michelson relaxed his usual severity and joined in, even managing to drink with apparent relish the sweet punch she had concocted.

Not long after the party he heard that Margarite's mother, with whom she had been living, had died rather suddenly, and that Margarite was thinking of giving up her career in physics. Sending for her immediately, he counseled her against such action. He suggested a change in her studies, advising her to go to Yerkes Observatory to work under the supervision of his friend Edwin Frost. He showed her a stellar map and suggested a part of the sky that might interest her. This was a turning point for Margarite, who later made some original scholarly contributions. In the spring after her graduation, she came to Michelson's office to say good-by. As a keepsake he gave her the broken fragment of the grating that he had used at his Nobel lecture.[9]

Michelson took advantage of his increased fame to ask the university administration to raise the salaries of Fred and Julius Pearson, who up until that time had each received $40 per month. He was successful in getting $35-a-month raises for both of them.

About this time Thomas Edison, not satisfied with his enormous success as an inventor, had developed a desire to be admitted to that holy of holies, the National Academy of Sciences. Relatively impoverished though they were, its members had the aura of a priesthood, and Edison wanted to belong. In most matters his judgment was based solidly on money values. He freely boasted: "I measure everything I do by the size of the silver dollar. If it don't come up to that standard then I know it's no good."[10] This view was not popular with the scientists.

Edison's name was brought up at a business meeting of the Academy in 1908 on the nomination of the Section of Engineering. A majority of physicists—Michelson included—were not enthusiastic and the nomination was defeated. Michelson explained his stand later to Mendenhall:

"The matter of presenting Edison's name for the Nat. Acad. was presented to my notice last year by Barker and I said, as I do now, that I should be willing to support his candidacy as an engineer but not as a physicist."[11]

Somewhat later Robert Millikan was persuaded by the engineers to endorse the proposal of Edison's name. After an eloquent speech recounting Edison's virtues, during which he rocked up and down, balancing on his toes "like the little lizards in the West," Millikan concluded: "I am sure there is no physicist who would not be glad to second the nomination to Academy membership of this great inventor."

A silence ensued. Then Michelson rose from his seat in the front row and said quietly, "I am such a physicist."[12] That settled the matter for some time to come. In 1927, however, the Academy reversed its views and Thomas Edison at long last was welcomed into the fold.

Most of the letters Michelson wrote to scientists were principally concerned with technical problems. His correspondence with T. C. Mendenhall was an exception. The two had much in common and shared a caustic view of the machinations of men in high position and of the operation of the Academy, of which each in turn became president.

Mendenhall had had his own troubles in a more serious situation. In 1890, as superintendent of the Office of Weights and Measures, he was put on a committee to check the weight of the coins at the Mint. Three days before the appointed day on which he was to weigh them, senators, congressmen, friends of the administration, and officials of the Mint began wining and dining him at a series of parties, in the hope of putting him in the "right" frame of mind. Mendenhall, however, pursued his task with determination, checking the weight of each coin with the utmost care and accuracy with the instruments he had brought from the Coast and Geodetic Survey. He was forced to report that the silver dime was somewhat short of its proper weight and some other coins were correspondingly underweight. His findings were suppressed from the report of the superintendent of the Mint and therefore never reached the public. Mendenhall was asked to resign from the committee before any investigation was made. He grew to expect chicanery of this kind in high office but he never became disillusioned.

In 1907 Mendenhall had retired to Italy because of ill health. Michelson wrote to cheer him up:

Chicago, Jan. 1, 1908

My dear Mendenhall,

Thanks for your very charming letter—I don't know when I've got one I enjoyed more—save for the regret it brings that you are no longer with us—and so far away that the chances of meeting are small.

I can fully appreciate all you say of the futility of ninety-nine hundreths of the so-called "advances" in modern civilization and know only too well that the peaceful appreciation of good music and real art—and the living 'midst lovely scenery and with *lazy* Italians—all these are privileges which cannot be too highly esteemed.

They are—alas—not for me—and in particular the atmosphere of Chicago is much less my ideal than that of almost any other spot on earth. Still I try to see some good in it and one thing I've learned—at the cost of many a hard knock—is that it doesn't pay to go around with a chip on the shoulder—and I've also found that human nature is not so abominable as I have sometimes thought.

This optimistic position is doubtless due in part to the fact that I've gotten the Nobel Prize as well as the Copley Medal and haven't found anything but the kindest and sincerest enthusiasm among all my colleagues—and have realized that I have many good friends when I thought I was nearly alone.

Another thing which helps along is the dear little family and no doubt that has helped to humanize me more than anything else. But I fear I'll never learn to "loaf." I get ennuyé when I'm not at work. More often than not the work is not the kind that counts—if it does all the better—but I must keep at it.

The last is a ten inch grating which gives very good results in the second order but I'm aiming at a fourteen inch which must be good in all the orders.

The "radium business" is I think very much over-worked. Its first results were wonderful but since then— nothing. Anyway it's not physics but chemistry. At least that's how I console myself for not being "in it."

Now, dear old colleague, don't talk so much about being "out of it" yourself. You've earned the right to rest and comfort and you've kept the warm regard of all your old friends, whose chief regret is that you are so far away that they don't get a chance to see you and to "reminisce" together.

If you should happen to find yourself in Turin, call on my son, Albert H. Michelson, who is the Consul for the U.S. at that place.

Write again—and as often as the spirit moves you and be sure your letters will be ever welcomed by

Yours cordially

A. A. Michelson[13]

CHAPTER 13

The Relativists of Göttingen

THROUGHOUT the academic year the Quadrangle Club provided a haven in which Michelson could relax when his work was done. He could always find a game of tennis when the weather permitted, or of billiards or chess otherwise. Dr. Preston Keyes in medical research was probably Michelson's closest friend. A wonderful dinner companion, he was always ready to talk philosophy, science, religion, or literature. He had a dry sense of humor, emphasizing his remarks with a funny little crooked smile. "That man Michelson," he once told the Quadranglers watching a game, "will never amount to much. Wastes all his time on light waves when he might have cut a national figure if he had only the ability to concentrate on billiards."

The game of chess held a fascination for Michelson even in his student years at the Naval Academy. He developed his pieces in a variety of unorthodox openings that often threw a conservative opponent off guard, but Frank James Marshall, the American chess champion, said, after a game, that the physicist played with more passion than skill.

Michelson never lunched with other club members at the long communal table, because he felt that having to make conversation interrupted his thinking. He preferred to eat alone at a small table which the waitress Anna held for him against any onslaught, even a crowd of football fans in the autumn. In his pocket he always carried a few white unlined cards, on which he made notes for his lectures. While he was waiting for Anna to bring him his luncheon, he would some-times entertain himself by sketching the characters sitting at other tables. He liked to pick a subject with some feature that lent itself to caricature, like a long, pointed nose, a receding chin, or the large bosom and flowered hat of the garden-club type of woman. Once in a while he was caught in the act. The subject would see him looking over frequently and take it for an invitation to come to his table for a chat. He learned to turn the card over deftly and jot down some inscrutable equations on the other side. Then he would smile innocently as though his mind were still lost in the abstract realm of pure science.

Following his instinct to simplify life by cutting out every extraneous activity, Michelson avoided committees and ad-ministrative duties as far as possible. He never attended meet-ings of the university senate or took any part in the forming of policy, which his position as head of a department entitled, if it did not enjoin, him to do. He went along with Harper in the understanding that they had great mutual respect but would not meddle in each other's affairs. Sometimes he dele-gated one of his assistants to attend in his place. In later years, Arthur Holly Compton asked Michelson if he and W. F. G. Swann, another young assistant, should attend a faculty meeting. "Since you ask me, you had better go," Michelson answered. It turned out that those two were the only faculty members present and were therefore given all the chores to do.[1]

On Sundays, Michelson often went downtown to the Chicago Academy of Fine Arts to join a class of creative painting and another in drawing from life, just to keep his hand in. Five-hour sessions were divided by a lunch hour during which he chatted with his teacher, Rudolph Weisenborn, at Huyler's Restaurant. On one of these occasions, lighting up one of Michelson's Corona-Coronas, the teacher began "pumping" him about the speed of light. Michelson jokingly said that he was paying good money to study painting with Weisenborn and if Weisenborn wanted to learn about physics, he could sign up for a course at the University of Chicago.

It was while Michelson was lunching at the club one day in February 1910 that Thomas C. Chamberlain, head of the department of geology, came over to his table with a proposition that was very much on his mind. Chamberlain was the author of a much-discussed theory on the origin of the universe, but at the moment he was more concerned with the interior of the planet earth. He came to Michelson to ask if he had any suggestion as to how the rigidity of the earth's interior might be determined by means of a physical experiment.

Geologists have always been curious about this subject. Because the temperature rises every few feet in the descent of a mine shaft, it had been assumed that the center of the earth was a molten mass like the sun. But Sir William Thomson's researches of 1863 made it clear that the earth must be considered as a very rigid body. Thomson had argued that it is not subject to tides caused by the sun or the moon as it would be if it were predominantly liquid. The idea of a boiling hell in the middle of the earth on whose crust we live should be abandoned. There had been numerous attempts to measure the rigidity of the earth, as well as its plasticity, by means of delicate pendulums, but no great degree of accuracy had been achieved.

Chamberlain managed to stir Michelson's interest in the problem. His solution struck other scientists as both highly original and very simple.[2] The experiment required two 6-inch iron pipes, 500 feet long, half-filled with water, to be laid in a trench 6 feet underground, one in a north-south and the other in an east-west orientation. Observation pits were to be dug at the ends where motion-picture cameras were installed. In Chamberlain's theory, if the earth had no rigidity, no tides should appear in the pipes, for the moon would attract the earth's mass as much as it attracted water. If, on the other hand, the earth were perfectly rigid, there should be tides of a few thousandths of an inch in the miniature seas within the pipes, which would follow the same schedule as do the tides in any body of water.

As soon as the ground had softened in the first spring thaw, Chamberlain and Michelson went out to Yerkes Observatory to talk with Edwin Frost about the idea, and the astronomer offered a piece of land near the observatory where the test could be made. A method of measuring changes in the water level was devised and the apparatus constructed in 1910. Michelson enlisted Henry Gale of the department of physics to supervise the installations and observations and the mathematical astronomer Forest Moulton to undertake the complicated tidal calculations.[3]

Michelson had to rely heavily on his own knowledge of physics as well as the help of his colleagues. Moulton was asked to solve three differential equations. In spite of his mathematical training, it took him several days to get results. When he presented his solutions, Michelson studied them for a moment and said, "The first two are right but the third is wrong." Moulton returned to his calculations. After a week he found his error and Michelson pronounced the answer correct. Moulton was irritated. "If you knew the answers why did you ask me to work them out?" Michelson replied that he knew them only from his experiments—an educated guess, he called it. He needed the mathematical proof.[4]

The results of this preliminary experiment were reported by Michelson at a meeting of the American Physical Society held at Ryerson Laboratory on December 1, 1913. Observations made from August 5 to September 2, 1910, had shown tides of a few thousandths of an inch. This result supported the theory that the interior of the earth has the same rigidity and elastic properties as steel. The physicists called the announcement the most important discovery of the year in their field, and Michelson was encouraged to make a more thorough investigation using an interferometer.

A new form of recognition came to Michelson with the offer of an exchange professorship at the University of Göttingen for the summer of 1911. That institution was a lively center for physicists and mathematicians during the early years of the twentieth century. A halcyon time, it has been called. In 1911 such men as David Hilbert, Felix Klein, Carl Riecke, and Waldemar Voigt were on the faculty.

Einstein's paper on the Special Theory of Relativity was beginning to be the subject of wide attention and speculation. At the time of its publication in *Analen der Physik,* 1905, the paper caused hardly a ripple in scientific circles and it remained almost unnoticed for several years. The article on "Aether" by Sir Joseph Larmor in the eleventh edition of the *Encyclopaedia Britannica* in 1908 made no mention either of Einstein or of relativity. Though the climate of opinion at Göttingen was beginning to be open to Einstein's ideas, men of science on the other side of the Atlantic were for the most part in violent reaction against them. In 1911 William Magie, president of the American Physical Society, addressed its members with a scorching attack on the new theory, denouncing the abandonment of the ether as a step backward. Insisting that relativity had not been necessary to explain the experiments of Fizeau and Mascart, he asked why the Michelson-Morley experiment was allowed to upset all the primary concepts of physics. "The principle of relativity accounts for the negative result of the experiment of Michelson and Morley," he said, "but without an ether how do we account for the interference phenomena which made that experiment possible?"[5]

A lost, uncomfortable feeling overwhelmed the conservative faction, although these ideas had long been suspected. Galileo had awakened grave doubts regarding the possibility of proving the earth's motion by any mechanical means. Newton had carried these suspicions a step further. "It may be," he wrote, "that there is no body really at rest, to which the places and motions of others may be referred."[6]

Hermann Minkowski, the great Russian mathematician at Göttingen, had died only two years before Michelson's arrival there, and his aura still lay over the institution where he had taught. Shortly before his death, Minkowski, taking as his subject "Space and Time," had delivered a beautiful speech in praise of relativity in which he discussed the fourth dimension and a hyphenated "space-time." This was the first prominent recognition of Einstein's Special Theory.

> The views of space and time which I wish to lay before you have sprung from the soil of experimental physics and therein lies their strength. They are radical. Henceforth space by itself and time by itself are doomed to fade away into mere shadows, and only a kind of union of the two will preserve an independent reality.[7]

Michelson's three experiments on ether drift were part of this "soil"; this was probably the reason he was invited to Göttingen.

Max Planck, author of the quantum theory published in 1900, also explained the overthrow of the classical theory of light by the very close linking of theory with experiment.

. . . it was the facts learned from experiments that shook and finally overthrew the classical theory. Each new idea and each new step were suggested to investigators, where it was not actually thrust upon them, as the result of measurements. The theory of relativity was led up to by Michelson's experiments on optical interference. . . .[8]

Planck also referred to the work of other experimenters, and in his *Scientific Autobiography* he added:

If physicists had always been guided by this principle [that is, that theory should foreshadow the feasibility of experiment], the famous experiment of Michelson and Morley undertaken to measure the so-called absolute velocity of the earth, would never have taken place and the theory of relativity might still be non-existent.[9]

Edna and the children, now four, six, and eight, were overjoyed when Michelson told them they would all be going to spend the summer in Germany. He had booked a June passage on the *Argentina*, a 16,000-ton steamer of the Atlantic Line sailing for Naples.

A few hours out of New York, the vessel hit the first of a series of storms. Edna collapsed into her berth and all three children were desperately seasick. Madeleine and Beatrice got themselves undressed but Dody slept all night in her checked spring coat and yellow straw hat, the elastic of which made a deep red mark under her chin. Michelson, undisturbed, dined heartily, trying out his Italian on the waiter.

On the second day, however, he took the girls in hand. With the help of a friendly stewardess, they dressed, had breakfast, and went up on deck, where Michelson and the ship's officers had rigged a swing from the yardarm. Beatrice, the most daring of the three, could pump so hard that she sailed high out over the railing with every motion of the swing. It was lucky for Edna's peace of mind that she did not see this performance. She remained in her cabin while the *Argentina* pitched and tossed in the Atlantic swells. Only when Gibraltar came into sight did she emerge and begin to enjoy the fine Mediterranean weather and the company of her fellow passengers. The Michelsons debarked in Naples and made the rest of the journey by train.

Göttingen was a charming old town surrounded by wooded hills and mountains. Medieval houses and shops, faced with white stucco and dark, heavy, wooden beams, lined the narrow winding streets. A generous number of beer halls, restaurants, coffee shops, and bakeries hummed with activity at almost all hours of the day.

The Michelsons rented rooms in the house of a faculty member, Professor Guericke, at Planckstrasse 1. Madeleine and Beatrice attended school, while Dody played in a sandpile with the neighbors' children down the street.

The university was housed on the outskirts of the town in the splendid halls of a seventeenth-century palace, remnant of the House of Hanover days. Soon after Michelson began his lectures, he discovered that the professors of physics and mathematics, as well as the students, were divided into radically divergent camps on the question of Einstein's theory of relativity. He ducked the issue successfully until one afternoon his colleagues invited him to a beer hall where they met every day after class. The relativists were all assembled at their *stamtisch*—the table where they always gathered—while those who clung to an ether concept sat around a table of their own. Since Michelson's experiment had been one of the factors that had triggered the new movement, both groups were waiting curiously to see which table he would join. Michelson paused for a moment and then made his position clear by taking a seat among the "old guard."[10] He was sixty, an age when it is difficult to alter the deep convictions of a lifetime. Having set the stage for the new theories, he made up his mind to stick with the things he knew, leaving relativity to the next generation.

Addressing the American Association for the Advancement of Science as retiring president in 1911 he expressed his viewpoint again:

The message[s] we receive from the depth of the stellar firmament or from the electric arcs of our laboratories, come they in a millionth of a second or in hundreds of light years, are faithful records of events of profound significance to the race. They come to us in cypher—in a language we are only beginning to understand.

Our present duty is to make it possible to receive and to record such messages. When the time comes for a Kepler and a Newton to translate them we may expect marvels which will require the utmost powers of our intellect to grasp.[11]

Max Born, then a young theoretician, later the author of a book on relativity, wrote in his diary about the Michelsons:

The next visiting professor (1911) was Albert Michelson from Chicago whose celebrated experiments are the main foundation of relativity. He came with his wife and three children, aged between six and ten [actually four and eight]. The lectures were for me, as a theoretician, not very interesting and did not bring me into close contact with him. Our friendship was accomplished on the tennis court where I happened to be his regular partner. He was a man of over 60, incredibly vigorous and an excellent, hard player. In the final tournament he beat us all and won the first prize.

On the tennis court I also met Mrs. Michelson and became much attached to her and the sweet little girls, particularly the second one, Beatrice, whom I still remember, a lovely child. I was sorry when at the end of the summer semester they had to return to America.[12]

Edna frequently took the children walking in the hills behind Göttingen. On these walks she taught them a little German, some history of the place, and a touch of botany.

The German forests in no way resembled the wild Michigan woods they knew. No tangle of vines, deciduous saplings, birch, or maple choked the paths. No swamps of sphagnum, bunchberries, reindeer moss, or rotting stumps lay underfoot. Reforestation had been carried on with typical Teutonic thoroughness. Every fir in the forest was planted in its row, allowing for the spread of its branches and the proper absorption of sunlight. The underbrush was cleared and the dead branches clipped and stacked for firewood.

In spite of her German heritage and her respect for conservation, there were times when Edna grew impatient with the Prussian mania for order. Wherever she went there were large black-lettered signs telling her what she could or could not do. She had been disturbed and worried by the frequent sight of Kaiser Wilhelm's spike-helmeted soldiers, goose-stepping through the streets of Göttingen. On one of these walks, emerging from the shadowy forest onto a meadow of forget-me-nots, she came face to face with a chain and a large sign blocking the path: DURCHGANG STRENGST VERBOTEN (PASSAGE STRICTLY FORBIDDEN).

"Oh, children," she said, "I think they just put these signs up to make themselves feel important." Ducking under the chain, she led them into the meadow and watched as they somersaulted down a grassy hill to where a stream gurgled over a rocky bed. There they opened their picnic basket and ate their sandwiches. Continuing the walk after luncheon, they came upon another large black sign. Edna was puzzled. "I really can't see why," she began but her voice trailed off into silence as she stared at the sign.

ACHTUNG, it read, WARNING—TARGET PRACTICE. They hurried away past the military installations, glancing fearfully at the giant howitzers.

"Children," she said when they arrived at home, "I think we had better not tell your father about the picnic today."

Kaiser Wilhelm II requested Michelson's presence at an audience on board the royal yacht, and Madeleine went along with her parents on a short cruise through the Kiel Canal. The Kaiser patted Madeleine on the head and was cordial to everyone. He was quite familiar with Michelson's work in optics,[13] and the audience would have been a great success except for a most peculiar accident. Michelson was stung on the tongue by a bee that flew into his mouth! He swore vigorously, Madeleine remembered, regardless of the royal presence. He never minded swearing, and certainly on this occasion nobody blamed him, for his tongue swelled up so that he was unable to eat or speak for two days.

Later, Michelson went to Italy for a visit with young Albert, still at Turin, and now a consul. They had a tennis game and afterward a good Italian dinner. He remembered the visit, his last with Albert, as a very happy one. The promising young diplomat died of pneumonia at his next post, Cologne, on June 9, 1915. When Michelson read the telegram announcing this, a look of shock came over his face. "Who is dead?" the little girls asked, but their father ignored them, wanting to be alone. Since they had never known Albert, they could not grieve.

When the 1911 summer semester was over, Michelson left Göttingen with his family to take up his duties in Chicago once again. But his pleasant association with Max Born did not end. On Michelson's invitation Born came to Chicago in the spring of 1912 to deliver a series of lectures on relativity. During the following summer the young physicist came to visit the Michelsons on Washington Island in the northern part of Lake Michigan. Chicago was so hot that Born left town on the overnight train without his overcoat. When he got out of his sleeping car the next morning to take the boat to the island, it was cold and raining. He was drenched and shivering when he arrived. Edna lent him her raincoat, and for two days, he said, he ran around in a female disguise.

"Edna was most kind to me," he wrote in his diary. "She tried to educate me and to change me from a lecturer at a little provincial German University into an American gentleman."[14]

When Born returned to the city, he began his lectures on relativity, for which Michelson showed little enthusiasm. In spite of their differences, Born was devoted to his host. "I have a vivid memory of his personality," he wrote; "his strong, rather small figure, his beautiful expressive face, his penetrating eyes and his quiet, deliberate way of speaking."[15]

Michelson showed him the ruling engine and explained how a grating was ruled. "The ruling of a grating is not a mechanical process in the ordinary sense, but involves microscopical, even molecular, properties of the materials."[16] Born was fascinated by the regularity found in certain spectra which he photographed. He noticed that Michelson was not inclined to attach much value to theoretical speculation about optical spectra, although this subject was then coming to the forefront of scientific development. He seemed to doubt the existence of simple laws governing the spacing of lines in the spectrum but was tremendously concerned with little deviations in the regularity of these lines.

Born confesses that he himself was not gifted at experimenting but what he learned from Michelson's way of looking at nature helped him to broaden his own research. He was too young and shy to discuss with his host the new theory of perturbation, but he noticed the gap between his own knowledge of and interest in atomic physics and the older man's. Nevertheless, he appreciated Michelson's reverence for the subject and his humility toward those who would one day understand what he knew he did not.

"Physics is much too difficult for physicists," said David Hilbert, the master mathematician of Göttingen.[17] Hilbert liked to tease his colleagues about the vagueness of their unproven principles but there was some truth in his words. Einstein's profound theory of relativity was called "mathematically awkward" by Minkowski, who had been his teacher, and Michelson's work had similar shortcomings. As he had done with Moulton's derivations for the theory of the earth's rigidity, Michelson often compensated for his sketchy mathematical background by an uncanny intuition—probably the same gift he had manifested before the examiners at the Naval Academy. This intuitive perception baffled one of his graduate students who came to him for help on an equation.

"Obviously the equation is thus and so," Michelson said, jotting it down. The student was skeptical and went away to figure out the mathematics. Three weeks later he came back sure that the equation was wrong. Michelson assured him it was right and, as it turned out, it was proven so when the result was verified. "How did you derive it?" the student asked. "Derive it? Derive it? I just wrote it down," said Michelson, smiling with satisfaction.[18]

Meanwhile the storm of controversy continued. The Michelson-Morley experiment was alternately cursed for upsetting Newtonian physics and blessed for introducing relativity. Other investigators made any number of tests, as incredulity mounted. Most of them confirmed the negative result. Still Einstein's theory was not fully accepted.[19]

Paul Ehrenfest, noted physicist and close friend of Einstein and Lorentz, opened his lecture on December 4, 1912, at the University of Leiden (where he followed Lorentz as professor of theoretical physics) on a note of alarm:

"Permit me to speak about a crisis . . . which at present seriously threatens a fundamental hypothesis of physics—the aether hypothesis. It seems to me that this crisis gives a vivid picture of the characteristic revolutionary mood which dominates theoretical physics at this moment."

And, in order to demonstrate the problem, he set up a miniature Michelson-Morley experiment for his students.[20]

Quantities of literature were put out to meet the popular demand for explanations of relativity and of the experiment which proved it. Michelson, feeling somewhat out of it by this time, remained unconvinced. He kept aloof from the discussions and turned with relief to the ruling of gratings, a task he found more rewarding.

There the long struggle was at last paying off. Significant improvements in technique brought him the longed-for result—an almost perfect grating of unequaled size. He employed an interferometer in conjunction with the ruling engine to determine residual errors of the screw to within a millionth of an inch.

Tempers had subsided with the passing of time since he had summarily withdrawn his application for assistance from the Carnegie Institution, but he had not had what he considered decisive evidence of a result—nothing to show for the institution's investment or his own time. At last, however, he had triumphed.

My dear President Woodward,

I have the honor to make the following report of work on the ruling of diffraction gratings—for which an appropriation of $2500 was granted by the Carnegie Institution about ten years ago.

My apologies are due for not sending an earlier report. . . .

I have recently ruled a ten inch grating which has a resolving power of over half a million.[21]

The feud was over—all was forgiven. President Woodward wrote a warm letter of congratulation on the achievement and asked Michelson for an account to be published in the yearbook for 1915.

As the German preparations for war began to threaten Europe, Michelson grew restless and impatient with the governments that failed to recognize the symptoms of aggression. After the invasion of Belgium, he asked Edna to drop her German friends and avoid speaking German in the house. This was somewhat awkward, as her closest friend, Mrs. William Nitze, was raising money for the German wounded. The beautiful Mrs. Nitze, wife of the professor of Romance languages at the University of Chicago, opened the German Bazaar at the Colosseum dressed as a circus rider complete with white ostrich plumes and mounted on the forehead of a gigantic elephant.

After France was overrun, Michelson worried about his British friends. "I hope you win and win thoroughly," he wrote to Sir Joseph Larmor.[22] In 1917, as America was being drawn into the war, he set out for Washington to see if he could still be of service to his country.

CHAPTER 14

Red Star in the Giant's Shoulder

WITH the outbreak of war in Europe in 1914, George Ellery Hale had written to William H. Welch, president of the National Academy of Sciences, urging him to offer the services of the Academy to President Woodrow Wilson in the event of war with Germany. Two years elapsed before the Academy was roused to action. Then Hale was made head of the National Research Council (NRC), a branch of the Academy through which scientists and engineers would bring their knowledge to bear on military problems in preparing the country for war.

Hale called Robert Millikan from Chicago in the summer of 1917 to head the Physics Division of NRC. As Millikan became involved in this job, his role at Ryerson dwindled. His aim was to turn the laboratory over to war work. In this connection he discussed with Michelson a plan for redesigning the range finder he had invented in 1890 and developing a new one badly needed for antisubmarine warfare. After the United States entered the war in April 1917, Michelson was commissioned a lieutenant commander in the Naval Coast Defense Reserve, and Millikan asked him to transfer his whole research operation from Chicago to the Bureau of Ordnance in Washington. Michelson reported to Rear Admiral Ralph Earle, Chief of the Bureau, on June 28, 1918, bringing with him Fred Pearson and Joseph Purdy, a younger man who was to prove very useful.

It was not easy for Michelson, now sixty-six, to leave his sanctuary where everything ran according to his wish, and where his mere presence inspired awe. In wartime Washington, younger men, many of them his former pupils and assistants, were in positions of high authority. Millikan had been Michelson's pupil in 1895, his assistant and associate for twenty years, and he had developed over this period certain admirable qualities that Michelson lacked entirely. He was tactful in handling colleagues and graduate students, a duty that had been thrust on his shoulders by Michelson. His gifts as an administrator had first brought him the position with the NRC and would later make him the head of the California Institute of Technology (he preferred to be known as "chairman of the executive committee" rather than "president"). Millikan's pride rose understandably with each new honor. He was frequently called to the White House, a circumstance he rather liked to publicize. But Michelson pursued his way serenely in his lesser role, smiling to himself or sharing the latest "Millikanism" with his wife at the dinner table.

S. W. Stratton, still head of the Bureau of Standards, was also in evidence. Seventeen years had passed since he and Michelson had worked together on the harmonic analyzer. Michelson's irritation over the Bureau of Standards episode had never quite disappeared, although he had to admit that Stratton had accomplished splendid work there, building the infant organization into an important department of the government. When they met again, Stratton welcomed his former boss cordially and offered to put the bureau at his disposal. Michelson asked modestly for a corner where he and Fred Pearson might carry on their work on the range finder.

When Michelson appeared at the Bureau of Ordnance for his orders, the officer of the day looked at him with disapproval. "Michelson, you're out of uniform," he said. "You should have a star on your cuff." Michelson went to his tailor to have the star sewed on. The following day a different officer greeted him. "Michelson, you're out of uniform, you have no right to that star on your cuff. Have it removed." Off went the star. This performance was repeated several times. Edna suggested that she should invent a star with a snapper so that he could wear it or not according to which officer was in charge.

Living quarters in Washington were almost impossible to find and Michelson did not have much time to look for them. He took the only house he could afford, in a Georgetown slum which became fashionable only many years later. When Edna saw the dilapidated "half house" which they had to share with another family, her spirits sank. It was built of mustard-yellow brick and stood in a treeless field in which the only other building was a dismal-looking orphan asylum. Beatrice and Dody were with their parents, attending the Holton-Arms School, but Madeleine was sent to boarding school at Farmington, Connecticut.

Several of Michelson's friends and associates found themselves in Washington during the war. Forest Moulton converted his skill at tracking celestial bodies across the sky to plotting the course of airplanes. Giorgio Abetti, a young Italian astronomer whom Michelson had met at the Yerkes Observatory, was now military attaché at the Italian Embassy. Arthur Gordon Webster of Clark University initiated a plan that could have been of enormous help to the American cause. Having studied ballistics in Germany under Helmholtz, Webster recognized the importance of this field of science in plotting the trajectory of a missile. He suggested setting up an "Institute" at Worcester for the study of the motion and impact of projectiles. The government gave him only partial support, and he was unable to make his point until the German guns were hitting Paris from a distance of 70 miles, while Allied guns had a range of 22. Only after Webster's death did his influence begin to be felt. Louis TenEyck Thompson, Webster's assistant at the Institute, became the Navy's first civilian ballistician and the technical director of the Naval Ordnance Test Station, now the Naval Weapons Center at China Lake, California. The handsome $8,000,000 laboratory there was dedicated to Michelson in 1948.[1]

When the range finder was ready for production, Michelson turned his attention to other projects. He experimented on the defects in optical glass, of vital importance for periscopes, telescopes, and gun sights. Now that German sources were cut off, inexperienced American manufacturers depended on Michelson's advice. The "striae," or flaws, had a different refractive index from the main body of the glass. Michelson photographed the detrimental effects of the striae, measured them with his interferometer,[2] and suggested correction of these flaws. He never perfected these lenses as he would have done had they been intended for one of his own instruments. Realizing the pressing need of the submarines he rushed them out with the minimum necessary preparation.

He also invented binoculars which could detect submarines at night or under poor illumination. The giant glasses, 6 inches high, 18 inches wide, and 24 inches long, were mounted on a tripod and could be rotated by levers in order to scan the sea and the horizon.[3]

Michelson lunched frequently at the Cosmos Club in Washington with his old friend George Ellery Hale, of whom he had seen very little since the astrophysicist had left Chicago in 1904.Through the Carnegie Institution, Hale had been able to realize his lifelong dream of building an observatory in the pure mountain air, about 6,000 feet above Los Angeles, on Mount Wilson. Now Hale renewed his efforts to persuade Michelson, after he was discharged from the Navy, to make a permanent break with the University of Chicago and come to Pasadena to live.

Hale had made this suggestion many times, and now Michelson was strongly tempted. He wrote Hale: "Regarding the possibility of coming to Pasadena after retiring—the only serious objection is the breaking of the many friendships the three daughters have made in Chicago and the East. We'll think it over a bit and perhaps even that objection may be overcome."[4]

The children did not realize at the time the sacrifice their father was making for them. Michelson promised Hale that he would soon come out for a visit. He was relieved from active duty in the Coast Defense Reserve on May 13, 1919, with the rank of commander, by Franklin Roosevelt, Acting Secretary of the Navy, and received commendation from Rear Admiral Ralph Earle, chief of the Bureau of Ordnance:

"While the Bureau could not approve all of the requests of its members for service at the front, I assure you that, in doing your utmost in the Bureau, your services, as an individual, had as great a share in defeating our enemies as if you had been in the front line trenches."[5]

Plans were made to leave Washington as soon as the Holton-Arms School closed. Michelson was gratified that he had been of use during the war, but now he longed for the serenity of his laboratory.

None of the Michelsons was sorry when the family headed for Chicago in June in an open Dodge touring car. Beatrice and Dody were wedged in the back seat with a number of suitcases while Michelson and his wife took turns at the wheel. Neither was a good driver. Michelson was apt to jerk from one gear to another with much racing of the motor between shifts, while Edna had a habit of letting her attention wander to some interesting piece of neoclassical architecture or a well-laid-out garden with an unfamiliar shrub. Her tendency was to drive toward the object of interest, paying little attention to the road or the ditches beside it. She usually recovered from her reverie in the nick of time, but they had some rather narrow escapes.

On reaching Chicago, they were all prostrated by a June heat wave. As soon as Madeleine had returned from boarding school, Michelson left with Edna and the children for one of his rare visits to their Canadian summer cottage at Desbarats on the neck of Lake Superior about thirty miles east of Sault Saint Marie. The cottage had been built by a local carpenter, Mr. O'Shaughnessy, with no more instructions from Edna than a suggestion that it should be "an awfully nice house for around $10,000." It had turned out fairly well: not handsome, but comfortable. O'Shaughnessy had carved the Stars and Stripes into a shield under the gable.

Michelson kept a small catboat on a mooring offshore and spent part of every day, as he had for many summers, sailing with his daughters. He had taught them to sail by standing on the end of the dock and calling out nautical directions through a megaphone as they rigged the boat and brought it up to the dock for a landing. His first rule was: "Never take your eye off the sail from the moment you get into the boat until you put it to bed." This was hard on young children, but it was what he had learned at the Naval Academy. Sometimes he would sing out, "Man overboard," which meant they must execute a rescue maneuver. Beatrice was the best sailor, thanks to his training, bringing home a silver cup in the races.

Toward sundown the brisk air often became chill, and Dody would light a fire. Michelson usually spent the evenings reading aloud to the family. They went through Alexander

Dumas, Walter Scott, James Fenimore Cooper, and Thackeray's *Vanity Fair*. *Pinocchio* was another of his favorites and he read it to the children, translating from the Italian as he went along. Edna filled in as a reader when her husband left for Chicago. For his own diversion, Michelson kept a pile of detective stories and novels by his bed. He read the same ones over every year, assuring Edna that he had absolutely no memory of the plots or dénouements; the books were simply soporifics.

As was often the case, Michelson's stay at Desbarats in 1919 was short, for in July he left in order to teach his summer classes at Yerkes Observatory. He also wanted to check on the experiment with the rigidity of the earth which Joe Purdy and F. M. Kannenstine were completing for him under Henry Gale's supervision. It required a very sensitive optical device especially designed to measure gradients, and Michelson had applied the interferometer to this problem with good results. He noticed that the instrument could record the slightest tremor of an earthquake, which would cause the fringes to disappear for ten minutes or half an hour. A more violent quake would make them vanish for about six hours.[6]

Kannenstine and Purdy had another use for the apparatus. They thought they might trace oil deposits in Texas, where they dreamed of making a fortune with the "oil smeller," as they christened it. Michelson did not care for the name or for the idea, but his two assistants did manufacture a gravity meter which met with some success.[7]

Michelson left Yerkes in August, heading west to San Francisco. Almost thirty years had elapsed since he had measured the satellites of Jupiter at Lick Observatory, and Holden had been dead some time. But Michelson went up to Mount Hamilton to talk with Lick astronomers on the feasibility of applying the technique he had developed on his former visit to the more difficult task of measuring the diameter of a distant star. This required a larger telescope than had been available at that time, but such a telescope now existed—the Hooker, on Mount Wilson.

Among the astronomers he met at Lick was Tracy Crawford, chairman of the astronomy department of the University of California, who invited him to lecture to a gathering of physicists, mathematicians, and astronomers at Astronomy Hall in Berkeley. Michelson accepted and the day was set.

Helen Crawford, the astronomer's wife, was an excellent pianist and she had urged Michelson to bring his violin to Berkeley. On the morning of the lecture, Crawford left the house at eight, instructing his friend to be at the hall at eleven. When her husband had left, Helen suggested playing some Mozart. Michelson agreed but when he opened his violin case, he was chagrined to find that the A string of the violin had snapped.

Some time was lost while he found his way to a music store to buy a new one. They began to play the A Major Sonata, and although Michelson was out of practice he soon fell into the mood of the music, guided by the graceful phrasing of the pianist. She stopped him sometimes from "playing out" when it was the piano's turn to carry the melody. He took her corrections in good grace, and the first movement was beginning to sound rather well when the telephone rang. Helen did not answer it. They were both so engrossed that they scarcely heard it.

Ten minutes later it rang again, and this time it did not stop even though Helen ignored it until they had finished the movement. When she finally answered, her husband's voice came over the wire with quiet fury. "Do you know where Professor Michelson is, Helen?"

"Oh, yes, dear," she answered, "he's right here beside me. We're playing a Mozart sonata. It's a pity you couldn't hear him, he's got the first movement almost under control. We'll play it for you this evening." An ominous silence followed.

"Helen, Professor Michelson is supposed to begin a lecture

in a few minutes. If he doesn't get here soon he will keep everyone waiting. What am I to tell them—that he is playing duets with my wife?"

The moment Michelson heard Helen speak to her husband, he realized what he had done. Leaving his fiddle on the piano, he dashed out to catch a taxi. The lecture hall was filled with impatient scientists when he arrived, and Crawford was anything but cordial. Later he forgave Michelson, even to the extent of asking to hear the sonata.[8]

On June 29, 1920, Michelson left for Pasadena. For several summers, he was to divide his time between the campus of the California Institute of Technology in Pasadena, where he repeated the experiment on the rigidity of the earth, and the observatory on Mount Wilson, where he carried out a new velocity of light test, a star-disk measurement, and a repetition of the ether-drift experiment. R. S. Woodward of the Carnegie Institution, of which Michelson had been made a Research Associate in May 1919,[9] took an immediate interest in these experiments and arranged to finance at least part of them.

At California Institute of Technology, Michelson had set up a series of underground pipes, partly filled with water, which were connected with his interferometer. Professor W. T. Whitney supervised these installations and the fluctuations of the tides were recorded by motion-picture cameras. This final experiment corroborated the earlier test in 1913.

Like most adopted Californians, Hale boasted shamelessly of the perfections of the state, and Michelson loved to tease him. He mentioned casually in a letter that his final experiments on the rigidity of the earth were likely to give valuable information concerning earthquakes. "I mean, of course, distant ones—I know you don't have them in California."[10]

At the observatory, Hale had collected a staff of brilliant men to work with him on the study of the sun, the moon, and other celestial bodies. He had installed cameras in the domes of the observatory to photograph solar and stellar phenomena and built a comfortable lodge for the men who operated these instruments.

Building the Mount Wilson Observatory had been a perilous operation. Every piece of lumber and stone had to be dragged laboriously up the mountain over a narrow footpath until a crude wagon road could be blazed. Hale himself had supervised the transport by mule team of the precious optical parts of the first solar telescope, the procession making its way up through steep ravines with only inches to spare between the towering cliffs and the precipices beneath. In 1919 there was a fairly good road up the back of the Angeles Crest and a funicular cable-car railway up the slopes above Altadena. A 60-inch reflector had been erected in 1908, and then the 150-foot telescope specifically designed to photograph the sun. The crowning glory of the observatory was the Hooker reflecting telescope, which had a large concave mirror at the bottom of the tube to reflect starlight. This glass, 100 inches in diameter, 13 inches thick, and weighing 4.5 tons, had required six years of polishing before installation. Until the 200-inch was built in the 1930s, it was the largest in the world.

Armed with these magnificent "eyes," Hale's intention was to launch an attack on the three great mysteries of astronomy: the evolution of stars, the structure of the universe, and the constitution of matter.

The mountain top with these powerful instruments comprised Hale's kingdom. In the pure mountain air, he felt released from mundane problems. Poetry, music, and art were an important part of his life, for he believed in the scientist as artist. He could quote Dante in Italian and recite from the classics or from the works of his contemporaries. Alfred Noyes, then poet laureate of England, had been his guest on Mount Wilson when the 100-inch glass of the Hooker telescope had been placed in its shaft and had written a poem about "the polished flawless pool."

Hale was anything but an ivory-tower scientist. In spite of intermittent illnesses that plagued him over the years, he lived a varied and active life. His passionate interest in archaeology took him to Egypt in 1911, and again in 1922, when Tutankhamen's tomb was opened. Hale and his family stood at the excavation site to watch its golden treasures being brought out.

It was perhaps through his ability to impart the romance of astronomical research that Hale won the help he needed from such millionaires as Andrew Carnegie, John D. Hooker, and Henry Edwards Huntington. A clever popularizer, he could make the average man share in the excitement of a great discovery.

Hale discouraged women astronomers and wives of the staff from invading his mountain-top "monastery." The atmosphere was reminiscent of the communities of those early Greek philosophers, the Pythagoreans, or that of Mount Athos where monks shut themselves off from the feminine world. But the monastic laws were relaxed for the benefit of Michelson's daughter, Beatrice, who arrived with her father for a visit during the summer of 1920. Hale thought a sixteen-year-old could hardly upset the mores. Michelson told Beatrice that she would have to be patient during the long hours of nocturnal observation, and she promised to be. But on the very first night she found an unexpected diversion.

Dick Seares, son of the assistant director of the observatory, was assisting Michelson in the velocity of light test, which had forty-five-minute intervals between observations. For these intervals, he had organized a nightly crap game among the assistants, which took place beneath the 100-inch telescope by the shaded light of a small flashlight. Every so often, one or another would have to leave the game to take readings. Beatrice would fill in for the absentee, hoping to bring him luck.

When the night's work was finished, Beatrice and her father went to look for their cabin. They were both rather sleepy and neither could remember which of the identical cabins was theirs. They woke the sleeping occupants of several others before they found their own.

Aside from the solar studies, observing on the mountain

took place during the night. Michelson enjoyed these nocturnal vigils. After dinner, while they waited for the daylight to
fade, it was the custom at the "monastery" to repair to the
billiard room where Alfred H. Joy, one of the astronomers,
often took Michelson on for a game. "We all marveled at his
superb skill with the cue," he wrote.[11] Throughout the night
there was coffee or hot soup and interesting talk at almost any
hour until the staff went to bed at dawn for a good day's rest.

Among the astronomers that Michelson came to know
were John Anderson, James Ritchey, Frederick Seares, Francis
Pease, Adriaan van Maanen, Edwin Hubble, and Milton
Humason, as well as Harlow Shapley, who was developing
radical theories on the nature of the spiral nebulae and the
scale of the universe. Hubble had detected one of the pulsating
stars called cepheids in the Andromeda nebula and as a result
was able to make the first measurements of the nebula's distance from the earth. It is easy to understand how Michelson
was drawn into this measuring game. He planned to use the
interference of light waves to attain the diameter of a star, a
totally new approach at that time.

His approach to astronomy was realistic—he left speculation to others. On a visit to Percival Lowell's observatory near
Flagstaff, Arizona, he was invited by Lowell, who believed he
had found evidence for life on Mars, to look through the telescope to see the planet's canals. Michelson looked but did not
see them. Lowell checked the image and saw them clearly.
Michelson looked again and still saw nothing but the red disk
with the white polar caps. Lowell protested, "The trouble with
you, Michelson, is that you're not sufficiently generous to your
imagination."[12]

For his star-disk measurement at Mount Wilson Michelson
chose Betelgeuse, the red star in the shoulder of the figure of
Orion, the brightest constellation of the northern sky. In selecting this star he took into consideration not only its brilliance but its size and its distance from the earth. Sirius, though

intensely bright, is comparatively small, its brilliance coming from the high radiation of its surface. Betelgeuse has a feeble surface radiation; its brilliance is due to its great size. Antares, which might have served as well for a first attempt with the interferometer, is not well placed in the California sky during the winter months when the measurements were actually made.[13]

Arthur Stanley Eddington had calculated the diameter of Betelgeuse from surface radiation. In his presidential address to the British Association for the Advancement of Science in 1920 he said: "Probably the greatest need of stellar astronomy at the present day, in order to make sure that our theoretical deductions are starting on the right lines, is some means of measuring the apparent angular diameters of stars."[14]

To measure Betelgeuse, Michelson redesigned his stellar interferometer, an ingenious arrangement of slits and movable mirrors at either end of a metal beam, and had it mounted on top of the Hooker telescope. The distance between the mirrors, about 20 feet, made possible a far greater resolving power than that of the 100-inch glass of the Hooker. The big mirror was blacked out for this experiment, so that light from the extremities of the star's diameter entered the telescope only through two slits. The two pencils of light were reflected to the focal image at the observer's station. Here Michelson was able to move the slits apart until he saw the interference fringes fade and disappear. He explained that in observing such an object as the disk of a star the distance between the two slits is measured when the interference fringes have just vanished, and the angular magnitude is then computed.[15]

By the end of the summer, although the interferometer was not yet provided with means for the complete separation of the slits, some preliminary observations had been made, and Hale predicted that Michelson's interferometer would play an important part in the future of sidereal astronomy. Not only did it have the advantage of a resolving power limited only by the length of the girder that can be constructed without undue bending or vibration, but also even in very poor seeing conditions the fringes may be quite distinct. The stellar interferometer is "probably the most important astronomical development of this century," wrote Ewart Williams in his book on interferometry.[16]

The beginning of the fall semester forced Michelson to return to his duties in Chicago before any final results could be attained. He left Francis Pease and John Anderson in charge of the work, instructing them to take the final readings. Michelson had complete confidence in Pease; as an observer at the telescope, the interferometer, or the velocity of light devices Pease's perseverance and devotion were beyond compare. But Michelson always felt a wrench on leaving a half-finished experiment.

On December 13, 1920, the news arrived. Pease telegraphed that with very good seeing, the fringes disappeared when the pencils were separated by 121 inches. This meant that Betelgeuse's angular diameter was 0.047 seconds of arc, or, in a linear measurement, 240×10^6 miles, a distance only slightly less than the orbit of Mars. Eddington's calculation proved very close to the mark; it was 0.051 seconds of arc.[17] Michelson was pleased to report this result to Dr. Woodward when he acknowledged the receipt of another $2,000 sent by the Carnegie Institution on December 21.[18]

Woodward replied: ". . . The result is staggering at first thought . . . the method you have added to astronomical resources is of the greatest importance. . . ."[19]

Astronomers were expecting these dimensions, but the press and the public had no notion of the colossal bulk of Betelgeuse; it is beyond ordinary comprehension. When word of Michelson's achievement leaked to the press before he was ready to announce it, excitement was intense. Unable to gain access to him at Ryerson, reporters flocked to the house to catch him at lunchtime. Dody found a group of them waiting on the front porch when she returned from school. Seizing an opportunity to show off her recently acquired knowledge, she launched breathlessly into a monologue she had prepared for her current events class the following day:

"He took light from either side of the star and brought it together again with mirrors in his interferometer. It's got a linear diameter of 240 million miles, almost as large as the orbit of Mars. Light from Betelgeuse would take 150 light years to reach the earth, and it is 2300 times larger than our sun."

When her older sisters arrived, her audience deserted her to besiege Beatrice and Madeleine with requests to arrange interviews with their father. When Michelson himself finally appeared, the reporters rushed at him as he came up the sidewalk. Before entering the house he paused just long enough to demand that they leave. The girls were upset, but their father told them that it was hopeless ever to talk with reporters. They didn't have enough background to grasp the subject and they were sure to get the facts all wrong and to give the information some sensational twist to catch the public interest. A newsman on a Pasadena paper, confusing the range finder with the stellar interferometer, had written: "[Michelson] is the inventor of a stellar range finder to measure the distance of the stars from the earth and from each other." In later years, however, Michelson grew more tolerant of the press.

Formal announcement of the star measurement was made by Michelson on December 29, 1920, at a combined meeting of the American Physical Society and the American Association for the Advancement of Science. Even this sophisticated audience was amazed to learn that the new device could measure with such precision an object 150 light-years from the earth.

Thomas J. O'Donnell had come to work for Michelson shortly after the war. His valuable training with range finders on the U.S.S. *Arkansas,* plus his Irish charm, won him the job against all other applicants. At Ryerson most of the instruments were made in the laboratory shops. Tom ran the furnace in the basement of the annex with the aid of Joe Purdy. There they melted down a mixture of copper and tin which they cast into plates of speculum for the gratings ruled on the ruling engine. Another painstaking task was the grinding and polishing of the slabs of glass used in the interferometer. The surfaces of these blanks had to be exactly parallel.

Michelson had complete confidence in his helpers and in their observations, which he never disputed. "He allowed no one to interfere with us, his brood," said Tom, "but, boy, could he let you know if you got off the beam. The Boss was strict and stern," he added, "but never sour. He was gentle to me even when I got on his nerves with my fast talking answers." Tom admitted that his tongue ran away with him sometimes when he thought he had found a solution to some problem. Michelson wanted him only to answer the questions put to him.

Tom was also in charge of testing the rotating mirrors for a new velocity of light experiment that Michelson was planning. These little mirrors were driven by a compressed-air turbine at dangerously high speeds, sometimes over 1,000 revolutions per second, to test their strength.[20]

One terrifying incident has been recorded by Tom:

THE FOUR-INCH QUARTZ VELOCITY OF LIGHT
OCTAGONAL ROTATING MIRROR BLOWUP

This was the big day—testing Michelson's largest octagon [rotating mirror]. My fears were getting the best of me. I got busy and built a heavy 2-inch thick cast iron barricade around the mirror mounting. Two portholes for observation were left open; No. 1 port at the level of the octagonal surfaces was used by Michelson for making angular displacement measurement of the returning image;

No. 2 port was used by Fred Pearson for observing Lissa-
jous figures projected by a single polished face of the
mirror's hold-down nut. A tuning fork furnished the vertical sweep, and the nut, the horizontal sweep of the strobo-
scopic setup which was used for determining the r.p.s. of
the mirror by Pearson.

I operated the throttle with step-by-step instructions
from Michelson as he observed the image displacements.
A glass mercury manometer which was used for determining the pressure of the air actuating the clockwise and
counterclockwise turbine drives was directly in front of
me. It reached from the floor almost to the ceiling. I called
out the pressures on Michelson's signal. The manometer
tube was constructed of [a] three-eighths-inch glass tube.
During this particular run the tube broke in four places
below the level of my shoulders. Dr. Michelson gave me
the most disgusting [disgusted] look. I was stunned too
and said loudly, "I didn't touch the manometer."

Michelson got up and still very much disgusted stared
down into the enclosure protecting us from the rotating
mirror. The mirror appeared to be still spinning. It took
some time for the spindle to come to a stop because our
air pressure was cut off. The Boss was still looking at the
rotating spindle. Then with a sudden jump he exclaimed,
"Where is the mirror?"

We all looked—the mirror had disintegrated. The explosion we heard was not the breakage of the manometer
but the explosion of the rotating mirror. Dr. Michelson
then said quietly, which was his usual manner, "We have
had it up to over 1000 r.p.s., why did it rupture at 600
r.p.s. on the way down?" The critical speed of a shade over
500 r.p.s. had not been reached. This is the speed that the
static and dynamic axis of the mirror and its spindle exchange positions and the unit vibrates excessively if held
at this speed for a few seconds. Michelson watched for this

critical condition and ordered us to speed up through or slow down through this region.

After some remarks and bewildered observations, I noticed Michelson's forehead was bleeding at several points. Then he noticed that both of my arms were bleeding close to the elbows. We took a look at Fred. He was also bleeding about his face. The injuries were not any more serious than one received in a desert sandstorm. We looked around the room for the remains of the quartz mirror. At first we found none. Then Fred noticed that the windows around the room were marked (sand blasted) with a white sandy streak at a level with the former octagon. I then examined the guard I built around the mirror and found a large packed quantity of white sand lodged in a corner of the protection shield. This lay in the direction between Michelson and Pearson. We weighed the sand and found it to be about one half the volume of the octagon. Then it was that this fear I had was shared by Michelson and Fred. In all the velocity of light set-ups before this time, no protection was used.[21]

Tom's "fear" was for the horrible fate they all would have suffered had there been no protecting shield this time between their faces and the mirror.

Joe Purdy, under Fred Pearson's supervision, also helped graduate students in their work with the instruments and prepared the optical equipment for Michelson's lectures to the advanced classes. But Joe, Fred, and Tom spent the major part of their time in the research laboratory at the west end of Ryerson, which was the home of the ruling engine.

Michelson, before going down the iron staircase to set up a grating in the temperature-controlled room, would change from his formal lecture attire into his work clothes; a pair of old trousers, stained and baggy, a shirt without a collar, carpet slippers, and a very disreputable old gray sweater with holes at the elbows. Only the chief and his trusted assistants had access to this sanctum sanctorum. Here they were seldom interrupted; if some misguided individual happened to knock at the door he was invariably turned away. The windows were fitted with light-excluding shutters and, outside, all cars and trucks took a detour to keep clear of the building. Pearson and Purdy often worked there in the dark, with only a tiny beam of light.

Michelson became so absorbed in his work that he sometimes kept them long after quitting time. Purdy especially would become bored with standing in the darkened room hour after hour, adjusting the mirrors at the chief's direction. When he complained to Fred, the older man would say, "It's all for the advancement of science." In retrospect, Purdy said, "The happiest years of my life were those spent at Ryerson Lab, especially those spent working under Michelson."[22]

Michelson did not always publish the results of experiments, though some of these were reported by others and thus got into the literature. One such experiment was the observance of fringes under poor seeing conditions. Certain of his observations were made on Mount Wilson, where seeing as poor as 1 on a scale of 10 was not considered very harmful. However, the accuracy of Michelson's results under such conditions was sometimes questioned. This was a challenge to him to prove that greater accuracy was sometimes obtainable during poor seeing than under more favorable conditions.

Tom O'Donnell described the observance at such times as being more accurate not from a scientific angle but from a psychological angle, "because of the mellowness of the field that you saw. You didn't have very sharp images or glaring this or glaring that. But the fringes just shone out so beautifully in the badly distorted field that you could easily see them disappear and come in again when you were making a measurement."[23]

In order to prove this theory, Michelson and his assistant

made a model simulating starlight with tiny pin pricks in a screen, much like the one he had made at Clark University. They asked some members of the biology department to measure these "stars" with their microscopes. Then Tom created artificial poor seeing by heating the air through which the measurements were taken. Michelson got a result with his stellar interferometer that was almost 1,000 times as accurate as that achieved by the microscopes.

He also made some very simple but beautiful experiments on elastic fatigue and other peculiar elastical behavior in metals. He found that quartz fiber will gradually bend under its own weight, but when the force of gravity is released by placing the fiber in another position, it will come back almost to its original shape. After completing his work Michelson read the literature on the subject and found that some results had already been obtained. Perhaps a third of his investigation was new and original, but in his view that was not sufficient to warrant publication. Why had he not read the relevant research before undertaking his experiment, he was asked. His reply was that too much reading before beginning work on a new idea threatened to kill all originality. When he tackled a problem he liked to do so from his own fresh viewpoint.

> If I go to the library first I am reading without any basis of perspective and I would undoubtedly be influenced by the writer's approach. If I have no basis of my own, my critical evaluation of what the author says is reduced. Whereas, if I spend six months experimenting on it, then I have some ideas of my own. After that, I read what the others say and I can really read them critically. If it's nonsense, it's obvious to me by then that it is nonsense. This way the reading really is valuable because you can still pick up things which you didn't think of at all. But you will not be influenced by the mistakes the other fellow just made, as you would if you began by finding out what had already been done.[24]

He often tackled problems that seemed impossible, or at least very difficult of solution and found the clue to lie in something relatively simple and obvious. Some of his colleagues said he never attempted an experiment unless it was so simple that everybody else had overlooked it.[25]

During the early years of Michelson's career as professor, his students for the most part found him an inspiring teacher. At the University of Chicago, however, relationships were more difficult. By that time his primary interest was in his own research and he must have grudged the time his courses required. The students became baffled and discouraged, and Michelson gained a reputation for being unapproachable, difficult, and dictatorial.[26] He could not be directed from a path once he had decided to take it. On one occasion, he started lecturing on physical optics when the subject for the course had been announced as "Mechanics and Wave Motion." One of the students rather timidly raised his hand and said that he had already attended the course in optics; could anything be done about it? "Yes," said Michelson, "you can take your card back to the registrar and he will cancel your registration."

His manner with the students was severe, almost military. Examining one pupil who confessed that he did not know his subject very thoroughly, he said, "I did not ask you if you were prepared, I asked you to recite."

Most of his students were more or less frightened by him. One girl was so panic-stricken that when her turn came to recite at the board, she was unable to utter a single word. Michelson finally said, "That will be all," and the poor creature sat down.

His lectures moved at a pace that was hard to keep up with. For example, the whole of the Fourier series, together with all its applications, on which a mathematician would normally spend a week, was covered in one lecture. One student said that Michelson could teach a year's course of undergraduate study in less than half an hour. "He could be lucid with fewer words than anyone I ever met." But it took the average student about five hours to digest what had been taught in each lecture. The students worked out a way to "handle" him. Two would work together, one of them taking notes while the brighter of the pair concentrated his whole attention on trying to comprehend what the professor was saying. Afterward they would combine forces.

His biases affected the content of his lectures. He did not stress thermodynamics because his aversion to the vagueness and extreme generality of the subject caused him to underestimate its importance. Although he was more sympathetic to the kinetic theory and molecular physics, he incorporated very little of these into his course. "Michelson tailored mathematics to fit physics," one student remarked. If the result of an equation came out negative, as it often did, he would look with disgust at the big minus sign on the blackboard staring him in the face; then walking over to the board, he would say, 'It should be plus." On the word "plus" he would draw a heavy vertical stroke through the minus sign, making it positive, then point his finger at the class and add: "You can verify it for yourselves."

A student could set his watch by Michelson's entrance into the lecture hall. He lectured in the German style after the manner of von Helmholtz—no interruptions, no questions. One morning he gave his students the problem of calculating the period of oscillation of a rocking stone, and told them the problem was worked out in Mascart's text on theoretical physics. At the next session of the class one of the new students raised his hand. Michelson glared at him in annoyance and asked what he wanted. "Professor Michelson," the student said, 'I have worked the problem on the rocking stone, but I don't get the same answer as Mascart does in the book." Michelson looked at him for a few seconds and said in a dry tone, "Well, one of you must be wrong." The lecture continued without further interruption.

Nevertheless, most of his students were grateful for the

training he gave them. Arnold Lieberman wrote: "I still remember my sense of delighted astonishment at the lucid clarity of his exposition. Over the span of almost four decades, I remember the man's quietness, humility and the perfect organization of his beautifully presented lecture, soft spoken manner and voice, enunciating clearly to the farthest corner of the room."

They admired his ability to draw neat, well-proportioned diagrams on the blackboard. He could draw a circle freehand almost as well as it could be drawn with a compass. His drawings of the sine curves were beautiful to look at, and even his handwriting had a decided flourish.

Stanislas Chylinski, a student in 1920, wrote: "To the class as a whole he presented the appearance of almost regal dignity and aloofness. He was a legendary figure and all of us were in awe of him. His punctilious politeness, however, tended on close contact to soften the first impression of almost Jove-like severity."

Chylinski had a more personal relationship with Michelson than did most of his students: "When he learned that I was of Polish origin, he told me of his Polish mother and of Strzelno where he was born, only about thirty miles from my own birthplace. At least twice a week he would send his emissary, Fred Pearson, over to my laboratory to invite me to a game of chess. It was like a royal command; I dropped everything and went."

When Michelson began teaching at the University of Chicago one of his duties was supervising the work of graduate students on their theses. For a few years he tried to do this, but with negligible success. The stumbling block was his inability to work with people. Although there were some exceptions, most of the graduate students tried his patience. By 1908 he reached the limit of his endurance. He called in his good-natured assistant Robert Millikan, who had been assigning some of the thesis subjects. According to Millikan's account, Michelson said:

> If you can find some other way to handle it I don't want to bother any more with this thesis business. What these graduate students always do with my problems, if I turn them over to them, is either to spoil the problem for me because they haven't the capacity to handle it as I want it handled . . . or . . . they get good results and at once begin to think the problem is theirs instead of mine, when in fact knowing what kind of a problem it is worthwhile to attack is in general more important than the mere carrying out of the necessary steps. So I prefer not to bother with graduate students' theses any longer. I will hire my own assistant by the month, a man who will not think I owe him anything further than to see that he gets his monthly check. You take care of the graduate students in any way you see fit and I'll be your debtor forever.[27]

Millikan agreed. Feeling liberated, Michelson returned to his research. It was a perfect solution. Millikan also took over the administrative and financial aspects of the department of physics and proved extremely capable. His success with the students was due to his uncanny sense of leads to problems that were likely to bear fruit for a doctoral thesis. About twenty-five of his students became brilliant physicists in pure science, applied science, or industry.

In 1920, Hale started a campaign to lure Millikan to California Institute of Technology. He wanted a man who could build that institution into America's leading research center for physics and chemistry and Millikan had the necessary drive and ability. Michelson was aware of the pressure being put on his friend. He wrote to Hale later:

> I can't say I hope you'll be successful in getting Millikan, important as I know his services would be to the Cal. Inst.

I shall sorely miss him if you succeed—but *then* I shall congratulate you in getting the very best man in the country if not in the world for the work.[28]

Hale did succeed. In the fall of 1921 Millikan became chairman of the Executive Council of the Institute, a position which he held for more than twenty years.

CHAPTER 15

The Spinning Prism

O NE of Einstein's predictions in connection with his General Theory of Relativity was that light from a star would be attracted by gravity to the sun so that the ray of light, bending as it passes, would make the star appear nearer the sun than it actually is. It is impossible to see the star's light while the sun is shining but astronomers believed that a photographic record of the displacement might be made during an eclipse. Eddington, noting that there would be a total eclipse of the sun on May 29, 1919, organized an expedition to view it from two vantage points, one group in Brazil and one in Principe, Gulf of Guinea, Africa. The astronomers felt themselves in luck because this eclipse took place against an exceptional patch of bright stars, the Hyades, a circumstance that would not occur again for a thousand years. The eclipse lasted 302 seconds, but clouds and poor weather obscured it and photographing was difficult. Nevertheless Eddington, on examining the plates from Africa, reported, "... a definite displacement in good accordance with Einstein's theory and disagreeing with the Newtonian prediction."[1] The evidence from Brazil supported the statement.

The result of this test helped to gain acceptance for Einstein's theories, but in the mind of Sir Oliver Lodge the question of the ether was by no means settled. In an address to the British Association for the Advancement of Science at Cardiff, Wales, in 1920, he said:

> ... why imagine that the success of the Einstein equation proves the observed velocity of light to be the same whatever the motion of the observer? If the observer thinks [Sir Oliver is not at all sure that he does], and if he is aware of the FitzGerald-Lorentz Contraction, he will know that such a proposition is not true; he will know that the velocity of light is not equal in all directions in a relatively drifting medium, that the wave front is not concentric to the observer, and that the Michelson experiment gives no proof of anything of the kind. . . .
>
> ... if on the strength of that remarkable achievement some enthusiasts proceed to formulate propositions which by ignoring the motion of the observer and all its consequences complicate the rest of the universe unduly, then, however much we may admire their skill and ability, I ask whether they ought not to be regarded as Bolsheviks and pulled up.[2]

That same year, during a visit to the United States, Lodge arrived at Ryerson Laboratory wearing a morning coat and a high silk hat. He discussed the whole subject with Michelson at length. Lodge declared privately that the theory of relativity, particularly in regard to the abolition of the ether, was "repugnant to common sense," and he was happy to find that Michelson shared this opinion,[3] as well as his antipathy to the Lorentz-FitzGerald contraction. The parting of the ways came only when Lodge, trying to assuage his grief over a son killed in the First World War, turned to a belief in psychic phenomena and extrasensory perception. When he reported holding long conversations with his son through seances, Michelson drew the line. Until this tragic "loss of reason," he had honored Lodge's scientific opinions.

Albert Einstein came to America in 1921 to promote the Zionist cause and to deliver a series of lectures at Princeton University which attracted many distinguished scientists. Dr. Ludwik Silberstein, a mathematical physicist with the Eastman Kodak research laboratories in Toronto, proposed to finance another experiment to test the theory of relativity. He persuaded Michelson to come to Toronto to discuss the possibility of another ether-drift test. In contrast to the Michelson-Morley experiment, which utilized the earth's motion in orbit, this one would involve the earth's rotation on its axis.

Michelson had contemplated this idea as early as 1905, but he was fairly sure that it would have the same negative result and was still extremely reluctant to spend time, effort, and money on it. The University of Chicago, however, brought pressure on him: ". . . this experiment has roused international interest to a very unusual degree as it is expected to furnish another check on the truth of the Einstein Relativity Theory. Professor Michelson's reputation will insure a very large amount of highly desirable publicity to the University if this experiment is carried out," Dean Henry Gordon Gale wrote to Vice President James Tufts.[4] Einstein himself was in favor of it because he said it might be a crucial test of the General Theory of Relativity.

During his Chicago visit on the Zionist tour, Einstein visited Ryerson Laboratory and discussed with Michelson the value of such an experiment. O'Donnell and Pearson showed him plans for the path of light to be projected in two directions around the rectangle. The execution of this experiment was delayed by other work; it was never very satisfying to Michelson.

During the early 1920s, Einstein came in for a great deal of public criticism, some of it prompted by anti-Semitism. Statements were falsely attributed to him; regarding one of these Michelson wrote to Silberstein: "I am glad to get your letter and especially pleased to know (what we all hoped to be true) that the statements attributed to Einstein were pure calumnies." Michelson must have made some public statement regarding this injustice, for he added a postscript to the letter: "I was very much pleased to have Einstein's appreciative note in your letter; and admire his work and especially his disinterested attitude in seeking truth."[5]

Edna gave a luncheon for Mrs. Einstein while their husbands were occupied with university functions. Her guests were curious and excited to meet the wife of a great celebrity, but they had some difficulty understanding her. Her English was halting and full of literal translations from German idioms.

At one point they were nonplused when Mrs. Einstein said that she had suffered in New Jersey from the snakes which bit her mercilessly. Everyone looked surprised. "Oh yes," she said, the snakes flew around her head and bit her face and hands and even flew up under her skirt to bite her ankles and legs. Her audience grew more puzzled and astonished as she embroidered the tale, but she told it with conviction and as she was the great man's wife, no one questioned it. In some ways it was no less strange than the theory of relativity, and that had to be accepted whether they liked it or not. But they looked to Edna for confirmation.

"Do you really mean that in Princeton snakes fly around in the air? And were you actually bitten by them?" Edna asked in German.

"*Ach nein!*" Mrs. Einstein explained. "*Ich spreche von Schnaken* [I'm talking about mosquitoes]!" It was an easy mistake and everybody had a good laugh.[6]

Michelson went to Brussels on April 1, 1921, to attend the Third Congress of Solvay at the invitation of H. A. Lorentz, the president, and Lord Rutherford. This was Michelson's first meeting with the Dutch physicist who had interpreted his ether-drift experiment in such a startling manner. Present also were other famous physicists whom he had previously known only by their works—Madame Curie, Pieter Zeeman, and Paul Ehrenfest—as well as Sir Joseph Larmor, an old friend whom he was delighted to see again.

The discussions at the congress covered a wide variety of subjects, none of them close to Michelson's sphere of endeavor. He listened politely, feeling somewhat lost, while Lorentz spoke on the theory of electrons, Rutherford on the structure of the atom, and Niels Bohr on the application of quantum theory to atomic problems.

On April 6 Michelson arrived in Paris to begin lecturing at the Sorbonne, where he had accepted an exchange professorship. The lectures were delivered in French, albeit somewhat haltingly. Michelson managed to make himself understood, however, as the scientific terms are universal. He had studied French as a child with his mother, an excellent French scholar who, he said, was not too pleased with her pupil.

Not long after the congress, Michelson saw Lorentz again. The Dutch physicist visited Hale at Mount Wilson, where he thoroughly enjoyed the good company of his host and the interesting solar and stellar observations. Returning by way of Chicago, Lorentz paid Michelson a visit. He had good news of the measurements of alpha Orionis, but he also gave Michelson the rather startling news that Millikan proposed to measure the velocity of light "in a long tube, exhausted of air." Michelson was quite upset. He dashed off a letter to Hale: "I merely wish to say that this was my original plan—before we decided on the present schedule; and that I thought I had this tube scheme in reserve."[7] Hale reassured him, explaining that the report was idle gossip.

The winter of 1921–1922 was an expensive one for the Michelsons. Dody was attending a private school on the North

Side; Beatrice, having made the honor roll at school, was now at Vassar College; and Madeleine, who had become engaged to a young architect, was planning a wedding reception at the house on December 22. Her fiancé, Philip Maher, shared an office with his father, one of Frank Lloyd Wright's early followers.

The household suffered the usual pre-wedding turmoil and everyone was edgy. Madeleine was afraid that her father would have an experiment on his mind and forget to give her away on the appointed day, or that Beatrice, now a Vassar intellectual, might decide to snub the more frivolous members of the bridal party. As for "the brat," she was sure Dody would trip over the bridal veil as she teetered down the aisle of the church on her first high-heeled shoes. Edna was worried because she had spent too much money and dared not ask for more. Michelson evaded her whenever she broached the subject. He promised Madeleine, however, that for her sake he would go through the whole "performance" on schedule.

When the wedding day came, he found he thoroughly enjoyed it. Madeleine was his favorite daughter and it was a delight to see her radiantly happy. When Madeleine and Philip were ready to leave, Dody was feeling so sentimental that tears ran down her cheeks. "Dody has had too much champagne," she heard her mother say, but her father only smiled at her instead of scolding. He was feeling nostalgic himself.

When his work was progressing well, Michelson was a delightful companion. He brought home delicacies for dessert to surprise his family—a bunch of hothouse grapes or some exotic South American fruit. "Happy Thoughts," the children called them. Or he would take the whole family downtown in a taxicab to luncheon at the University Club and afterward to a matinée. But there were days when Edna warned the children that their father was in "one of his moods." These usually indicated that the ruling engine was misbehaving, or that another "negative" result had been obtained. Michelson would glower throughout the entire meal and no one dared speak. Sometimes his rage would cause him to rise from the table, go to the lavatory in the hall, clear his throat noisily, and spit.

In one of his bitter outbursts he told his family that human beings were utterly unimportant in the universal view—"a skin disease upon the face of the earth." Dody had occasionally suffered from severe attacks of poison-ivy infection which spread over her body in itching welts, blisters, and finally an oozing crust. She conceived a hideous image of the world erupting in similar festering boils with germlike people crawling over them as the diseased planet whirled through space. It also occurred to her that, however this ghastly situation had come about, nobody seemed to care.

From her father's cynicism Dody eventually developed a suspicion that all patterns for Utopia are harmful, stemming perhaps from a lack of courage to acknowledge and face the truths of life and of death. But from her father she inherited also an insatiable curiosity and enormous powers of enjoying the natural world about her. Humans to her were just one more infinitely fascinating manifestation of the natural world.

Edna's reaction to her husband's nihilistic view had been to turn for comfort to her neglected Episcopal church. The daughters were hastily baptized and confirmed, and, dressed in flowing white robes topped with nunlike headdresses, they sang in St. Cecilia's choir at the Church of the Redeemer. Michelson never accompanied his family to church. He had the faculty of forgetting all human trivia in the engrossing solace of his work, the congenial company of his assistants at the laboratory, a hard game of tennis, or his watercolors.

On January 27, 1923, a farewell dinner was given by the university for Martin Ryerson, retiring chairman of the Board of Trustees. Ryerson had been an unusual donor. Unlike the trustees of Case or Clark, he had attached no strings to his gifts.

Although his interests lay more with the arts than the sciences, Michelson had found him sympathetic to the needs of the laboratory, with a personal pride in Michelson's achievements.

The son of a millionaire who had made his fortune in pine lumber, Ryerson had attended public school in Chicago. Later his father had sent him to Paris, where he began collecting the paintings that he eventually gave to the Chicago Art Institute. He was a shy, quiet fellow with a fine sense of values. Much of his time had been spent traveling in Europe with his wife. They had no children. From time to time the Michelsons were invited to Lake Geneva, where the Ryersons entertained weekend guests on their estate. A ride around the lake on their steamboat and a visit to Yerkes Observatory were always part of the program.

Dody had been sent to boarding school in the fall of 1922, and the following months were lonely ones for Edna. She found the rambling old house on Kimbark Avenue strangely quiet with all her children gone. Now that she and her husband were alone together, the differences in their tastes and habits became more apparent. He was nineteen years older than she, content to sit reading or thinking, while she yearned for companionship and the stimulus of young people around her. She poured out her loneliness in letters to her daughters, and before the winter was over she had evolved a plan to break the monotony. In the fall of 1923 she sailed for Europe with Beatrice and her Vassar roommate, Virgilia Peterson, who became known as an author and critic after the Second World War. All three enrolled in classes at the University of Grenoble.

Michelson was not particularly pleased to have his wife disappear for a year, but he realized that she needed a change. When he returned from Pasadena, he moved to his old bachelor haunt, the Hotel del Prado, and sank his mind in work. He emerged from his solitude only when Dody came home from boarding school for Christmas. They spent the holiday with Madeleine, her husband, and their baby boy.

More than fifty years after Michelson's graduation from Annapolis, he received, in the spring of 1924, an invitation to lecture at the Naval Academy. Since the date coincided with Dody's Easter vacation, he took her with him to visit Commander Wilbur R. van Auken, an officer on the base. There were very few landmarks that Michelson could recognize, as he and Dody walked over the filled-in land by the old sea wall where he had first measured the speed of light. Michelson Hall, the handsome new science building, now stands on this site.

Michelson was introduced at the lecture by an admiral of the brass-hat variety whose voice thundered to a climax at the end of his introduction: "Who knows but if Michelson had remained in the Navy, he might have been an ADMIRAL!" Only one man dared to laugh out loud at this conceit: young Earl Thomson, a civilian physicist with a broader view of life's attainments.[8]

Before leaving for Europe in 1923 Edna had persuaded her husband to build a new house behind the old one on the land facing 58th Street. Dining with Madeleine and her husband on the eve of her departure, she had said to her son-in-law, "Philip, I am going to Europe and Mr. Michelson to Mount Wilson. While we are gone, I want you to build us a nice little house on the back lot."

Philip Maher had never encountered such a casual client. He sketched a plan on the back of an envelope, and the Michelsons approved it without further question.

On her return the house was almost finished. Built of brick with high-pitched slate roofs in the style of a French Provincial manor house, it had a round turreted tower in which a circular stairway led to the second story. The only change Edna made was to add to the dining room a little conservatory, which Tom O'Donnell helped to build, where she grew tuberous begonias, maidenhair ferns, and several varieties of lilies. The house suited both the Michelsons to perfection and in it began a new era of drawing together that lasted through their remaining years.

The National Academy of Sciences had been formed in 1863 by men of ambition and high ideals; among them were Louis Agassiz, Joseph Henry, Alexander Bache, and Benjamin A. Gould. At the height of the Civil War they secured a charter from President Lincoln and Congress to form a "Company of Scientists" who would advise the federal government, upon request, on matters of science relating to public policy. Members served without pay, an elite group chosen by internal invitation. Their charter marked the first recognition by the United States government of the importance of abstract science.

Michelson had become a member in 1888, when the membership consisted of only fifty scientists. Meetings were held twice a year, usually in Washington or at one of the eastern universities. New members to fill the places of those who died or resigned were selected on the basis of some distinguished piece of original scientific research. This was in contrast to the policy of the American Association for the Advancement of Science, which counted among its members anyone interested enough to pay dues. However, the AAAS reserved the title of Fellow for members of an inner council who had some claim to scientific knowledge.

Michelson had been through ups and downs in his feelings regarding the Academy. In 1909, he had had a falling out with Ira Remsen, professor of chemistry at Johns Hopkins. Michelson, wishing to encourage a more active membership in the Academy, had proposed a rule which would bring before the Council for action the name of any member who was absent from meetings for five consecutive years. He blamed Remsen not only for the defeat of this proposal but for the way in which he had been "hooted out of the meeting." After that incident, Michelson availed himself of the "privilege" of staying away.[9]

Hard feelings were forgotten by 1916 when the Academy awarded Michelson its highest honor, the Draper medal. Elected president in 1923, he presided, on April 29, 1924, at the first meeting held in the rotunda of the new five million-dollar building just completed for the Academy by the architect Bertrand Goodhue. A neoclassical edifice on the north side of the Mall along Constitution Avenue in Washington, it had been dedicated by President Calvin Coolidge at an impressive ceremony. A large group of high-ranking scientists turned out to hear Ernest Fox Nichols give a lecture on "Joining the Infra Red and the Electric Wave Spectra" which proved to be the culmination of his life's work.

Michelson felt a warm affection for Nichols, although they had seen little of each other in recent years. He admired the elegance of Nichols's exposition proving that a light beam can exert minute pressure on an object in its path and also his new work bridging of the gap in the spectrum between electromagnetic and infrared rays.

Nichols had set up on the stage a radiometer which he had designed and built especially for demonstration at the lecture. Mounting the semicircular marble platform he began his talk, showing slides of the spectra of electromagnetic and infrared rays. Nichols had determined the wavelengths of these rays by means of Michelson's echelon grating. "I think this will interest our president, Dr. Michelson," he said, then motioned for the next slide. "I shall . . ." He took a step or two, sank quietly onto the bench, and put his head down. After a minute, Michelson went over and touched him gently. He was dead. Michelson sadly adjourned the meeting and the scientists formed a double line while Nichols's body was carried from the building and the flag was lowered to half-mast.[10]

Nichols's death was not the only one to sadden the members of the National Academy on that April day of 1924. Michelson had announced the loss of three other members, particular friends of his, whom he would miss.

One was Jacques Loeb, the physiologist whose pioneer experiments in artificial fertilization had brought him fame; he had shared a makeshift laboratory with Michelson when the University of Chicago was in its infancy.

Thomas Corwin Mendenhall had died in Italy at the age

of eighty-two. His life had been a good one, full of action and interest, so that his friends could not feel deep regret or grief over his death, but for Michelson he was one of the few congenial spirits with whom he could share thoughts. In the years to follow he would often think of something to interest Mendenhall and then remember with a start that his friend was dead.

The third death that Michelson had to announce was the suicide of Arthur Gordon Webster, his former assistant at Clark —a tragic loss to science which shocked the members of the Academy.

In comparing Webster's life to Michelson's, the biographer cannot help wondering at the difference in their careers. Webster's light (a veritable beacon) remained under a bushel, while Michelson's shone to the world. Michelson had met instant success with his first experiment, while Webster remained for thirty years at an institution that had not the means or the vision to advance his talents.

A certain reticence derived from his Puritan ancestry kept the New Englander from playing the kind of game that is necessary to gain advancement in almost every field of endeavor. He disdained to exploit his great gifts in applied science, although such activities had made his Serbian friend Michael Pupin, professor of electro-mechanics at Columbia, a millionaire. At the memorial service held in 1925, Pupin spoke with some bitterness of the drudgery Webster underwent to earn the barest subsistence in a society burgeoning into conspicuous wealth.

When, during the war, Webster had broken his precedent and offered his knowledge of ballistics to the armed services, the response had been half-hearted. He had been appointed chairman of the Naval Consulting Board, a group of unimaginative engineers (Webster called them imperfectly educated physicists), who refused to back him. The unrewarded compromise with his ideals so mortified him that he sank into a deep depression from which he could not recover.

Two years after Webster's death Michelson decided to

throw his weight behind a movement to raise funds for scientific research. As president of the National Academy of Sciences, he wrote Herbert Hoover, then Secretary of Commerce, a letter which shows that Webster's tragedy was still fresh in his mind.

Dear Mr. Hoover,

It is a great satisfaction to know that you have undertaken to act as Chairman of the Trustees of the National Research Endowment. . . .

There can be no doubt that the situation would be immensely improved if the prospects of the more promising men who have the talent and ability and the taste for the pursuit of scientific investigation could be made comparable with those of say a successful physician or lawyer. It is too much to expect our more gifted scientific investigators to forego the advantage of a comfortable living, one which, more or less deservedly, actually does command the respect of the community, for a position in which he cannot hope to give his family the education and the surroundings which he could approve, and for which he would have to struggle to maintain at the expense of time, thought and labor which could be far better spent in uninterrupted pursuit of his scientific work.

It is a great satisfaction to know that in the distribution of the income from the funds which we hope to raise, the greater emphasis will be given to research in pure science. . . .

While not wishing to appear too free in suggesting details of methods of administering the funds, may I express my earnest hope that especial importance be attached to the work of individual workers rather than to organized cooperative investigations.[11]

The last sentence embodies the spirit of the individual scientist, a breed of which Michelson himself was almost the last. There were already many teams of researchers preparing the road toward nuclear physics.

In the summer of 1924, Michelson had attended a meeting of the American Physical Society, in Chicago, where he met the young Niels Bohr, already one of the principal architects of the physical atom and the quantum theory. Physicists, in their struggle to explore the atomic structure of electricity, approached the problem mainly from the point of view of spectroscopy. Bohr persuaded Michelson to show him the ruling engine which was turning out the gratings coveted by all spectroscopists and expressed a keen desire to procure a grating for his Institute in Copenhagen. Michelson explained the tedious and time-consuming process of constructing a grating and told him that there were none available at the moment, that his own work, he said, had to be delayed while a grating was being ruled. Bohr, however, was not to be discouraged. On his return to Copenhagen he wrote to Michelson with such tact, not to say cunning, that he achieved his purpose. He was well aware of Michelson's devotion to the wave theory in spite of the popularity of the newer discoveries in quantum mechanics.

> First of all I want to thank you for all the kindness you showed me during the meeting of the Physical Society in Chicago. My visit to America was a most refreshing and instructive experience to me and I need hardly say that one of the things I remember with greatest pleasure was the opportunity of making your personal acquaintance and learning about your general attitude toward the troubles with which physicists are struggling in the present years.
>
> It may perhaps interest you to hear that it appears to be possible for a believer in the essential reality of the

quantum theory to take a view which may harmonize with the essential reality of the wave theory conception, even more closely than the views I expressed during our conversation. In fact, on the basis of the correspondence principle it seems possible to connect the discontinuous processes occurring in atoms with the continuous character of the radiation field. . . .

After repeating his request, Bohr continued:

I hope you will not consider my request as too presumptuous but the purpose of my question was just to learn whether there might be a possibility for us to benefit in this way from your unique experience without being at the same time a disturbance to yourself. I hope therefore that you will excuse my daring in writing to you about this matter.[12]

The harmony Bohr predicted between the two seemingly incompatible theories has apparently been achieved. In any case, Michelson obliged him by sending a grating.

Ever since joining the summer staff at Mount Wilson, Michelson had been preparing for a new determination on the speed of light. This one was to be made between Mount Wilson and Mount San Antonio, or "Old Baldy," 22 miles away. By June of 1924 he was ready to go forward with a "preliminary measurement." He hesitated to call any of these a final figure.

Preparations had been carried out while he was in Chicago. Fred Pearson had erected a stone base to support the rotating mirror and the arc lamp. The reflecting mirror had been laboriously emplaced at a site on Baldy.

The terrain between Mount Wilson and Baldy was fearfully rough, and Hale thought it might be impossible to measure it along the surface of the ground. But Michelson had drawn the United States Coast and Geodetic Survey into the act: He wrote to Colonel E. L. Jones:

THE SPINNING PRISM

On invitation of Dr. George E. Hale, Director of the Mt. Wilson Observatory, I am preparing to make a redetermination of the value of the velocity of light. I am hoping to obtain an order of accuracy from ten to twenty times that obtained in my previous work (at Annapolis in 1878 and in Cleveland in 1885). This constant is not only of theoretical importance in Physics and in Astronomy, but may have an immediate bearing on the work of the Coast Survey in furnishing a means of measuring distances which may furnish a valuable check on the results of trigonometric surveys.[13]

Colonel Jones was quick to accept the undertaking. No doubt he realized that with an accurate constant he could reverse the process for measuring light velocity. When that value and the speed of the rotating mirror are known, the distance can be calculated with very little effort. The system developed into what was later called radar (radio detecting and ranging) which proved most valuable in the Second World War for locating enemy aircraft and submarines.

Jones sent Major William Bowie out to supervise the work in 1922, and Clement L. Garner, a geodesist, was put in charge of the difficult task of laying down the baseline. Garner had to detour around some private property and a number of orange groves, across stream beds and deep ravines. It was impossible to run a straight survey line but he was able to triangulate all deviations in order to reduce the measurement to those of a theoretically straight base. New 50-meter Invar tapes helped him to accomplish this feat because they were almost impervious to temperature changes and therefore held their length without much perceptible stretching. These tapes were suspended between portable towers built high enough to pass over most obstructions. There was one house, however, that could not be circumvented. Its owner kindly allowed Garner to pass the tape through the windows and doors (fortunately in line) to measure his base. Rainstorms and strong winds made the work on the high line between the mirrors on the mountains even more difficult, but finally it was completed. Coast and Geodetic Survey headquarters in Washington analyzed the results and proclaimed that Michelson's baseline was 35,-385.53 meters long with a probable error of one seven-millionth of the whole—perhaps one-quarter of an inch.[14] This standard of accuracy had never before been reached by geodetic survey and the whole staff took pride in the achievement. It was an example of the energy and devotion that Michelson inspired by his attitude toward the beauty of accuracy.

In designing the experiment, he reverted to a plan somewhat resembling the arrangement in which Fizeau intercepted light with the cogs of a toothed wheel. Michelson used a multifaceted mirror of eight, twelve, or sixteen sides, made of glass or steel, which revolved at just such a speed that it presented a different facet to the returning beam. During the time the beam of light flashed across the 22 miles to Baldy and back (0.00023 seconds) the mirror would turn through such an angle that the observer saw the image exactly as he would if the rotating mirror were at rest. No displacement of the image occurred and therefore only two measurements were required: the speed of rotation, and the distance between mirrors. This proved to be a vast improvement over earlier tests.

For measuring velocity of light, Michelson needed a powerful arc lamp, which was a very expensive item. The Mount Wilson staff cast about for a means to beg or borrow one for the time while the tests were carried out. Dr. Walter S. Adams wrote to the Army Corps Area Commander at the Presidio in San Francisco to inquire if this could be arranged. The adjutant replied that it was contrary to an act of Congress to lend government property, but that he wished to cooperate in every way possible. If the lamp could be accompanied by one of their men and the transportation and subsistence paid, it might be furnished.

THE SPINNING PRISM

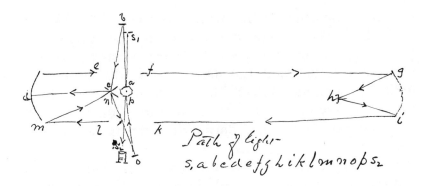

Sketch by Michelson of the velocity of light apparatus used in his 1922–1927 experiments at Mount Wilson

At this point, the War Department learned of the plan and offered to send Major Edward B. Stephensen of the Engineer Officers Reserve Corps to assist Michelson with the operation of the arc light. Stephensen was interested in searchlight development and would combine this study with that of the velocity of light.

Two days after this offer reached Adams, Michelson wrote that E. A. Sperry himself had offered a lamp, the one that was finally used.

> From the interviews with Sperry (and a second one only yesterday, here) it really seems as if the Sperry arc light will give a *very much* brighter intensity per square millimeter than the usual arc and it is to be expected that the chances of success will be materially increased. I am preparing two revolving mirrors, one of 12 faces and the other the same (small) mirror, whose faces are to be corrected.[15]

When Michelson arrived in Pasadena he drove up to Mount Wilson, where Dr. Pease and Fred Pearson had been preparing the octagonal rotating mirror, heart of the experiment. The nickel-steel prism, machined and polished with extreme care, was ready for a test. Pearson started it spinning with the air turbine and regulated the speed with a tuning fork until the eight-sided prism rotated 529 times a second. The rotation speed was such that the prism turned through exactly one-eighth of a revolution during the light passage to Baldy and back.

Michelson soon saw that three operators were needed to run the apparatus and asked William R. Smythe, formerly a student of his, to help. Smythe later described the experiment:

> One observer watched the face of the spinning prism through a telescope and, at a signal from the second observer, noted the displacement of the beam from the distant mirror, from its position with the prism at rest. This measured the amount by which the transit time differed from one-eighth of the rotational period.
>
> The second observer controlled the speed of the prism with an air valve while he watched the reflection in his telescope . . . of an oscillating beam from the mirror on a vibrating tuning fork. When this appeared stationary, the tuning fork period was an exact multiple of that of the prism, and he signalled the first observer.
>
> The third observer compared the period of the tuning fork with that of a gravity pendulum. . . . The friction of this pendulum was so small that, once set in motion, it would swing for nearly a day before coming to rest. . . .[16]

The real activity on Mount Wilson began after sunset. By 8 p.m. the eyepieces were focused, the slits adjusted, and the tuning fork warmed up. When the prism began to rotate, the howl of the turbine blades passed through and beyond the audible range. But the faces of the prism striking the surrounding air maintained a steady shriek. Between 9 and 11 p.m., before the night wind took over from the day wind, there was usually about an interval of half an hour during which the air mass between Mount Wilson and Mount San Antonio was quiet. This period yielded the best measurements.

The huge arc lamp that furnished the light beam took nearly all the direct current that Mount Wilson generators could supply. Its powerful violet rays lit up the mountain top with a lurid glow. The electrician in charge, although protected with welders' gloves and helmet, had been severely burned through his shirt by these rays and the pattern of the crossed strap of his overalls was still vividly depicted on his skin.

Michelson felt uneasy as he watched the three men take up their posts, facing the uncovered prism only 2 feet away. More than once such prisms had exploded from centrifugal force during preliminary tests. Metal or glass fragments, like a shotgun blast, could riddle everything in their plane. There were some shields around the prism but it was open in the direction of the observer's eyepiece. Any intervening plates or mirrors would have given confusing reflections.

Pearson tried to hold the prism steady while Michelson watched for the appearance of the reflected beam, an iridescent boiling blob of light, at first bearing no resemblance to a line. After about an hour of careful adjustments this image took on a symmetrical shape. Pearson steadied the prism and Smythe reported that at last the tuning fork had settled down. Then measurements began.

The main difficulty lay in maintaining a constant blast of air on the prism to keep it revolving. Michelson was sure that this could be remedied in another series of tests, but these would have to wait for another summer. The preliminary figure for this series was 299,820 kilometers per second *in vacuo*. This velocity was correct to one part in 10,000.[17]

CHAPTER 16

─────────────────

Absolute Motion?

M ICHELSON had been persuaded to carry out the experiment on the effect of the earth's rotation on the
velocity of light suggested by Dr. Silberstein in 1921
as a way to test Einstein's theories. During the summer of 1923
some preliminary tests were run in the open air at Mount
Wilson, but the interference fringes were so unsteady that it
was decided to make the test in a vacuum pipe and to do so
in Chicago.

After months of preparation the experiment took place at
Clearing, Illinois, on the prairie some ten miles west of the
university, in the bitterly cold weather of early December,
1924. Dr. F. M. Kannenstine carefully surveyed and staked out
a rectangular tract of land. The city of Chicago furnished a
pipeline a foot in diameter and about a mile long, for the
vacuum tube through which the light beam would travel. This
was valued at $16,000. The university contributed $17,000.
Silberstein, who had offered to finance the whole experiment,

gave only $500, which did not even cover the cost of one eyepiece.

As Michelson later explained the principle:

> . . . Imagine a rectangle about which two beams of light are reflected, one going in a clockwise and the other in a counterclockwise direction. If the earth were stationary, these two beams would come back to the starting-point at exactly the same moment. But if the earth is revolving, one of the two beams would have to go a little farther than the other to reach the starting-point. The difference would be greatest at the pole, and about half as great at the latitude of Chicago . . . the effect to be expected is of the order of a quarter of a light-wave. . . . If this displacement should turn out to be zero, or even less than this calculated value, it would be exceedingly difficult, if not impossible, to account for the Einstein theory.[1]

Michelson, who was not well at the time, depended on his research assistant, Dr. Henry Gale, to direct operations. Gale was a huge man, both tall and wide, who had starred on the Chicago football team in 1896. Perhaps he could never forget the heights of glory achieved in those days of his youth. Having been a hero he was understandably spoiled. He developed a keen grasp of physical optics, better than Millikan's (the two collaborated on a textbook), but he did practically no research on his own. However, he made excellent use of Michelson's powerful spectroscopic tools, the gratings and the echelon interferometer, and the two men worked well together.

From the little shack that sheltered the apparatus, Michelson and Gale deployed their helpers. Tom O'Donnell, Joe Purdy, and another assistant, Charles Stein, were posted at the various mirrors at the corners of the rectangle. Everyone agreed that Stein should take the coldest station because, being a Russian who had escaped from Siberia, he was thoroughly accustomed to subzero temperatures. Michelson spoke to his assistants over field telephones that had been installed at each station by courtesy of the local Bell Telephone Company.

Dr. Silberstein arrived from Rochester at a time when Michelson was not well enough to meet him. Henry Gale took Silberstein out to Clearing and disliked him immediately. According to Tom, things were handled in a very strange way during the Boss's absence. Silberstein brought a prohibited bottle of Scotch to Clearing, as well as an unwelcome covey of reporters. Everyone except Gale had a drink "or two or three," said Tom. "Gale loved his liquor, but disliked Silberstein and would only drink with 'friends.' " The subzero weather contributed to their discomfort. Tom summed up the day's observations: "And so for this and that and for the leak in the pipe, and everything else, they didn't get to see the displacement of the fringes."[2] They kept these difficulties from the Boss.

In December 1924, at a crucial point of the experiment, Michelson, suffering from a bladder infection, became so ill that he was taken to the Presbyterian Hospital. A prostate operation was necessary.

Henry Gale took over the final testing and supervision. He had volunteered for the killing job of making the visual observations every four hours. Michelson at first refused to let him undertake this strenuous routine which allowed him only three and one-half hours of sleep at a stretch. But Gale actually begged for the work, and this dogged devotion was one of the reasons Michelson insisted that the results be published under their joint authorship.[3]

They decided to prepare an announcement for the press to counteract some of the wild publicity with which the experiment had been dramatized. "Einstein on Trial," the headlines had proclaimed; "Michelson Leads Flank Attack Upon the German Scientist." This kind of reporting made Michelson very unhappy. "I should have conducted my observations in some obscure corner without all this publicity," he said. And again, in a moment of irritation, "All we can deduce from this experiment is that the earth rotates on its axis!"[4]

Michelson was released from the hospital in time for

Christmas. Madeleine drove him home in her new Wills St. Clair roadster. Fred Pearson and Joe Purdy were waiting in front of the house on Fifty-eighth Street to help him out of the car. Fortunately it was not snowing.

Michelson, pale and shaking from the exertion, managed with their support to walk through the gate and up the little path to the house. At this point, from behind the shrubbery, two reporters startled him by clicking their cameras in his face. Joe and Fred promptly chased them away.

Edna was overjoyed to have him at home again. Now she could plan his meals exactly as he liked them, free from the hospital rules and regulations. In a few days he showed marked improvement but was still very weak. Too weak, Edna thought, to get up on January 8, 1925, in response to a request from the university to deliver a full-scale lecture[5] on the most interesting aspects of his work. But the invitations had been sent out and Michelson was not to be restrained. He sent Tom and Fred down to Orchestra Hall the morning of the lecture to set up the optical equipment.

As they were working on the stage, they heard a loud voice with a heavy German accent protesting from the rear of the auditorium. "I heff a concert this afternoon. I can't allow this paraphernalia upon my stage." Frederick Stock, conductor of the Chicago Symphony Orchestra, strode down the aisle. "Who iss dis Michelson?" he roared.

Tom answered him. "A thousand years from now, Mr. Stock, his name will be remembered."

"Ach so . . . " the conductor's voice trailed off. That afternoon the orchestra played a children's concert against a background of curious instruments.

In the evening, the University of Chicago took over the Hall. Edna wrote to Dody:

Last night was the great occasion of your father's public lecture—the first he ever gave here—and almost anywhere at that. It was by invitation. I mean the University which is engaged in an expansion campaign asked three men, your father, Mr. James Henry Breasted the famous Egyptologist who had recently discovered Tuten Kamen's [sic] Tomb and Mr. Laing [chairman of the Latin Department and general editor of the University of Chicago Press] to give lectures, and invited enough people to simply pack Orchestra Hall up to the topmost seat. About 800 applied for tickets and were turned away. Everyone gave dinners before it and all the North Siders were there. When it was over the audience applauded and applauded. I thought they would never stop. He had made everyone love him besides admiring him.[6]

The excitement of the occasion carried Michelson through the evening, and it was only after he was safely home that the strain began to show. He lay in bed all the following day, dozing and resting in a darkened room, trying to regain his strength. Infection following his operation caused discomfort. Edna was worried. When the pain grew sharp she got him into a hot bath to relieve it and telephoned his doctor. She felt needed now that her husband depended on her, and she canceled all engagements in order to nurse him. A closeness sprang up between them that had not been there for many years, if ever.

"I was to have met Beatrice for tea and to see some paintings at the Art Institute," she wrote to Dody, "but I have just sent word that I don't think I ought to leave him. Even if he only dozes in the next room. He might need me. But it is very lonely."

Michelson was in and out of the hospital throughout the spring. He was still far too ill to attend the April 27, 1925, meeting of the National Academy of Sciences, and Arthur Holly Compton read his paper. "The latest test of Einstein's theory has proven two things," Michelson had written. "First, that the earth's rotation has no effect on the velocity of light, and secondly that the ether-drag hypothesis is definitely disproved."[7] Thus Sir George Stokes's theory of an ether stirred into motion with the earth could no longer be invoked to explain the Michelson-Morley experiment.

Little by little the patient improved. It was gratifying to Edna to find him able to enjoy himself. A currently popular limerick delighted him:

> There was a young lady named Bright,
> Whose speed was far faster than light:
> She set out one day
> In a relative way
> And returned home the previous night.[8]

In June of 1925 Edna brought him the good news that he was being appointed the first Distinguished Service Professor of the University of Chicago.

While the pros and cons of relativity were being thrashed out at levels ranging from understanding to irrational hysteria, Dayton C. Miller had been eagerly preparing what he hoped would be definitive evidence to disprove the theory and reestablish familiar paths of thought. He had been invited by Hale in 1921 to come to Mount Wilson to repeat the Michelson-Morley experiment at a 6,000-foot altitude. Miller set up an enormous interferometer near the edge of the mountain. After four years of labor against great difficulties and many discouraging setbacks, Miller's experiment revealed a slight positive result which he thought he had perceived even at the outset. In 1922 Max Born had written to Einstein that he had heard about Miller's success in revealing a positive effect. "I do not believe a word of the rumour" was his comment, but he urged Einstein to find out for sure and send him word on a postcard.[9]

Miller made his final announcement to an astonished audience of the American Physical Society, of which he was then president, at Kansas City, December 29, 1925. He told the meeting that he had discovered an ether-drift of 10 kilometers per second, indicating that the earth is moving at that rate toward the head of the constellation Draco.[10] He assured his audience that no corrections need to be applied to these observed values. "Absolute motion" had been measured! For those who wanted to believe, hope sprang up anew.

The American Association for the Advancement of Science awarded Miller a $1,000 prize for his "discovery of absolute motion" in 1925, but the National Academy of Sciences was more conservative. Attacks on relativity were no longer admitted by most physicists.

Later, in 1925 and 1926, Born went to Mount Wilson to see demonstrations. Miller allowed him to operate the gigantic interferometer, which Born found "very shaky and unreliable." A slight cough or a movement of the hand would throw the fringes out of view so that readings were not possible.[11] Since Born was not an experimental physicist, he was hardly qualified to condemn the experiment, but he was right about its results.

Miller persisted in making a final test in 1926. After much anguish over the recalculations he convinced himself and a few others of the accuracy of his results. In consequence, a number of ether-drift experiments were performed in various countries around the world. Perhaps the most dramatic was that of Professor Auguste Piccard who took an interferometer 7,000 feet up in his balloon.

Michelson was even persuaded to build a bigger interferometer than had ever been made before. For this instrument, the mirrors were prepared in a new manner: "We have found that plane parallel plates, properly sputtered with platinum or gold, answer almost if not quite as well as the prisms," he wrote to Walter Adams.[12]

Adams was no supporter of Miller's theory of a positive effect. He wrote Michelson: "In view of Dayton Miller's rather exasperating statements on this subject I should like to see your work published in sufficient detail to cut the ground from under him. . . .[13]

With few exceptions, the ether-drift tests made with new and different types of interferometers reinforced the negative result of the 1881 experiment. Miller might have been wiser to have concentrated on his valuable research in acoustics and the exquisite tone of his flutes.

In the political spectrum, Michelson's opinions were definitely conservative. Edna, who had retained her progressive outlook, loved to tease him about this. She had a splendid opportunity one morning as the family sat at breakfast and the maid appeared with a roll of papers addressed to Michelson. The wrapper was covered with stamps of the USSR. Burning with curiosity, the children watched him examine the exterior of the packet and lay it down, unopened, near his plate.

"Are you receiving secret documents from the Bolsheviks, Albert?" Edna queried. "I thought you disapproved of them."

The revolutionary government had been in control for seven years at this time, but Michelson never changed in his opposition to any movement to recognize the Soviet Union.

"Please open it, Pahdie," Beatrice begged. His indifference to mail was baffling. All sorts of interesting-looking letters went into the fire or the waste basket unopened. Michelson was deeply engrossed in his morning copy of the *Chicago Tribune*. Without looking up he said, "You may open it if you wish."

Madeleine and Beatrice began at once to peel off the wrappings. They unrolled a beautiful parchment, decorated with ribbons and seals. Edna looked at the scroll, trying to make out the Cyrillic letters.

"Why, Albert," she said, "it's from the Russian Academy of Sciences in Leningrad. I believe they have made you a member." Michelson went on reading his paper. "I suppose you'll have to refuse it, feeling as you do. Shall we send the announcement back to them?" A mischievous smile played at the corners of her mouth.

Slowly, Michelson looked up from his newspaper. "No, I think I'll accept it." And there the matter was dropped.

Mrs. Rockefeller McCormick, a daughter of the founder of Chicago University, often entertained members of the faculty in her gray stone "palace" on Lake Shore Drive. On one occasion the Michelsons were invited to dinner and the opera. Michelson was seated on his hostess's right, while on his right was a beautiful creature with "very little above the eyebrows," according to Edna.

"Oh, Professor Michelson," gushed the young lady, "I think it's perfectly marvelous the way you were able to measure the diameter of that star"—much batting of long black eyelashes—"but there is one thing I don't quite understand." A look of bewildered innocence puckered her forehead under the curls. "May I ask you a very personal question?" Michelson nodded encouragingly. "*However* do you find out the name of the star when it's *so* far away?"

Michelson was thoroughly enjoying his dinner when he noticed his hostess looking nervously at the watch placed beside her on the table. She did not wish to be late for the opening curtain of *Aida,* with Mary Garden in the title role. At her signal, the waiters stepped forward to remove each guest's plate, whether he had finished or not. But Michelson had no intention of relinquishing his squab en brochette until he had savored the last delicious mouthful. Placing both hands on the solid gold plate, he held it obstinately against any attack. The waiter finally retreated, while Michelson finished his main course. The rest of the guests were rushed through dessert and coffee; then Mrs. McCormick rose from the table in a frosty silence and swept the party into limousines. In private, Michelson's friends congratulated him on his audacity, but several years elapsed before he had another invitation from Mrs. McCormick.

Times had changed since the publication of his book, *Light Waves and Their Uses,* in 1903. Michelson made a valiant effort to allow for the new thinking, but it was uphill work. "I am perfectly willing to accept the consequences of Einstein's theory, but not his premise," he said, and he would continue to hold his belief in the ether because it explained every phenomenon of light except the one dealt with by relativity. "We know that light is a vibration of something—of what?—that 'what' we call ether."[14]

However much Michelson may have wished Einstein disproved, he nevertheless forced himself to keep an open mind. He had been cautious at first, as was natural for a man schooled in nineteenth-century thinking, but as soon as he considered the evidence conclusive, he accepted the theory of relativity. "He never deviated from an unflinching search for the truth, regardless of personal considerations or life-long convictions," Hale wrote of his friend.[15]

Collecting his thoughts for another slender volume, in 1927 Michelson wrote *Studies in Optics,* a beautiful eulogy of wave motion, which alone can explain the phenomena of interference, polarization, and transverse waves. His antipathy toward modern concepts, although he tried to keep it under control, is evident in the first chapter when he directs an insult at his old enemy, the corpuscular theory of light. This, he points out, has long been considered dead and should have been forgotten. Had it not been resuscitated in a modified and complicated manner, he would not have bothered to mention it.

The occasion for such a return to an exploded idea is a supposed difficulty brought to light by the theory of relativity, according to which, as many of its supporters maintain, not only is a medium unnecessary, but it is even inconsistent with its fundamental assumptions. But even if we admit the difficulty, it is doubtful if this is a valid reason for rejecting a theory which has yielded such splendid results.[16]

The book is a loving testimonial to the wave theory and the miracles that can be performed with light waves.

Over the summers of several years Michelson returned to the Monastery on Mount Wilson to refine his measurements on the velocity of light. He was a familiar figure to young Harold Babcock, who was usually working with Hale at the solar observatory. One morning in the summer of 1926, Babcock appeared, rather timidly, at Michelson's office with a grating in his hands. Dr. John A. Anderson, who was away, had put Babcock in charge of the Mount Wilson ruling engine during his absence, with instructions to show the grating to Michelson if the ruling was completed. Michelson, looking it over with his naked eye, told Babcock he had made a good one and wished him luck. Babcock admired a watercolor lying on the table. "I played hooky yesterday," Michelson explained with a mischievous smile.[17]

When the summer was over Michelson felt his results were good. Before leaving he wrote, on August 29, 1926, to Major Bowie at the Coast and Geodetic Survey:

You will be interested to know that the measurements of the velocity of light with the 22 mile base have just been completed with results which have been rather unexpected in accuracy. The mean value of five series of measurements including about 1600 separate observations comes out 299800 $\pm$ 1 kilometer per second. The $\pm$ 1 may be accidental, but I feel quite confident at any rate of a probable error less than one in 100,000.[18]

The final velocity of light figure for the Mount Wilson–Baldy tests was 299,796± 4 kilometers per second, [19] (186, 285 ± 2 1/2 miles per second). This figure, attained in January 1927, was considered by Michelson himself to be his most accurate determination and it is the one closest to the currently accepted value of 186,282.3960 miles per second. It has stood against measurements made by electronic methods long after his death.[20] But, being a perfectionist, Michelson was not satisfied. Adams, who became director of the observatory after Hale's retirement, urged him to accept these figures as final. "The accordance of your separate series of observations is so extraordinary that it is a case of 'gilding the lily' to attempt to reduce it very much further."[21]

Adams encouraged him, however, to try a longer measurement over a different area. Michelson now turned his attention to measuring the velocity of light over a far greater distance than had ever been used before. With the aid of his friends of the Coast and Geodetic Survey, the distance between stations on Mount Wilson and Mount San Jacinto, 82 miles away, was painstakingly measured, as was also the distance between Mount Wilson and Santiago Peak 50 miles away.

Neither of these tests gave much promise of success because of the hazy atmosphere and the smoke from constant forest fires. An idea for eliminating these difficulties had been taking shape for some time, and in March of 1927 Michelson wrote to Major Bowie:

The work at Mount Wilson is correctly reported to have been so seriously interfered with by weather conditions that practically nothing has been done with the San Jacinto line. . . . I am, however, considering two other possibilities: one, the situation of a station near Tucson, Arizona, and the other an attempt through a long pipe line either exhausted or filled with hydrogen. . . .[22]

(319)

In July of 1928 his stay in Pasadena was cut short because of an infection that gave him great physical discomfort and necessitated his return to Chicago for an operation. Recuperation was slow. He had to cancel an appointment to lecture in Lima, Peru. To pass the time, he asked Edna to read aloud to him, and when he felt up to it, he dictated letters to her. As he improved he was allowed to receive visitors. Arthur Holly Compton and Preston Keyes came frequently. They had been sorely worried. Michelson's daughters came to the hospital one at a time. When Dody entered the room one day she found him engrossed in making a sketch of monkeys scampering up and down the screen at the foot of his bed. To each monkey he had given the face of one of the doctors or interns. "These are the fellows who are tinkering with my insides," he told her. They were excellent caricatures. A pretty little nurse was shaking with laughter as she identified them. She was a Catholic and told Dody that she had been trying to save her father's soul, without much success. "I'm helping Professor Michelson to see the light," she explained, as they both went into gales of laughter over the *double entendre*. She must have made some impression on him, however, because among the trinkets on his bureau was a little crucifix she had given him; he kept it until he died.

September found him back in Pasadena. The climate did wonders for his health, but haze blocked his work on the mountain. "I have definitely given up a repetition in the open but am considering a trial in vacuo," he wrote to Bowie.[23]

This bold scheme was occupying more and more of his thoughts. In a vacuum there could be no smoke or haze, but instead perpetually "good seeing," a controlled environment. But a mile-long vacuum? Very difficult to build—it would cost a lot of money.

On November 1, 1928, Michelson attended a very happy celebration in Washington. It was the annual meeting of the Optical Society of America, and was called the Michelson

Meeting in honor of the fiftieth anniversary of his first publication on the velocity of light.[24] Addressing several hundred physicists and members of the Optical Society, Michelson described his latest techniques and announced a variance of only one part in several hundred thousand in his latest figure.

In successive meetings in the auditorium of the Bureau of Standards on November 2 and 3, Michelson, speaking without a prepared paper, explained his three experiments on ether drift by drawing diagrams on a blackboard.

He did not offer any conclusions. "I am merely pointing out a fact," he said, "and that is that the results of my experiment, conducted with greater scientific care, and improved apparatus and refined technique, with the intention of eliminating every possible source of error, are again negative. It is for physicists to study and explain these results and reconcile them with the existence of the hypothetical ether."[25]

Dayton Miller was asked to express his views. He merely repeated, "All I can say is that my own results have been positive."[26]

Paul R. Heyl of the Bureau of Standards then discussed the nature of light. His simple statements marked the progress of twentieth-century thinking. Waves behave like particles, and vice versa, he told the physicists. Modern thought blends the two ideas of waves and quanta. Matter equals energy. Curved space acts like a mechanical surface of constraint. If space can be bent or straightened, can it not vibrate like ether?[27] Michelson was pleased to hear these comforting words at the end of Heyl's talk.

In a sense, Michelson's technique of painting a watercolor was illustrative of his method of attacking a scientific problem. His strong artistic sense, rather than empirical knowledge, was what led him to the heart of the problem. The same elegant simplicity appears in the design of his instruments. He was a reasonably happy man because he could derive enormous satisfaction from his work, which he often called his "play."

South of Chicago at the foot of Lake Michigan lay the Indiana sand dunes. The Michelsons often drove down the lake shore toward the village of Miller for a picnic. On one of these outings Michelson accompanied his family with the idea of painting a watercolor. He walked up and down a few dunes carrying his small easel and paintbox, looking for a spot which "composed." Now and then he paused to frame a view in his hands, half closing his eyes to imagine the scene on paper. When he had found a good subject he set up his easel, opened his paintbox, and filled the little water cup from a bottle he had brought with him.

He blocked out the sketch first in pencil and then with a large flat brush he put in a wash across the rough paper for the sky, leaving the snowy shape of the cumulus clouds dry. The sand dunes he painted a pearly gray on their shadowy side and a rich, golden ocher where the light struck them. The scrub pine and dry grass in the foreground and the leaden color of Lake Michigan gave the picture a wintry look in spite of the pale sunshine. Michelson rose from his stool to look at his picture from a distance. He was not quite satisfied with the way the paints had dried while he was still trying to work them around, and he wished he could avoid muddying the colors. Taking out his small bone-handled pocket knife, he ran the blade around the edge of the block of paper, carefully removing his first attempt in order to start a fresh one.

Trial and error in time produced results. In 1928, he was persuaded to lend his pictures to the Renaissance Society for a one-man show at Ida Noyes Hall; two of his watercolors were shown at the Chicago Art Institute. Although these watercolors are unpretentious and lack the shock value of many paintings of the era, viewers felt their charm. One woman told Michelson he should never have given up art for science. "I did not have to choose," he answered, "because for me they are inseparable."

During this period, Michelson noticed that when reporters got a chance to talk to him, they usually asked if he was the brother of the famous newspaperman Charlie Michelson. Charlie was rapidly becoming a legend. When he was still very young, Hearst had sent him to Cuba to cover the revolution. There he played poker with another reporter, Winston Churchill. After a short term in a Cuban jail, Charlie left for Buffalo, where President McKinley's assassin was being tried. He was in San Francisco for the 1906 earthquake and fire and in Veracruz for the landing of U.S. troops in 1914. He covered the trial of Harry K. Thaw for the murder of the architect Stanford White in 1906 and that of John T. Scopes for teaching Darwinian theory in Dayton, Tennessee, in 1925. For several years he was managing editor of the *Chicago Examiner;* later he became Washington correspondent for *The New York World.* Charlie had developed a crackling newspaper style. His fearless handling of people and events soon put him in the forefront of correspondents in the capital. He made no personal enemies, and people took good-naturedly his jibes which cut and cleansed but left no scar.

In 1928, he became director of publicity for the Democratic National Committee. Needling Republicans became his daily pastime. The Depression played into his hands and he became known as "Hoover's gadfly." His column entitled "Dispelling the Fog," under the letterhead of the Democratic National Committee, should, according to his Republican opponents, have been called "Laying a Smoke Screen." His efforts were partly responsible for Franklin D. Roosevelt's victory in 1932. Occasionally, however, he felt some pangs of conscience for selling his talent to the Democrats instead of retaining his independence as a reporter: "My sister is a distinguished writer, my brother a tremendous physicist, and I am the family prostitute."[28]

He was also a practical joker, and in 1928 Albert was the butt of one of his younger brother's pranks. Charlie had blown into Chicago with the usual flurry of excitement. He lived in a whirlwind of activities altogether foreign to the scientist's serene existence. For some time Charlie had been longing to disturb this academic calm, and an idea came to him in Michelson's office at Ryerson. They were going to Washington together, and there was a little time to kill before leaving. Albert was concentrating on some letters. Charlie, unobserved, stepped up on a chair, and set the hands of the wall clock thirty minutes ahead. He then waited impatiently until his brother noticed the time. "Good God," said Michelson, "we've missed the train."

"Oh, don't worry about that," Charlie answered, "I'll have it held for you." He telephoned the station master and pretended to give instructions for holding the train. Bewildered, Michelson got into a cab with his brother. They arrived at the station to find the train still at the platform. It was some time before Albert observed Charlie's mischievous grin and realized that he had been gulled.

He himself was not devoid of the art of teasing, which seemed to run in the family. His fun was often derived at the expense of his friend Arthur Holly Compton, whose work on the change in wavelength of X rays when scattered by electrons later became famous as the Compton Effect. Compton was away from home when an emissary from the Swedish Consul came to alert him that he was to receive the Nobel Prize. He returned to Chicago to read in the *Tribune* that he was to share the 1927 Physics prize with the Scottish physicist C. T. R. Wilson. The honor was unexpected, and Compton's first instinct was to consult with Michelson. The latter, who was delighted at the news, had been about to telephone congratulations when Compton appeared at the door of his office. Looking quite bewildered, Compton began to inquire anxiously what sort of ceremony took place in Sweden and how one behaved before royalty.

Michelson saw that Compton, who was known to be a teetotaler, had qualms about the toast to the king at the banquet. It was a situation that Michelson relished and he made the most of it. He welcomed Compton with a broad smile of fatherly pride and expressed his delight in the achievement. Then his face took on a serious look. "You must be very cautious, Compton. When I was there they gave me a banquet that lasted until long after midnight. First we drank a very strong punch. There's no way of avoiding that. The Swedes are touchy and easily offended if you don't drink with them. Then finally we sat down to dinner. Between the courses there were speeches. With each dish and for each toast they served a different colored wine. At my place they had a wine for every color in the spectrum!

"Now here's where you must really be careful, Compton. The spectrum, as you know, has many more colors nowadays than it did in 1907. You will be asked for a report on your work shortly after the second round of liqueurs."

Compton went away suspecting Michelson's story but rather ill at ease nevertheless. At the royal banquet, he told it on himself, much to the amusement of the Swedes.[29]

CHAPTER 17

The Work Is Done

M ICHELSON's health continued to plague him, and the Chicago climate increased his vulnerability to colds. He became seriously ill in September of 1929, and his condition deteriorated steadily. The surgeon, Dr. Karl Kretchmer, decided to operate on the bladder, in spite of the danger that pneumonia might set in. Michelson's fever went to 103 degrees, and the newspapers announced that he was near death.

He recovered from that operation but just as he was beginning to heal, the doctors told him a second operation was necessary. Edna was distraught. She suppressed her inclination to blame the surgeon for her husband's misery, but she remarked that he seemed to get an enormous amount of publicity out of the case. "Kretchmer Saves Michelson for Science," the newspapers said.

The turning point came in October. One evening the

fever remained below normal and by daylight Kretchmer told the family that Michelson's fighting spirit had won the battle. He continued to improve and soon he was out of danger.

Word of Michelson's condition had reached Mount Wilson, causing serious doubts as to whether he would ever be able to finish the experiments. Dr. Adams informed him that all preparations had ceased.

From his hospital bed, Michelson dictated to Edna a letter to Adams:

> I shall have to confess that I was rather disappointed at your letter stating that everything had been brought to a standstill on the work on the velocity of light.
>
> If it does not annoy you too much I would very much like to have some sort of explanation. Not that I have the least desire to criticize any action which you may have considered necessary, but in order to prepare myself for the work of next year. . . .
>
> You will be pleased to hear, that in response to your suggestion that I apply for an additional $10,000.00, I have just received a reply from Dr. Merriam [of the Carnegie Institution] granting this amount. . . .
>
> Dr. Kretchmer encourages me to think that I shall be out of the hospital in a month or so and I look forward to resuming work in Pasadena some time in May.[1]

This letter must have brought a positive reaction because on November 22, 1929, Michelson's spirits were soaring. He was so pleased with the "extremely favorable results of the preliminary work," that he felt tempted "to go out to California even in my present crippled condition, to see the work finished."[2]

New tennis courts had been built in Pasadena and Adams told him that all his old opponents were waiting for a match with him. Michelson replied that he hardly hoped to try out the courts this year.

One of his first visitors after Dr. Kretchmer dismissed him from the hospital in November was Harold Babcock from Mount Wilson. Babcock had heard Adams express the wish that Michelson would move to Pasadena. Seeing him now still rather miserable in the "vile Chicago weather," Babcock urged him to cut his ties and join the Mount Wilson staff. Michelson and his wife had already almost decided that it would be best for him to move to the milder climate of California. His retirement from the University of Chicago was long overdue, but every year, at the president's request, Michelson had agreed to stay on. Now, however, the decision was made. The Michelsons arranged to sell their house and move to Pasadena permanently.

If it was hard for Edna that June day in 1930 to walk out of her home for the last time, leaving the conservatory and garden she had cherished, it was even more of a wrench for Michelson to leave the laboratory that had been the scene of his research for thirty-five years.

A sum of $30,000 from the Carnegie Institution of Washington and the University of Chicago had been put at Michelson's disposal for further measurements on the velocity of light. Before leaving Chicago he called in Arthur Compton for a last visit. During their talk Michelson confided that he had grave misgivings about carrying on further research on this subject when perhaps a younger man, "more in the swim," might make better use of the grant. "It's so much money!" he said. "Why don't you use it?"

Compton, struck by his humility, reassured him of the importance of the physical constant and convinced him that he must continue his experiments on the speed of light.[3]

Forest Moulton, Michelson's good friend for most of their years at Chicago, noticed as Michelson grew older that he came to accept life more gracefully. He was like the sea on a summer's day, Moulton wrote, serene, illimitable, unfathomable. Unlike some of the more harassed professors in their orbit, he did not allow himself to be encumbered by university duties and no longer drove himself to complete laborious tasks.

> . . . he never feared that science, the University, or mankind was at a critical turning point; he never trembled on the brink of a great discovery. . . . He never rushed into print with immature work. He was not in the habit of publishing the same thing over and over again in slightly varying form. He did not run around the country, posing as a genius and addressing minor scientific organizations. He never invited the press to carefully timed dramatic announcements before the major scientific societies. He never proclaimed the explosion of the Universe. He never attracted popular attention and approval by claiming to find support for theological dogmas or the doctrine of the freedom of the will in the laws of falling bodies or in any other scientific principles. Instead, he pursued his modest and serene way along the frontiers of science, entering new pathways and ascending to unattained heights as leisurely and as easily as though he were taking an evening stroll.[4]

The five-day train trip to California was exhausting and Edna was deeply grateful to Hale for meeting them at the station with a car. They settled temporarily at the Maryland Hotel in Pasadena while Michelson recovered his strength and Edna looked around for a house. She found a comfortable one at 1717 San Pasqual Street, not far from the office of Mount Wilson Observatory.

Old friends welcomed the Michelsons to Pasadena. The Italian astronomer Giorgio Abetti and his wife had come to Mount Wilson from Florence on a Rockefeller grant. The Abettis were most congenial friends, with whom Michelson and his wife could discuss subjects quite apart from physics: roses, music, theater, travel, children, or the world situation. They were a boon to Edna, who did not care for the California life style. On a Sunday drive along Wiltshire Boulevard she noticed a roadside display of papier-maché fireplaces with mantel pieces. "There you see how flimsy California life can be. The hearth, symbol of the home, is for sale beside the road. They buy one and bring it back with them, stand it up next to a wall in the parlor, not at all troubled by the lack of a chimney."

Michelson had to laugh, but having grown up in the West he did not miss, as she did, the changes of seasons, the sense of history, or the intellectual point of view of the East. Now a permanent resident of California, Michelson on June 20 took charge of his last velocity of light test. Ever since 1927 work had been in progress. Rockefeller and Carnegie money at his disposal now amounted to $67,500.

A site had been selected on a piece of land 6 miles southwest of the town of Santa Ana. This property had originally been part of an enormous Spanish land grant. Its owner, James Irvine, Jr., generously allowed the observatory to use part of it. The terrain was well suited to Michelson's purpose, varying only a few feet in elevation over the distance of a mile.

A $50,000 contract had been drawn up with the California Corrugated Culvert Company to furnish the 36-inch steel pipe in 60-foot lengths. Fred Nichols, a capable engineer on the Mount Wilson staff, had worked out the electrical circuit and devised an original manner for sealing the pipe at each joint with the inner tube of a tire covered with several coats of rubber paint.

In testing the apparatus on a short length of pipe at the Ross Flying Field near California Institute of Technology, Michelson found that ample light was available after the beam from the source had been reflected three times from end to end of the pipe. Increasing the length of the light path to five reflections, however, dimmed the image to such an extent that he called off the tests until he was able to procure a more powerful lamp. By spring of 1930, the complete mile-long pipeline had been built on the Irvine Ranch and the optical system installed. It was hoped that the effects of ground shifting (caused by those unmentionable earthquakes) would be eliminated by the vacuum inside the tube. As the temperature and pressure were constant, the distance remained constant.

A small rotary pump driven by a 5-horsepower motor was used to draw out the 40,000 cubic feet of free air. As the density in the air diminished, the pump worked harder and harder. At first squeaks and hisses were heard along the pipe from certain joints that were not quite airtight, but these leaks were gradually eliminated. Every problem was worked out as it arose. There were no precedents to go by.

An arc light placed outside the tube was used instead of sunlight to shine through a window onto the polished surfaces of the small rotating steel mirror. Several of these mirrors, with 8, 16, or 32 facets, were tried out with closely similar results. A 32-sided mirror had been cut with extreme precision, accurate to within one part in a million, a painstaking task that Fred Pearson had accomplished. It would rotate at 1,000 revolutions per second. Pearson also completed work on the delicate tuning fork that controlled and measured the revolutions of the mirror by pitch determination.

Michelson was troubled by the rapid tarnishing of the mirrors. He corrected this difficulty by coating them with fluorite.

For setting up the vacuum-tube experiment Michelson wanted to send Tom O'Donnell to Santa Ana. Tom had had experience with similar apparatus used in the "rotating earth" experiment at Clearing, Illinois. From this point of view, his presence in California was invaluable, but he was a difficult man to get on with. With certain apprehensions, Michelson wired Dr. Pease: "I am sending Tom O'Donnell to assist in the velocity of light work and hope you will see that he will feel at home when he arrives."[5]

Tom was an outspoken Irishman, and he never hesitated to tell a man to his face that the work in the instrument shop was not being done "correctly," by which Tom meant according to the way Michelson had trained him.

In one instance, he had been making a trial run on the vacuum-tube experiment. After days of work, the image he sought was still not returned to the observer's eyepiece. The reason, according to Tom, was that the mirror at the far station had been made concave instead of convex. This, he thought, was a shocking error that involved enormous waste of time and money.

Fired with righteous indignation, Tom left the site at 3 A.M. and drove to the Maryland Hotel in Pasadena where the Michelsons were staying. He did not hesitate to wake the Chief, although it was then 4:30 in the morning. Michelson threw on a robe and came down to the lobby, where they talked earnestly for a couple of hours, as O'Donnell drew diagrams on a Chinese laundry card and pointed out his theory of the error.

"The mirror at C_2 should be convex instead of concave. Pease designed it but he's too stubborn to agree that for the multi-round set up, the mirror will have to be changed to convex."

Michelson replied that it made no difference as far as the Mount Wilson runs were concerned, but he assured Tom that he was theoretically correct. Tom thought Michelson was covering up for Pease. He retorted: "This is one case where Einstein's Relativity raises hell with your multi-round trip circuit!"

Both were too engrossed to notice that daylight had arrived and early risers were stirring in the lobby. A little group of curious people gathered near them to listen. Among these, a reporter nosed his way in and asked what the trouble was. Michelson became aware of his audience for the first time. Embarrassed at being seen in public in his night clothes, he fled to his room before the cameras could catch him.

Tom went back to Santa Ana to take it out on Fred Pearson and Dr. Pease for the mistake, which he felt was a betrayal of the trust that the Chief had placed in them. A major row ensued.

In the end, a convex mirror was substituted and Tom was convinced that all was well again.[6] He was always the hero of his own stories.

It was difficult for Michelson to find out who was really to blame in these quarrels. As his health weakened he was less and less able to cope with disagreements among his assistants. Pease and Pearson eventually managed to get Tom sent back to Chicago and finished the experiment without him.

One evening Pease and Garner, who had made the geodetic measurements, went to make a report to Michelson at a small hotel in Santa Ana where he sometimes stayed while he was making observations. They found him propped up in bed, quite alert but showing signs of physical weakness. He made no mention of this nor did they. On learning of their difficulties, he said: "Regardless of other progress, it is quite an accomplishment to obtain so much vacuum in a mile long, three foot diameter, corrugated iron pipe."[7]

Michelson could no longer apply his talent for putting his finger on the source of error. There were large, unexplained discrepancies, due perhaps to unstable, alluvial soil or to the rapid changes of temperature when the sun was shining on the tube. In their later determinations, Pease and Pearson found fluctuations up to 12 miles per second, the cause of which could not be discovered.

William Smythe said of this impasse, "I have always felt . . . that if the chief . . . had lived the results would have been different."[8]

Physicists who are familiar with these experiments believe that textbooks on optics should refer to Michelson's 1927 Mount Wilson result as his most precise measurement, instead of citing the Santa Ana figures, as they frequently do.[9]

In March 1931, Dody arrived in Pasadena, shortly before her father made his last visit to the Irvine ranch. He was determined to inspect the work that had been done and to try out a new and more powerful pump to create the vacuum. Dody accompanied him on the long drive, which tired him visibly. He forced himself to overcome his fatigue during the many hours he spent with Fred on the fine adjustments of the instruments. Exhaustion overtook him in the middle of his observations. His face was ash-gray by the time he finally had the satisfaction of seeing the image return clearly after three reflections through the pipe, a distance of 6 miles.

Edna announced the next morning that Professor and Mrs. Einstein were coming to luncheon. "How does Father feel about that?" Dody asked, remembering that a certain coolness had existed between the two men. Edna assured her that this was all in the past. Einstein had heard that Michelson was ill and he wished to come over to cheer him up. "Please don't get him started on the subject of the ether," she whispered to Einstein when he arrived.

The coolness on Einstein's part had stemmed from a time in his youth, in the beginning of his career, before he became known in the United States. He had hoped for approval and acceptance of his Special Theory of Relativity from four men in particular; that approval was in each case long denied him.[10] One of these was his early mentor, Ernst Mach. H. A. Lorentz, Henri Poincaré, and Michelson were the other three. While it was not in Einstein's nature to harbor a grudge, he had for the most part avoided direct confrontations with his critics. This attitude registered with Michelson as a kind of professional snub, although it is possible that he imagined it. Michelson was aware, toward the end of his life, that the new trends in mathematics were over his head, which made him humble but at the same time rather sensitive. When Lorentz invited him to the April 1921 Solvay Congress, he had accepted with reluctance: "It was not my intention to attend the Brussels Meeting and indeed I feel that the modern developments to be discussed are quite beyond my limited range of ideas."[11] In connection with the relation of relativity to his own experiment, Michelson told a French friend, Émile Picard, with a touch of humor, *"Je n'ai pas voulu cela* [That was not what I had in mind.]"[12]

By 1930 physics had become so complex that no two men in slightly different fields could fully follow each other's thinking. But as relativity gained in popularity, Einstein became the center of attraction and Michelson withdrew from the controversy. He was sorry that he had been in any way responsible for this "monster." Einstein understood how he felt: "He told me more than once that he did not like the theories that had followed from his work."[13] But even at this time, when the law of probability became popular, Einstein himself felt the discomfort of new concepts.

"Even the great initial success of the quantum theory does not make me believe in the fundamental dice game, although I am well aware that our younger colleagues interpret this as a consequence of senility.[14]

It was in April 1931 that this extraordinary man entered Michelson's home with both hands outstretched in friendship. Michelson attempted to rise from his chair to welcome his guest, but weakness prevented him. It was an emotional meeting for both. Einstein drew a chair up close to Michelson's and they talked to each other, exchanging the compliments that only physicists know how to pay to other men in their field. Einstein had recently acknowledged Michelson's contribution at a dinner given by the California Institute of Technology:

... You, my honored Dr. Michelson, began with this work when I was only a little youngster, hardly three feet high. It was you who led the physicists into new paths, and through your marvelous experimental work paved the way for the development of the theory of relativity. You uncovered an insidious defect in the ether theory of light, as it then existed, and stimulated the ideas of H. A. Lorentz and FitzGerald, out of which the special theory of relativity developed. These in turn pointed the way to the general theory of relativity, and to the theory of gravitation.[15]

Although Einstein's manner to the older man was one of great deference and respect, their conversation all through the luncheon with the Michelsons had wit and humor. Michelson was twenty-seven years older than Einstein. They had a few laughs at Millikan's expense. Outside his office, an enormous sign posted by one of the religious sects read JESUS SAVES. Beneath this message some students had added:
BUT MILLIKAN GETS THE CREDIT!
At luncheon, as the wine was poured, the subject of prohibition came up, with speculation as to whether repeal would pass the next session of Congress. Einstein thought that the saloons should be re-established, because he equated them with the German *biergarten* where intellectuals had their tables reserved at the popular hour for erudite argument. Edna corrected this impression. The American saloon of pre-prohibition days was often the scene of much conviviality and a pleasant escape from the daily grind, but it was not famous as the background for philosophical exchanges.

Mrs. Einstein regaled the Michelsons with stories of the extraordinary gifts that had been showered upon them as a result of the blast of publicity accorded Einstein's arrival in the United States on December 12, 1930. One company had presented them with a freshly killed salmon flown in from Alaska. Armour and Co. had sent a prize ham, while a rival meatpacker, not to be outdone, had sent a Stradivarius violin, loaned for the duration of Dr. Einstein's stay in America.

They were living, Mrs. Einstein said, in "*so einem kleinen Bungaleuchen* [sort of a little bungalow]," in which there was not one inch of space to spare, and if more gifts arrived, they would both have to move out.

Dr. Einstein wore his hair in what was then a rather astonishing style. It rose from his forehead in a vigorous white mane and fell almost to his shoulders. In 1931 this was definitely conspicuous. While they were lunching Edna found herself describing a person she had recently encountered. "He had an incredibly bushy head of hair," she said, using both hands to show just how incredible it was. In the middle of her sentence her eyes rested on Dr. Einstein's equally incredible hairdo, and her voice trailed off in some embarrassment. Not knowing how to extricate herself, she hastily rang for the waitress to pass the vegetables. Dody could hardly keep from laughing.

When luncheon was over the Einsteins, fearing that Michelson had tired himself talking, took their leave. Einstein pressed Michelson's hand warmly at parting, with a gentle look of sympathy in his large, round, sorrowful eyes.

Toward the end of April, Michelson was confined to the house by his physician, Dr. Walter Parks Bliss, who hoped to build up his patient's slow circulation and weakened heart with rest and diet. Michelson stayed in his bedroom most of the day, reading over the reports of the Irvine ranch experiment and checking the figures and observations made by his assistants against the findings of earlier tests. As time went on Dr. Bliss came to the house more often. He suggested that a trained nurse be engaged and advised Edna never to leave her husband unattended. Another physician was called in consultation when Michelson was no longer able to move his arms and legs. Edna was told that her husband's condition was critical and was forced to accept the fact that he was dying. All visitors had long since been turned away and the house had grown ominously quiet. Dody walked on tiptoes past her father's room where nurses whispered quietly with Edna.

During the last weeks of Michelson's life, Pease and Pearson worked feverishly to bring in a definite series of figures so that the experiment might be concluded before he died. The Coast and Geodetic surveyors were still working on their preliminary measurements when Pease telegraphed to Garner on April 14: "Michelson is very low. We are hurrying. Send value of distance so that we can let him know."[16]

On the seventh of May, Pease came to Michelson with the latest figures for the new determination of the speed of light: 299,774 kilometers per second. Michelson's face lighted up with an almost childlike pleasure. Knowing that he did not have long to live, he told Pease to pull up a chair and open a notebook at once so that he might start dictation.

> ### Measurement of the Velocity of Light in a Partial Vacuum by A. A. Michelson, F. G. Pease, and F. Pearson
>
> The following is a report on the measurement of the velocity of light made at the Irvine Ranch, near Santa Ana, California during the period of September 1929 to . . .[17]

The effort exhausted him, and after dictating the first paragraph he fell into a peaceful sleep while Dr. Pease watched with mounting concern.

On the morning of May 9, 1931, Michelson died.

"The master is gone," said his friend Dr. Theodore G. Soares, pastor of the Pasadena Union Liberal Church, who conducted a simply ritual at the gathering of Michelson's family and those few friends who were asked to the house on the day of his funeral. A violinist played Michelson's favorite passage from Bach's works for unaccompanied violin, and two poems—Edwin Markham's "Revelation" and Wordsworth's "Lines composed a few miles above Tintern Abbey"—were read. When the ceremony was over, six men from Mount Wilson, who had worked with Michelson, came forward to pick up his closed coffin. Carefully they lifted it to their shoulders and carried it out of the house to be taken away for cremation as he had wished.

Postscript

MY father's medals were locked in the safe of Ryerson for many years after his death. Mother, who outlived him by only six months, offered them to the University of Chicago with the following letter to Henry Gale, who succeeded Michelson as head of the Physics Department.

Sept. 17, 1931

Dear Henry,

My husband's wish was to have Ryerson have his medals, should they be disposed to accept the gift. I had intended to talk it over with you but am submitting to a major operation tomorrow at the Emergency Hospital, Washington, D.C., so that I am trying to settle outstanding things up a little.

Will you wire me whether Ryerson (or the University) can accept such a gift? The medals are in the safe deposit box of the Continental Illinois Bank. If you get in touch with my lawyer . . . he can arrange turning them over to you. . . .[1]

My mother died a few days later. No effort was ever made to display the medals. In time, the Manhattan Project moved into Ryerson and all material not immediately pertinent to the creation of the atomic pile was thrown out. Ruling engine records, polarization of light records, butterfly and insect specimens, prisms, gratings, books, notebooks, and looseleaf records of his work were all stolen or lost.

Tom O'Donnell showed me the spot where the contents of Michelson's desk were dumped. Students rifling the letters had found a number of canceled checks bearing his signature, which were selling for a fair price even then. Tom swears that there were letters from Röntgen, Rayleigh, Kelvin, Larmor, Lodge, Gibbs, and many others, which were destroyed before the scavengers could lay hands on them. This is why in so many instances I have found Michelson letters in the files of these men, but have not found their answers, unless by good fortune they were methodical enough to make duplicates, a laborious process before the days of typewriters and copying machines.

Surreptitiously, Tom created his own little Michelson museum in the rear of the laboratory, with the instruments he had salvaged. He continued to demonstrate the velocity of light and ether-drift experiments to the students of nuclear physics, proudly showing them how the Boss had told him to drill through the roof of Ryerson to pass the light beam up onto a higher level, fearing the ether might be trapped in a basement room below ground.

Much of this historic material went to the junkyard. When, in 1948, the U. S. Navy dedicated Michelson Laboratory at the Naval Ordnance Test Station in China Lake, California, all the remaining instruments, documents, letters, and medals were sent there "on permanent loan" from the University of Chicago. D. T. McAllister, curator of the museum, has almost completed the task of cataloging all this material and has collected the only complete file of Michelson's published papers.

The lost documents never reappeared. But Michelson's memory continues to shine, even from the dark side of the moon.

"I was the one who suggested naming a crater for your father," Dr. Donald H. Menzel wrote me from the Harvard Observatory. "It is indeed a magnificent crater, 75 miles in diameter, with lots of smaller craters inside it. I wanted your father to have a good one. . . ."[2]

Concerning the influence of Michelson's work on the progress of science today, Charles H. Townes, inventor of the laser, has pointed out that with the purer light of this new technique, it is possible to obtain measurements of a precision of one part in a million millions but the method is still essentially the same as that invented by Michelson. His use of interference phenomena may be applied to the detection of motion of a satellite at interplanetary distances, to a precision of a fraction of an inch. Dr. Townes also mentions radar as having evolved from the precise knowledge of the speed of light. Michelson's stellar interferometer has been improved by the use of microwaves and the separation of the telescopes by a whole continent, but again the technique is the same.

Dr. Townes has repeated the Michelson-Morley experiment with laser light, producing the same negative result. But, undeterred, he states that he hopes with the newer refinements of laser technology to push the experiment to still further accuracy because ". . . there still may be, even if one believes completely in special relativity, some motional effects which can be detected if one measures precisely enough."[3]

Michelson would have rejoiced at these words and at the spirit of persistence, one after his own heart.

Reference Notes

Chronology

For Further Reading

Acknowledgments

Index

REFERENCE NOTES

In these notes, material at present in the author's own files is cited as A.F.; all such material will eventually be located at the American Institute of Physics in New York City. Copies of most of the papers referred to in these notes may be found in the Michelson Museum, China Lake, California, here cited as M. Mus.

Introduction: Quest for My Father

1. This subject is discussed in A. A. Michelson, *Studies in Optics* (Chicago: University of Chicago Press, 1927; paperback, Phoenix Science Series, no. 514, 1962), chapter XV, "Metallic Colors in Birds and Insects."
2. Harvey B. Lemon, "Albert Abraham Michelson: The Man and the Man of Science," *American Physics Teacher*, vol. IV, no. 1 (February 1936).
3. Quoted in R. S. Shankland, "Michelson-Morley Experiment," *American Journal of Physics*, vol. XXXII, no. 1 (January 1964), p. 35.
4. Elsa Michelson Meeres to the author, February 22, 1962 (A.F.).
5. "Michelson at 76 Outlines 3 New Tasks," *The New York Times*, January 18, 1929, p. 24.

1. Strzelno to the Golden West

1. *Torun Gazette*, July 11, 1963 (translated by Stanley Cuba, Polish Institute, New York, N.Y.).
2. Dates and other information about Michelson's family in Poland are from documents of the Circuit Court Archives of Inowroclaw and Strzelno (photocopies A.F.).
3. "Pioneer Letters" (The Historical Society of Southern California, March 1939).
4. Richard Coke Wood, *Murphys, Queen of the Sierra* (Angels Camp, Calif.: *Calaveras Californian*, 1948). See also G. F. Wesson, *A Memorial and Biographical History of the Counties of Merced, Stanislaus, Calaveras, Tuolumme and Mariposa, California* (Chicago: Lewis Publishing Co., 1892), and Kenneth M. Castro and Doris Castro, *Murphys, California, Short History and Guide* (Murphys, Calif.: privately printed, 1972).
5. Bret Harte, *The Luck of Roaring Camp* . . . (New York, Franklin Watts, 1968).
6. Miriam Michelson, *The Wonderlode of Silver and Gold* (Boston: Stratford Co., 1934), pp. 50, 108–109.
7. National Archives, Records of the Department of the Navy: Naval Academy Records, Register #1817, Commissions, vol. II.
8. Thomas Fitch, "Letter to the Editors," *Inland Empire* (Hamilton, Nev.), June

15, 1869; enclosed with his letter to the President; ref. 10, Records of the Department of the Navy . . ., *op. cit.*

9. *Annual Register of the United States Naval Academy at Annapolis, Md., for the Academic Year 1872–'73* (Washington: U. S. Government Printing Office), p. 48.

10. Thomas Fitch to the President of the United States, June 17, 1869, Records of the Department of the Navy . . ., *op. cit.*

11. Appointments were actually made by the Secretary of the Navy from nominations by Senators, Congressmen, or the President ("Regulations Governing the Admission of Candidates into the Naval Academy," *Annual Register . . . 1869–'70*, pp. 31–33.

12. Harold D. Carew, "Putting the Stars in Place," *Touring Topics*, vol. XXII, no. 9 (September 1930), p.26. There are many versions of this story; I have told my father's, which is very close to what he told Carew.

13. *Annual Register, . . . 1869–'70*, pp. 18–19.

2. Appointment to Annapolis

1. "Midshipman" was the designation for students from the founding of the Academy until July 1870, when it was changed to "cadet-midshipman." After graduation, May 31, 1873, he had the rank of Midshipman (Patrick F. Clausey, Head, Special Collections Library, U. S. Naval Academy, Annapolis, Md., to the author, May 9, 1972).

2. Park Benjamin, *The United States Naval Academy* (New York and London: G. P. Putnam's Sons, 1900), p. 267.

3. *Ibid.*, pp. 276–278.

4. *Ibid.*, pp. 280–281.

5. *Annual Register of the United States Naval Academy at Annapolis, Md., for the Academic Year 1869–'70* (Washington: U. S. Government Printing Office), pp. 36–37.

6. *Annual Register . . . 1870–'71*, p. 16.

7. National Archives, *Records of the Department of the Navy; Naval Academy Conduct Rolls re. Michelson, vol. 374*, p. 145.

8. A. A. Michelson, as told to the author.

9. *Ibid.*

10. Bradley A. Fiske, *From Midshipman to Rear-Admiral* (New York: Century Co., 1919), pp. 15–16.

11. *Annual Register . . . October 1, 1873*, p. 9.

12. A. A. Michelson, as told to the author; see also *The New York Times*, May 10, 1931, p. 1.

13. Miriam Michelson, *The Wonderlode of Silver and Gold* (Boston: Stratford Co., 1934), pp. 315–316.

14. John Tyndall, *On the Study of Physics, Fragments of Science, A Series of Detached Essays, Addresses and Reviews.* 2 vols. 6th ed. (New York: Appleton & Co., 1897), vol. I, p. 295.

15. Ludovico Geymonat, *Galileo Galilei, A Biography and Inquiry into His Philosophy of Science,* trans. Stillman Drake (New York: McGraw-Hill, 1965), pp. 119–120.

16. *Ibid.*

17. A. A. Michelson, as told to the author.

18. Robert A. Millikan, *Biographical Memoir of Albert Abraham Michelson, 1852–1931* (Washington, D.C.: National Academy of Sciences, Biographical Memoirs, vol. XIX, Fourth Memoir, 1938), pp. 130–131; also letter from Elsa Michelson Meeres to the author (A.F.).

19. Elsa Michelson Meeres to the author (A.F.).

3. The Speed of Light

1. AGySgt Mel Jones, "U. S. Frigate Constellation," *Leatherneck Magazine,* vol. XLIII, no. 6 (June 1960), pp. 34–37.

2. Bradley A. Fiske, *From Midshipman to Rear-Admiral* (New York: Century Co., 1919), p. 12.

3. *Annual Register of the United States Naval Academy at Annapolis, Md., October 1, 1873. First Class Examination Papers, "Light," May, 1873* (Washington: U.S. Government Printing Office), p. 79.

4. Galileo Galilei, *Dialogues Concerning Two Sciences* (1638), trans. Henry Crew and Alphonso de Salvio (New York: Macmillan, 1914; paperback ed., New York: Dover Publications, 1954), p. 44.

5. W. Doberck, "Ole Römer," *Nature,* vol. XVII (1877), p. 105.

6. W. H. McCrea, "James Bradley 1693–1762," *Quarterly Journal of the Royal Astronomical Society,* vol. IV (1963), p. 40. See also D. E. Blackwell, "Discovery of Stellar Aberration," *ibid.,* pp. 44–46; and Sir Richard Wooley, "James Bradley, Third Astronomer Royal," *ibid.,* pp. 47–52.

7. Armand Hippolyte Louis Fizeau, "Sur une expérience relative à la vitesse de propagation de la lumière," *Comptes Rendus de l'Académie des Sciences,* vol. XXIX (1849), pp. 90–92; Jean Bernard Léon Foucault, "Méthode générale pour mesurer la vitesse de la lumière dans l'air et les milieux transparents . . .," *ibid.,* vol. XXX (1850), pp. 551–560; Marie Alfred Cornu, "Détermination expérimental de la vitesse de la lumière entre l'observatoire et Montlhéry," *Annales de l'Observatoire de Paris, Mémoires,* vol. XIII, pp. A.1–A.315, plates 1–VII (Paris: Gauthier-Villars, 1876). See also *Encyclopaedia Britannica,* 11th ed., vol. XVI, pp. 623–624.

8. Jean Bernard Léon Foucault, "Détermination expérimental de la vitesse de

la lumière; parallaxe du soleil" and "Description des appareils," *Comptes Rendus*... , vol. LV (1862), pp. 501–503, 792–796.

9. A. A. Michelson, "Experimental Determination of the Velocity of Light made at the U. S. Naval Academy, Annapolis," U. S. Nautical Almanac Office *Astronomical Papers*... , vol. I, part III (Washington: Navy Department, 1882), pp. 115–118.

10. A. A. Michelson, "Experimental Determination of the Velocity of Light," *Proceedings of the American Association for the Advancement of Science*, vol. XXVIII (1879), p.124.

11. Albert A. Michelson, "Experimental Determination of the Velocity of Light," *Scientific Monthly*, vol. XXVII (1928), p. 563.

12. Michelson, "Experimental Determination ... made at the U. S. Naval Academy ...," *op. cit.*

13. Fragment of a letter, Simon Newcomb Papers, Library of Congress, Manuscript Division.

14. Simon Newcomb Papers.

15. Simon Newcomb to A. A. Michelson, April 30, 1878, Simon Newcomb Papers.

16. *Ibid.*

17. Simon Newcomb Papers.

18. Simon Newcomb, "On a Proposed Modification of Foucault's Method of Measuring the Velocity of Light," Appendix E, *Report of the National Academy of Sciences* (1878), p. 23.

19. *Ibid.*, p. 25.

20. A. A. Michelson, "On a Method of Measuring the Velocity of Light," *American Journal of Science and Arts*, third series, vol. XV, no. 89 (May 1878), pp. 394–395; see also A. A. Michelson, "Velocity of Light," *Nature*, vol. XVIII, June 20, 1878, p. 195.

21. Michelson, "Experimental Determination of the Velocity of Light," *Proceedings, A.A.A.S.*, vol. XXVII (1878), pp. 71–77.

22. Michelson, "Experimental Determination of the Velocity of Light," *Proceedings, A.A.A.S.*, vol. XXVIII (1879), p. 157.

23. A. A. Michelson, "Supplementary Measures of the Velocities of White and Colored Light in Air, Water, and Carbon Disulphide," U.S. Nautical Almanac Office *Astronomical Papers* . . ., vol. II, part IV (Washington: Navy Department, 1882), p. 244.

24. Michelson, "Experimental Determination ... made at the U. S. Naval Academy ..." *op. cit.*, p. 120.

25. Virginia City, Nev., [*Evening*] *Chronicle*, May 14, 1879 (photocopy M. Mus.).

26. Simon Newcomb, "Measures of the Velocity of Light made under Direction of the Secretary of the Navy during the years 1880–'82," U.S. Nautical Almanac Office, *Astronomical Papers* . . ., vol. II, part III, p. 120.

27. Nathan Reingold, ed., *Science in Nineteenth Century America* (New York: Hill and Wang, 1964), p. 276.

28. A. A. Michelson, "On the Modification Suffered by Light on Passing Through

REFERENCE NOTES

a Very Narrow Slit," *Annual Report of the National Academy of Sciences* (Washington: U.S. Government Printing Office, 1880), p. 15. See also unpublished notes in files of the National Academy of Sciences.

29. G. L. deHaas-Lorentz, ed., *H. A. Lorentz, Impressions of His Life and Work* (Amsterdam: North Holland Publishing Co., 1957), pp. 94–95.

30. A. A. Michelson to Simon Newcomb, February 12, 1880, National Archives, Records of the Department of the Navy, Records of the Naval Observatory (RQ 78), Velocity of Light, July 1874–1885.

31. Wolcott Gibbs to Julius Hilgard, July 19, 1880, M. Mus.

32. A. A. Michelson to Alfred H. Mayer, June 26, 1880 (copy M. Mus.).

4. The Luminiferous Aether

1. Adolphe Ganot, *Elementary Treatise on Physics, Experimental and Applied*, trans. and ed. E. Atkinson. 9th ed. (New York: Baillière Brothers, 1863), p. 3.

2. "Light," *Encyclopaedia Britannica*, 11th ed., vol. XVI, p. 612.

3. Quoted in A. E. Bell, *Christian Huyghens and the Development of Science in the Seventeenth Century* (London: Edward Arnold & Co., 1947), p. 111.

4. Christian Huyghens, "Traité de la lumière" (The Hague, 1690; reprint ed., Leipzig: Gressner and Schramm, n.d.), pp. 4–19.

5. Thomas Young, "Outlines of Experiments and Inquiries Respecting Sound and Light," *Philosophical Transactions*, vol. LC (1800), pp. 106–150; see especially pp. 125–130.

6. Augustin Jean Fresnel, "Lettre de M. Fresnel à M. Arago, sur l'influence du mouvement terrestre dans quelques phénomènes d'optique," *Annales de Chimie et de Physique*, vol. IX (1818), p. 57–66.

7. Dominique François Jean Arago, "A record of some spoken comments," *Comptes Rendus . . .*, Vol. VIII (1839), pp. 325–327; see also Edmund Whittaker, *A History of the Theories of Aether and Electricity*, rev. ed. (London: Thomas Nelson and Sons, 1951), vol. I, p. 109.

8. Armand Hippolyte Louis Fizeau, "Sur les hypothèses relatives à l'éther lumineux et sur une expérience qui paraît démontrer que le mouvement des corps change la vitesse avec laquelle la lumière se propage dans leur intérieur," *Annales de Chimie et de Physique*, vol. LVII (1859), pp. 385–404.

9. A. A. Michelson, *Light Waves and Their Uses* (Chicago: University of Chicago Press, 1903; paperback ed., Phoenix Science Series, No. 508, 1961), Lecture 8, p. 152.

10. George B. Airy, "On a Supposed Alteration in the Amount of Astronomical Aberration of Light Produced by the Passage of the Light through a Considerable Thickness of Refracting Medium," *Proceedings of the Royal Society*, vol. XX (November 23, 1871), pp. 35–39. See also "Additional Note," *ibid.*, vol. XXXI

(January 16, 1873), p. 121, cited in Loyd S. Swenson, Jr., *The Ethereal Aether* (Austin & London: University of Texas Press, 1972), p. 26.

11. James Clerk Maxwell, *A Treatise on Electricity and Magnetism*. 2 vols. (Oxford: Clarendon Press, 1873), vol. II, p. 437.

12. James Clerk Maxwell, "Aether," *Encyclopaedia Britannica*, 9th ed., vol. VIII, p. 769.

13. J. C. Maxwell to David Peck Todd, March 19, 1879, *Nature*, vol. XXI (1880), pp. 314–317.

14. H. A. Lorentz, "Conference on the Michelson-Morley Experiment," *Astrophysical Journal*, vol. LXVIII (December 1928), pp. 349–350; see also R. S. Shankland, "Michelson-Morley Experiment," *American Journal of Physics*, vol. XXXII, no. 1, 16–35 (January 1964), p. 26.

15. A. A. Michelson to Simon Newcomb, November 22, 1880, Simon Newcomb Papers, Library of Congress, Manuscript Division.

16. A. A. Michelson to C. A. Bell, December 22, 1880, Alexander Graham Bell Papers, National Geographic Society Archives, Washington.

17. A. A. Michelson, "The Relative Motion of the Earth and the Luminiferous Ether," *American Journal of Science*, vol. XXII, no. 128 (August 1881), p. 125–126.

18. *Ibid.*, p. 124.

19. Arthur Stanley Eddington, "Professor A. A. Michelson, For[eign]-Mem[ber] R[oyal] S[ociety]," *Nature*, vol. CXXVII, no. 3213 (May 30, 1931), p. 825.

20. Michelson, "Relative Motion . . . ," pp. 128–129.

21. *Ibid.*

22. A. A. Michelson to Alexander Graham Bell, April 17, 1881, Alexander Graham Bell Papers.

23. *The Sidereal Messenger of Galileo Galilei, and a Part of the Preface to Kepler's Dioptrics*, trans. Edward Stafford Carlos (London: Rivingtons, 1880), p. 86.

24. A. A. Michelson, unpublished transcript of the opening remarks of his lecture on "Application of Interference Methods to Astronomy" at the Carnegie Institution of Washington, April 25, 1923 (photocopy M. Mus.).

25. George F. Barker to John N. Stockwell, March 22, 1881, Case Western Reserve University Archives.

5. Foundations Tumble

1. Quoted in Herbert R. Young, Case archivist, "The Founding of Case Institute of Technology," Case Western Reserve University Archives.

2. A. A. Michelson to Simon Newcomb, June 15, 1882. National Archives: Records of the Department of the Navy, Records of the Naval Observatory (RG. 78) Velocity of Light Letters July 1874—Jan. 1885.

3. A. A. Michelson to Simon Newcomb, September 6, 1882, Records of the Naval Observatory, Velocity of Light Letters.

REFERENCE NOTES

4. *Ibid.*

5. A. A. Michelson to Simon Newcomb, September 12, 1882, Records of the Naval Observatory, Velocity of Light Letters.

6. A. G. Bell to his wife, July 25, 1883. Alexander Graham Bell Papers, National Geographic Society Archives, Washington.

7. Undated letter from George Barker to A. G. Bell, Alexander Graham Bell Papers.

8. "Michelson mixed tennis with physics at Case," *Cleveland Plain Dealer*, May 10, 1931.

9. R. S. Shankland, "The Michelson-Morley Experiment," unpublished paper (copy A. F.)

10. *Ibid.*

11. *Ibid.*

12. J[ames] Clerk Maxwell, *Matter and Motion*, ed. Sir Joseph Larmor (New York: Dover Publications, n.d.), p. 81; cited in Loyd S. Swenson, Jr., *The Ethereal Aether* (Austin & London: University of Texas Press, 1972), p. 30.

13. Lord Rayleigh, "President's Address," *Report of the Fifty-fourth Meeting of the British Association for the Advancement of Science* (London, 1885).

14. J. Young and G. Forbes, *Nature*, vol. XXIV (1881), p. 303.

15. A. A. Michelson, "Letter to the Editor," *Nature*, vol. XXIV (1881), pp. 460–461.

16. Montreal *Gazette*, August 28, 1884.

17. *Ibid.*, September 3, 1884.

18. Told to the author by Professor Richard Cox, Johns Hopkins University.

19. Letter from William H. Crew to the author, July 12, 1966, quoting Henry Crew's diary (A.F.).

20. Lord Kelvin, *The Baltimore Lectures* (London: C. J. Clay & Sons, 1904), p. vii.

21. Silvanus P. Thompson, *The Life of William Thomson, Baron Kelvin of Largs* (London: The Macmillan Company, 1910), vol. II, p. 879 and pp. 1021–1025.

22. H. A. Rowland, "Bericht betreffend Versuche über die elektromagnetische Wirkung elektrischer Convection," *Annalen der Physik*, vol. CLVIII (1876), p. 487; also *American Journal of Science*, vol. XV (1878), p. 30.

23. Henry Crew Diary, entries of October 14 and 17, 1884, Niels Bohr Library, American Institute of Physics, New York, N.Y.

24. R. S. Shankland, "Michelson-Morley Experiment," *American Journal of Physics*, vol. XXXII, no. 1 (January 1964), p. 25.

25. "Coefficients" letter to Lord Kelvin, June 15, 1896. T. C. Mendenhall Collection, Niels Bohr Library, American Institute of Physics, New York, N. Y.

26. A. A. Michelson to J. Willard Gibbs, December 15, 1884, Gibbs Collection, Yale University Library.

27. Armand Hippolyte Louis Fizeau, "Sur les hypothèses relatives à l'éther lumineux et sur une expérience qui paraît démontrer que le mouvement des corps change la vitesse avec laquelle la lumière se propage dans leur intérieur," *Annales de Chimie et de Physique*, vol. LVII (1859), pp. 385–404.

28. E. W. Morley to his father, September 17, 1885, Edward W. Morley Papers, Library of Congress, Manuscript Division.

29. E. W. Morley to his father, September 27, 1885, Edward W. Morley Papers.

30. A. A. Michelson to E. W. Morley, October 12, 1885, Edward W. Morley Papers.

31. Letter from Dr. Allan Hamilton to Edgar Stanton, December 8, 1891 (courtesy Francis Stanton, Chicago, Ill.).

32. A. A. Michelson to H. Rowland, November 6, 1885, Henry Augustus Rowland Papers, Eisenhower Library, Johns Hopkins University.

6. The Michelson-Morley Experiment

1. A. A. Michelson and E. W. Morley, "Influence of Motion of the Medium on the Velocity of Light," American Journal of Science, vol. XXXI (May 1886), pp. 377–386.

2. A. A. Michelson and E. W. Morley to Sir William Thomson, quoted in Silvanus P. Thompson, The Life of William Thomson, Baron Kelvin of Largs (London: Macmillan, 1910), vol. II, p. 857. See also R. S. Shankland, "Michelson-Morley Experiment," American Journal of Physics, vol. XXXII, no. 1 (January 1964), p. 28.

3. Sir William Thomson to A. A. Michelson and E. W. Morley, quoted in Silvanus P. Thompson, vol. II, p. 857.

4. Michelson and Morley, "Influence of Motion . . . ," p. 386.

5. Miriam Michelson, The Wonderlode of Silver and Gold (Boston: Stratford Co., 1934), p. 111.

6. Charles Michelson, The Ghost Talks (New York: G. P. Putnam's Sons, 1944), pp. 67–76.

7. Interview with Eckstein Case, Cleveland Plain Dealer, May 10, 1931.

8. The News and Herald (Cleveland), October 28, 1886, p. 8.

9. Letter from the Adelbert faculty to the Case faculty, signed by Edward Morley, Secretary, reproduced in ibid.

10. Rayleigh Archives, Airforce Cambridge Research Laboratory, Cambridge, Mass.

11. E. W. Morley to his father, April 17, 1887, Edward W. Morley Papers, Library of Congress, Manuscript Division.

12. A. A. Michelson and E. W. Morley, "On the Relative Motion of the Earth and the Luminiferous Ether," American Journal of Science, vol. XXXIV, no. 203 (1887), pp. 335–336; 338–339.

13. Edward W. Morley and Dayton C. Miller, "Report of an Experiment to Detect the FitzGerald-Lorentz Effect," Proceedings of the American Academy of Arts and Sciences, vol. XLI, no. 12 (August 1905), p. 323.

14. A. A. Michelson to Lord Rayleigh, August 17, 1887, Rayleigh Archives.

15. H. A. Lorentz, "L'influence du Mouvement de la Terre sur les Phénomènes Lumineuse," Archives Néerlandaises (Harlem, 1887), p. 21.

16. H. A. Lorentz to Lord Rayleigh, August 18, 1892, *Lorentz Microfilm* (Niels Bohr Library, American Institute of Physics, New York, N. Y.)

17. George F. FitzGerald, "Report of Activities of the Physical Society," *Nature*, vol. XLVI (1891), p. 165. See also Oliver J. Lodge, "Aberration Problems," *Royal Society of London, Philosophical Transactions*, vol. 184-A (1893), pp. 749–750.

18. H. A. Lorentz, *Versuch einer Theorie der electrischen und optischen Erscheinungen in betwegten Körpern* (Leiden: E. J. Brill, 1895), pp. 37, 125.

19. Leopold Infeld, *Albert Einstein*, (New York: Charles Scribner's Sons, 1950), pp. 20–21.

20. *The Cleveland Leader*, October 12–14, 1887.

21. A. A. Michelson, "A Condensed Autobiography," November 30, 1907 (part of his diary) (photocopy M. Mus.).

22. Victor F. Lenzen, "The Contributions of Charles S. Peirce to Meterology," *Proceedings of The American Philosophical Society*, vol. CIX, no. 1 (1965), p. 43.

23. A. A. Michelson and E. W. Morley, "On a Method of Making the Wave-length of Sodium Light the Actual and Practical Standard of Length," *American Journal of Science*, vol. XXXIV, no. 204 (December 1887), p. 429.

24. O. H. Tittmann, U.S. Coast Survey Office, Washington, D.C., to Dr. J. René Benoît, October 22, 1890, B.I.P.M. Archives (copy M. Mus.)

25. John A. Brashear to E. S. Holden, April 5, 1889, The Brashear Archives, The Brashear Association, Pittsburgh, Pa.

26. A. A. Michelson, "A Plea for Light Waves," *Proceedings of the American Association for the Advancement of Science*, vol. XXXVII (1889), pp. 1–14.

27. George E. Hale, "Some of Michelson's Researches," *Publications of the Astronomical Society of the Pacific*, vol. XLIII (1931), p. 176.

7. Clark versus Hall

1. G. Stanley Hall, *First Annual Report of the President to the Board of Trustees, October 4, 1890* (Worcester, Mass.: Published for the University, 1890), pp. 10, 11; also "Decennial Address," in *Clark University 1889–1899 Decennial Celebration* (Worcester, Mass: Printed for the University, 1899), pp. 48, 49; Clark University Archives.

2. A. A. Michelson to E. W. Morley, June 29, 1889, Edward W. Morley Papers, Library of Congress, Manuscript Division.

3. Michelson to Morley, December 3, 1889, Edward W. Morley Papers.

4. Michelson to Morley, March 6, 1890, Edward W. Morley Papers.

5. Michelson to Morley, May 12, 1891, Edward W. Morley Papers.

6. Elsa Michelson Meeres to the author, February 22, 1962 (A.F.).

7. A. A. Michelson, Descriptions of Lecture Courses given at Clark University in 1889–1892, Clark University Archives.

8. *Arthur Gordon Webster . . . In Memoriam* (Worcester, Mass.: Clark University Library, vol. VII, no. 4, March, 1924) pp. 17–18.
9. Letter from Dr. Robert G. Hall, son of G. Stanley Hall, to the author, June 8, 1966 (A.F.).

8. The Satellites of Jupiter

1. A. A. Michelson, "On the Application of Interference Methods to Astronomical Measures," *American Journal of Science*, vol. XXXIX (February, 1890), pp. 579–590.
2. George E. Hale, "Some of Michelson's Researches," *Publications of the Astronomical Society of the Pacific*, vol. XLIII (1931), pp. 175–85.
3. A. A. Michelson to E. C. Pickering, July 6, 1890, Letters from Eminent American Astronomers, Harvard University Archives.
4. Michelson to E. C. Pickering, July 14, 1890, *ibid.*
5. William L. Bryan, a student at Clark in 1891 and later president of Indiana University, quoted in George H. Blakeslee, "An Historical Sketch of Clark University," Clark University Library Publications, vol. 8, no. 9 (June 1937).
6. A. A. Michelson to E. S. Holden, April 11, 1890, Lick Observatory Archives.
7. Patent No. 452060, May 12, 1891, application filed November 7, 1890.
8. William M. Folger, Chief of the Bureau of Ordnance, Navy Department, to A. A. Michelson, June 25, June 30, July 14, 1891, National Archives, Washington, D.C.
9. The information and quotations on this dispute are taken from "Deposition of the Faculty," Clark University Archives.
10. G. Stanley Hall, *Life and Confessions of a Psychologist* (New York: D. Appleton and Company, 1923), p. 298.

9. Convocation in Chicago

1. B. A. Gould to G. Stanley Hall, January 17, 1892, Clark University Archives.
2. A. A. Michelson and G. Stanley Hall agreement, April 14, 1891, Clark University Archives.
3. Letter from A. G. Webster tó his wife, June 20, 1892 (copy A.F.)
4. A. A. Michelson to J. R. Benoît, April 25, 1892, International Bureau of Weights and Measures Archives, Paris.
5. Letter from Elsa Michelson Meeres to the author, June 26, 1962 (A.F.).
6. "Introduction Historique," *La Création du Bureau International des Poids et Mesures et son oeuvre* (Paris: Gauthier-Villars, 1927), pp. 1–31.

REFERENCE NOTES

7. A. A. Michelson, "Détermination Expérimental de la Valeur du Métre en Longueurs d'Ondes Lumineuses," *Travaux et Mémoires du Bureau International des Poids et Mesures*, vol. XI (Paris: Gauthier-Villars et Fils, 1894). See also Jean M. Bennett, D. Theodore McAllister, and Georgia M. Cabe, "Albert A. Michelson, Dean of American Optics: Life, Contributions to Science and Influence on Modern Day Physics," *Applied Optics*, vol. XII, no. 50 (October 1973).

8. Charles H. Townes, "Our Greatest Precision Tool," address at the Case Western Reserve University Albert A. Michelson/Edward W. Morley Award Dinner, October 15, 1970 (copy A.F.)

9. A. A. Michelson to W. M. Folger, October 16, 1892, National Archives, Washington, D.C.

10. Frederick T. Gates, "The Need of a Baptist University in Chicago, as Illustrated by a Study of Baptist Collegiate Education in the West," paper read before the Baptist Ministers' Conference, Chicago, October 15, 1888, Frederick T. Gates Correspondence, 1888–1906, Box 1, folder 2, University of Chicago Special Manuscript Collection.

11. Letter from Leonard B. Loeb, Emeritus Professor of Physics, University of California, to the author. Loeb was a student of Michelson's who also taught under him at Chicago, and his father, Jacques Loeb, had been an intimate friend of Michelson's during these years. This story, however, has been questioned.

12. A. A. Michelson to W. R. Harper, July 3, 1892, President's Papers, Regenstein Library Archives, University of Chicago.

13. A. A. Michelson to G. E. Hale, August 17, 1892, Hale Observatories Archives, Pasadena, Calif.

14. G. E. Hale to A. A. Michelson, September 2, 1892, *ibid.*

15. T. C. Mendenhall, draft manuscript, T. C. Mendenhall Collection, Niels Bohr Library, American Institute of Physics, New York, N.Y.

16. A. A. Michelson, notebook (1891–1895), Hale Observatories Archives.

17. Robert A. Millikan, *The Autobiography of Robert A. Millikan* (New York: Prentice-Hall, Inc., 1950), p. 24.

18. Robert A. Millikan, *Biographical Memoir of Albert Abraham Michelson, 1852–1931* (Washington, D.C.: National Academy of Sciences, Biographical Memoirs, vol. XIX, Fourth Memoir, 1938), pp. 124–125.

19. A. A. Michelson to Henry Rowland, September 5, 1889, Henry Augustus Rowland Papers, The Eisenhower Library, Johns Hopkins University.

20. Helen Wright, *Explorer of the Universe, A Biography of George Ellery Hale* (New York: E. P. Dutton, 1966), p. 116.

21. George Ellery Hale, Henry Gordon Gale, and Edwin Bryant Frost.

22. Ogden Rood to A. A. Michelson, October 16, 1894, M. Mus.

23. A. A. Michelson to W. R. Harper, May 16, 1895, President's Papers, Regenstein Library Archives, University of Chicago.

24. *Chicago Sunday Times Herald*, January 19, 1896.

25. A. A. Michelson, "Theory of X-Rays," *American Journal of Science*, vol. CLI, no. 4 (April 1896), pp. 312–314; and A. A. Michelson and S. W. Stratton, "Source of X-Rays," *Science*, vol. III, no. 71, pp. 694–696.

26. A. A. Michelson to W. R. Harper (undated) 1897, President's Papers, Regenstein Library Archives, University of Chicago.

27. A. A. Michelson, "Recent Progress in Spectroscopic Methods," *Science*, vol. XXXIV, no. 887 (December 29, 1911), pp. 893–902.

28. A. A. Michelson to R. S. Woodward, Chairman of the Advisory Committee on Physics, Carnegie Institution of Washington, Carnegie Institution Archives.

29. A. H. Compton in an interview with the author in 1960.

30. Michelson, "Recent Progress in Spectroscopic Methods," p. 901.

10. The Lowell Lectures

1. *Chicago Tribune*, October 21, 1897.

2. A. A. Michelson, *Light Waves and Their Uses* (Chicago: University of Chicago Press, 1903; paperback ed., Phoenix Science Series, no. 508, 1961), p. 72.

3. Oliver Lodge, *The Ether of Space* (New York: Harper & Bros., 1909), p. 70.

4. Oliver Lodge, *My Philosophy* (London: Ernest Benn, 1933), pp. 189, 192, 200, and 197.

5. Sir Edmund Whittaker, *A History of the Theories of Aether and Electricity, The Classical Theories* (London: T. Nelson and Sons, 1951), pp. 391–392.

6. Joseph Larmor, *Aether and Matter*. Adams Prize Essay (Cambridge: The University Press, 1900), p. 16.

7. A. A. Michelson, "The Relative Motion of the Earth and the Ether," *American Journal of Science*, vol. III (June 1897), p. 478.

8. H. A. Lorentz, *Versuch Einer Theorie der electrischen und optischen Erscheinungen in bewegten Korpern* (Leiden: E. J. Brill, 1895), p. 121.

9. R. S. Shankland, "Conversations with Albert Einstein," *American Journal of Physics*, vol. XXXI, no. 1 (January 1963), p. 55.

10. H. A. Lorentz, "Conference on the Michelson-Morley Experiment," *Astrophysical Journal*, vol. LXVIII (December 1928), pp. 349–350.

11. Lord Kelvin, "Nineteenth Century Cloud over the Dynamical Theory of Heat and Light," *American Journal of Science*, vol. 4, no. 12 (November 1910), pp. 391, 392.

12. Michelson, "Relative Motion of the Earth and the Ether," p. 478.

13. Michelson, *Light Waves and Their Uses*, pp. 162–163.

14. *Ibid.*, pp. 1–2.

15. A. A. Michelson to W. R. Harper, March 11, 1899, President's Papers, Regenstein Library Archives, University of Chicago.
16. Hugh F. Newall, "Albert Abraham Michelson 1852–1931," *Obituary Notices of Fellows of the Royal Society* (London), no. 1 (December 1932), pp. 18–25.
17. A. A. Michelson, "Radiations in a Magnetic Field," *Philosophical Magazine*, vol. XLIV (1897), pp. 109–115.
18. A. A. Michelson, "The Echelon Spectroscope," *Astrophysical Journal*, vol. 8 (1898), pp. 37–47.
19. Guest book register at Terling (letter from Lady Rayleigh to the author, October 3, 1971).
20. Rexmond D. Cochrane, *Measures for Progress, A History of the National Bureau of Standards* (Washington: National Bureau of Standards, U. S. Department of Commerce, 1966), p. 654, *n*. 3.
21. Henry A. Rowland, "The Highest Aim of the Physicist," *Bulletin of the American Physical Society*, vol. I, no. 1, 1900, pp. 4–5.
22. Told to the author by Earl W. Thomson, Senior Professor of Physics, Emeritus, U.S. Naval Academy, who attended the meeting.

11. Departure from Symmetry

1. Letter from Elsa Michelson Meeres to the author, June 26, 1962.
2. Edna Stanton Michelson was the source of most of the personal and family material in this chapter.
3. A. A. Michelson, "Form Analysis," *Proceedings of The American Philosophical Society*, vol. XLV (1906), p. 115.
4. A. A. Michelson to R. S. Woodward, April 24, 1902, Carnegie Institution of Washington Archives.
5. Michelson to Woodward, December 11, 1902, *ibid.*
6. Charles D. Walcott to A. A. Michelson, March 11, 1903, *ibid.*
7. E. W. Morley and Dayton C. Miller, "Report of the Experiment to Detect the FitzGerald-Lorentz Effect," *Proceedings of the American Academy of Arts and Sciences*, vol. XLI, no. 12 (August 1905), p. 321.
8. G. E. Hale to A. A. Michelson, July 8, 1904, Hale Observatories Archives, Pasadena, Calif.
9. Hale to Michelson, June 24, 1904, *ibid.*
10. Charles Scribner, Jr., "Henri Poincaré and the Principle of Relativity," *American Journal of Physics*, vol. XXXII, no. 9 (September 1964), p. 672.
11. Henri Poincaré, "The Principles of Mathematical Physics," *The Monist*, vol. XV, January 1905, pp. 6, 16, 20.
12. A. A. Michelson to G. E. Hale, December 28, 1904, Hale Observatories Archives.

12. The Nobel Prize

1. William Pickering to A. A. Michelson, November 12, 1903, Harvard University Archives.
2. Svenska Dagbladet, November 11, 1907.
3. Count Wachtmeister, at Nobel Prize Award Ceremony, Dagens Nyheter and Svenska Dagbladet (Stockholm), December 10–13, 1907.
4. Told to the author by A. A. Michelson.
5. A. A. Michelson, "Recent Advances in Spectroscopy" (Nobel Lecture), Les Prix Nobel en 1907 (Stockholm: P. S. Norstedt & Soner, 1909), p. 5. See also The Albert A. Michelson Nobel Prize and Lecture, Publications of the Michelson Museum, No. 2, U.S. Naval Ordnance Test Station, China Lake, Calif., March 1966, p. 11.
6. K. B. Hasselberg to G. E. Hale, December 29, 1907, Hale Observatories Archives, Pasadena, Calif.
7. A. A. Michelson to reporters, Dagens Nyheter (Stockholm), December 11, 1907.
8. Silvanus P. Thompson, The Life of William Thomson, Baron Kelvin of Largs. 2 vols. (London: Macmillan and Co., 1910), vol. I, p. 499, and vol. II, p. 907.
9. G. R. Harrison to the author, February 10, 1962. Margarite Crowe gave the fragment to Professor Harrison at the Massachusetts Institute of Technology, where he sometimes showed it to his students as a "relic of Michelson."
10. Matthew Josephson, Edison, A Biography (New York: McGraw-Hill, 1959), p. 283.
11. A. A. Michelson to T. C. Mendenhall, October 28, 1909, T. C. Mendenhall Collection, Niels Bohr Library, American Institute of Physics, New York City.
12. Charles Greeley Abbot, Adventures in the World of Science (Washington, D.C., Public Affairs Press, 1958), p. 77. See also letter from C. G. Abbot to Frederick Seitz, June 29, 1964, National Academy of Sciences Archives, Washington, D.C.
13. A. A. Michelson to T. C. Mendenhall, January 1, 1908, T. C. Mendenhall Collection, Niels Bohr Library.

13. The Relativists of Göttingen

1. A. H. Compton in interview with the author, 1960.
2. Harvey B. Lemon, "Albert Abraham Michelson: The Man and the Man of Science," American Physics Teacher, vol. IV, no. 1 (February 1936), p. 7.
3. A. A. Michelson, "Preliminary Results of Measurements of the Rigidity of the Earth," Astrophysical Journal, vol. XXXIX, no. 2 (March 1914), pp. 105–138.
4. Harvey B. Lemon, Michelson Anecdotes (unpublished; A.F.)
5. William F. Magie, "The Primary Concepts of Physics," Science, vol. XXXV

(February 23, 1912), p. 290; cited in Loyd S. Swenson, Jr., *The Ethereal Aether* (Austin & London: University of Texas, 1972), p. 177.

6. *Sir Isaac Newton's Mathematical Principles of Natural Philosophy and His System of the World*, trans. Andrew Motte, revised with commentary by Florian Cajori, vol. I, p. 8 (paperback, Berkeley, Calif.: University of California Press, 1966).

7. Herman Minkowski, "Raum und Zeit," address given September 21, 1908, *Physikalische Zeitschrift*, 10 (1909), p. 104; included in *Gesammelte Abhandlungen von Herman Minkowski* (Leipzig, 1911), which was reprinted as *Gesammelte Abhandlungen* (New York: Chelsea Publishing Co., 1967), p. 431.

8. Max Planck, *The Universe in the Light of Modern Physics* (New York: W. W. Norton, 1931), p. 60.

9. Max Planck, *Scientific Autobiography and Other Papers* (New York: Philosophical Library, 1949), p. 139.

10. Letter from Stanley Goldberg, a student of Gerald Holton, to the author, April 13, 1965. The story was originally told to Holton by Professor Philipp Frank.

11. A. A. Michelson, "Recent Progress in Spectroscopic Methods," *Science*, vol. XXXIV, no. 887 (December 29, 1911), pp. 901–902.

12. Quoted in a letter from Max Born to the author, March 28, 1961 (A.F.)

13. Letter from Kristoffer Glimmes (a student in physics at Göttingen in 1911) to Olav Overagaard, December 2, 1965 (copy A.F.)

14. Quoted in Max Born's letter of March 28, 1961.

15. *Ibid.*

16. Letter from Max Born to the author, December 7, 1962 (A.F.).

17. Constance Reid, *Hilbert* (New York and Berlin: Springer-Verlag, 1970), p. 127.

18. Told to the author by Thomas O'Donnell, who was present.

19. Stanley Goldberg, "In Defense of Ether: The British Response to Einstein's Special Theory of Relativity, 1905–1911," in Russell McCormmach, ed., *Historical Studies in the Physical Sciences*, vol. II (Philadelphia: University of Pennsylvania, 1907), pp. 96–100.

20. Martin J. Klein, *Paul Ehrenfest* (Amsterdam, London: North Holland Publishing Company, distributed by American Elsevier, New York, 1970), vol. I, p. 2.

21. A. A. Michelson to President R. S. Woodward, Carnegie Institution, Washington, D.C., March 12, 1915, Carnegie Institution Archives, Washington, D.C.

22. A. A. Michelson to Sir Joseph Larmor, March 1, 1916, Royal Society Archives, London (copy, A.F.).

14. Red Star in the Giant's Shoulder

1. Albert B. Christman, *Sailors, Scientists and Rockets*, (Washington, D.C.: U. S. Government Printing Office, 1971), p. 14.

2. A. A. Michelson, "Optical Conditions Accompanying the Striae Which Appear

as Imperfections in Optical Glass," *Scientific Papers of the Bureau of Standards,* vol. XV, no. 333 (Washington, D.C.: Department of Commerce, 1920), pp. 41–45.

3. Letter from Alva Bennett, an assistant to Michelson, to the author, February 25, 1962 (A.F.).

4. A. A. Michelson to G. E. Hale, October 6, 1919, Hale Observatories Archives, Pasadena, Calif.

5. Rear Admiral Ralph Earle to A. A. Michelson, n.d. (photocopy M. Mus.).

6. A. A. Michelson and Henry Gale, "The Rigidity of the Earth," *Astrophysical Journal,* vol. I, no. 5 (December 1919), p. 336.

7. Joseph Purdy, tape recording (A.F.)

8. Letter from Helen Crawford to the author, November 6, 1971 (A.F.); also a personal interview.

9. Letter from A. A. Michelson to R. S. Woodward, May 8, 1919, Carnegie Institution Archives, Washington, D.C.

10. Michelson to Hale, December 20, 1916, Hale Observatories Archives.

11. Letter from Alfred H. Joy to the author, October 9, 1961 (A.F.).

12. Jo Hickox, technician at Mount Wilson, in a conversation with the author.

13. Letters to the author from Harold D. Babcock (November 25, 1962) and Frederick Seares (undated) (A.F.). Both were astronomers on the Mount Wilson staff at the time of the Betelgeuse measurement.

14. A. S. Eddington, "Presidential Address to Section A of the British Association at Cardiff, August 24, 1920," *Observatory,* vol. XLIII (1920), p. 349.

15. A. A. Michelson, *Light Waves and Their Uses* (Chicago: University of Chicago Press, 1903), p. 137; paperback ed. (Phoenix Science Series, no. 509, 1961), p. 136.

16. W. Ewart Williams, *Applications of Interferometry* (4th ed. New York, John Wiley & Sons), p. 21.

17. Eddington, "Presidential Address . . . ," p. 349.

18. A. A. Michelson to R. S. Woodward, December 24, 1920, Carnegie Institution of Washington Archives.

19. R. S. Woodward to A. A. Michelson, December 27, 1920, *ibid.*

20. Thomas J. O'Donnell, in a conversation with the author (tape recording A.F.).

21. O'Donnell, unpublished manuscript (A.F.)

22. Joseph H. Purdy in a conversation with the author (tape recording A.F.).

23. O'Donnell, in an interview with the author.

24. Michelson gave this explanation to Norman Hilberry, director of the Argonne National Laboratory in Chicago, who reported it to the author (tape recording A.F.).

25. Neil M. Clark, "Michelson Holds the Stopwatch on a Ray of Light," *American Magazine,* January 1926, p. 24.

26. Information and quotations relating to this period of Michelson's teaching are taken from letters to the author from some of Michelson's former students, Stanislas Chylinski, R. L. Doan, Newell S. Gingrich, W. V. Houston, Harvey Lemon, Arnold Lieberman, John S. Millis, G. D. Shallenberger, Alfred Simon, W. R. Smythe (A.F.).

27. Robert A. Millikan, *Biographical Memoir of Albert Abraham Michelson*, 1852–1931 (Washington, D. C.: National Academy of Sciences, Biographical Memoirs, vol. XIX, Fourth Memoir, 1938), p. 126.
28. Michelson to Hale, June 7, 1921, Hale Observatories Archives.

15. The Spinning Prism

1. Arthur Stanley Eddington, *Space, Time and Gravitation* (Cambridge: The University Press, 1920), p. 116.
2. Oliver Lodge, "Popular Relativity and the Velocity of Light," *Nature*, vol. CVI (November 4, 1920), p. 326.
3. Letter from Richard Cox, author of *Time, Space and Atoms*, to the author, November 14, 1969 (A.F.); see also Oliver Lodge, *My Philosophy* . . . (London: Benn, 1933), chapter vi, especially pp. 49–50.
4. H. G. Gale to Vice President James A. Tufts, February 13, 1924, Michelson Correspondence, University of Chicago Archives.
5. A. A. Michelson to L. Silberstein, September 19, 1921 (photocopy M. Mus.).
6. The author was present at this luncheon.
7. A. A. Michelson to G. E. Hale, March 18, 1922, Hale Observatories Archives, Pasadena, Calif.
8. Earl W. Thomson, Senior Professor of Physics, Emeritus, Naval Academy, in conversation with the author, March 23, 1961.
9. Letter from A. A. Michelson to T. C. Mendenhall, October 28, 1909, T. C. Mendenhall Collection, Niels Bohr Library, American Institute of Physics, New York City.
10. E. L. Nichols, *Biographical Memoir of Ernest Fox Nichols* (Washington, D.C.: National Academy of Sciences, Biographical Memoirs, vol. XII, 1929), pp. 99–131; see especially p. 122.
11. A. A. Michelson to Herbert Hoover, November 28, 1925, National Research Endowment Archives, Washington, D.C.
12. Niels Bohr to A. A. Michelson, February 7, 1924, Nils Bohr Institute of Theoretical Physics, Copenhagen (copy American Philosophical Society, Philadelphia, Pa.).
13. A. A. Michelson to Colonel E. L. Jones, May 1, 1920 (photocopy M. Mus.).
14. William Bowie, "Measurement of Length of Line used in Determination of Velocity of Light," *Astrophysical Journal*, vol. LXV, no. 329 (1927), pp. 14–22.
15. A. A. Michelson to Walter S. Adams, May 8, 1924, Hale Observatories Archives.
16. Letter from William R. Smythe, professor of physics, California Institute of Technology, to the author, November 21, 1961 (A.F.).
17. A. A. Michelson, "Preliminary Experiments on the Velocity of Light," *Astrophysical Journal*, vol. LX, no. 4 (November 1924), p. 261.

16. Absolute Motion?

1. A. A. Michelson, "Light Waves as Measuring Rods for Sounding the Infinite and the Infinitesimal," *University Record* (Chicago), vol. XI, no. 2 (April 1925), pp. 150–153.

2. Tom O'Donnell, in an interview with the author.

3. Harvey Lemon, in an interview with the author.

4. Quoted by A. H. Compton in interview with the author.

5. Michelson, "Light Waves as Measuring Rods . . ."

6. Edna Stanton Michelson to the author, January 9, 1925 (A.F.).

7. A. A. Michelson and H. G. Gale, "The Effect of the Earth's Rotation on the Velocity of Light," part II, *Astrophysical Journal*, vol. LXI (1925), pp. 139–145.

8. Arthur H. P. Buller, *Punch*, December 19, 1923.

9. Letter from Max Born to Albert Einstein, August 6, 1922, and related commentary, in Max Born, ed., *The Born-Einstein Letters*, trans. Irene Born (New York: Walker, 1971), pp. 73–74.

10. D. C. Miller, "Significance of the Ether-Drift Experiments of 1925 at Mount Wilson," *Science*, vol. LXIII, April 30, 1926, pp. 433–443.

11. Letter from Hedwig Born to Albert Einstein, April 11, 1926, *Born-Einstein Letters*, pp. 89–90.

12. A. A. Michelson to Walter S. Adams, March 18, 1927, Hale Observatories Archives, Pasadena, Calif.

13. Walter S. Adams to A. A. Michelson, January 27, 1930, Hale Observatories Archives.

14. The author remembers Michelson expressing these views.

15. George Ellery Hale, "Some of Michelson's Researches," *Publications of the Astronomical Society of the Pacific*, vol. XL (1931), p. 184.

16. A. A. Michelson, *Studies in Optics* (Chicago: University of Chicago Press, 1927; paperback, Phoenix Science Series, no. 514, 1962), p. 4.

17. Harold D. Babcock in an interview with the author.

18. A. A. Michelson to Major William Bowie, August 29, 1926, Hale Observatories Archives.

19. A. A. Michelson, "Measurements of the Velocity of Light Between Mount Wilson and Mount San Antonio," *Astrophysical Journal*, vol. LXV, no. 1 (January 1927), p. 12.

20. Charles H. Townes, "Our Greatest Precision Tool," address at the Case Western Reserve University Albert A. Michelson/Edward W. Morley Award Dinner, October 15, 1970.

21. Letter from Walter S. Adams to A. A. Michelson, April 2, 1927, Hale Observatories Archives.

22. A. A. Michelson to Major William Bowie, March 15, 1927, Hale Observatories Archives.

23. Michelson to Bowie, September 20, 1928, Hale Observatories Archives.

24. *Supplement to the Journal of the Optical Society of America and Review of Scientific Instruments*, vol. XVII, no. 4, part 2 (October 1928).

25. *The New York Times*, November 3, 1928, p. 21.

26. *Ibid.*

27. Paul R. Heyl, "The History and Present Status of the Physicist's Concept of Light," in "Proceedings of the Michelson Meeting of the Optical Society of America," *Journal of the Optical Society of America*, vol. XVIII, nos. 1–6 (March 1929), pp. 183–192.

28. Quoted by Ernest Cuneo, lawyer for the Democratic National Committee, in an interview with the author.

29. A. H. Compton, in an interview with the author.

17. The Work Is Done

1. A. A. Michelson to Walter S. Adams, October 31, 1929, Hale Observatories Archives, Pasadena, Calif.

2. Michelson to Adams, November 22, 1929, Hale Observatories Archives.

3. A. H. Compton in an interview with the author.

4. Forest R. Moulton, "Albert Abraham Michelson," *Popular Astronomy*, vol. XXXIX, no. 6 (June-July 1931), pp. 308–310.

5. A. A. Michelson to F. G. Pease, April 27, 1929 (A.F.).

6. Letter from Thomas O'Donnell to the author, December 6, 1969, and taped interview with the author (A.F.).

7. Letter from Clement L. Garner to the author, January 30, 1962 (A.F.).

8. Letter from William R. Smythe to the author, November 21, 1961 (A.F.).

9. R. S. Shankland, "Final Velocity-of-Light Measurements of Michelson," in "Letters to the Editor," *American Journal of Physics*, vol. XXXV, no. 11 (November 1967), pp. 1095–1096.

10. Gerald Holton, "Einstein, Michelson and the 'Crucial' Experiment," *Isis*, vol. LX, pt. 2, no. 202 (Summer 1969), pp. 133–197.

11. A. A. Michelson to H. A. Lorentz, March 22, 1921 (copy, A.F.).

12. Émile Picard, *L'Évolution des idées sur la lumière et l'oeuvre d'Albert Michelson* . . . (Paris: Gauthier-Villars, 1935), p. 26.

13. R. S. Shankland, "Conversations with Albert Einstein," *American Journal of Physics*, vol. XXXI, no. 1 (January 1963), p. 57; and "Conversations with Albert Einstein II, *ibid.*, vol. XLI, no. 7 (July 1973), pp. 895–901.

14. Letter from Albert Einstein to Max Born, September 7, 1944, *The Born-Ein-*

stein Letters, trans. Irene Born (New York: Walker and Company, 1971), pp. 148–149.

15. Albert Einstein, speech at The Athenaeum Dinner given in his honor on January 15, 1931; translation published in *Science,* vol. LXXIII, no. 1893 (April 10, 1931), p. 379.

16. F. G. Pease to Clement Garner, April 14, 1931, Hale Observatories Archives.

17. A. A. Michelson, F. G. Pease, and F. Pearson, "Measurement of the Velocity of Light in a Partial Vacuum," *Astrophysical Journal,* vol. 82 (1935), p. 26.

Postscript

1. Edna Stanton Michelson to Henry Gordon Gale, September 17, 1931 (A.F.).

2. Donald H. Menzel to the author, January 11, 1971 (A.F.).

3. Charles H. Townes, "Our Greatest Precision Tool," address at the Case Western Reserve University Albert A. Michelson/Edward W. Morley Award Dinner, October 15, 1970.

CHRONOLOGY

1852   Albert Michelson born in Strzelno, German-occupied Poland, December 19.

1856   Michelson family crosses the Atlantic and the Isthmus of Panama; arrives at Murphys Camp, California.

1864–1869   Albert attends school in San Francisco.

1869–1873   Attends U.S. Naval Academy.

1873–1875   Two years at sea.

1875   Becomes instructor in physics at Naval Academy.

1877   Marries Margaret Heminway.

1878   First measures velocity of light.

1879   Transferred to Nautical Almanac Office.

1880–1882   Studies in Berlin and Paris; performs first ether-drift experiment; for which he invents interferometer.

1882   Resigns from Navy; appointed first professor of physics at Case School of Applied Science, Cleveland, Ohio.

1885   With Edward Morley repeats Fizeau experiment on light in moving water; made a Fellow of the American Academy of Arts and Sciences.

1887   Repeats ether-drift experiment with Morley (the Michelson-Morley experiment).

1888   Receives gold and silver Rumford medals.

1889   Leaves Case; appointed to first chair of physics at Clark University, Worcester, Massachusetts.

1890   Measures diameter of a satellite of Jupiter at Harvard and Lick observatories.

1892   Measures the meter in terms of a light wave for the International Bureau of Weights and Measures at Paris.

1894   Appointed to first chair of physics at the University of Chicago.

1895   Begins building an engine to rule diffraction gratings.

1898   Divorced from Margaret; invents echelon spectroscope and, with S.W. Stratton, harmonic analyzer.

1899   Delivers the Lowell Lectures; elected president of American Physical Society; marries Edna Stanton.

1903   *Light Waves and Their Uses* published.

1907   Receives Copley Medal of Royal Society and Nobel Prize in Physics.

1911   Exchange professorship at the University of Göttingen.

1914   Measures the rigidity of the earth.

1915   Rules 10-inch high-resolution grating.

1918–1919   Lieutenant Commander in the Naval Reserve in Washington.

1919   Returns to University of Chicago.

THE MASTER OF LIGHT

1922   Measures the diameter of Betelgeuse with stellar interferometer at Mount Wilson.

1923   President of the National Academy of Sciences.

1925   Attempts to measure the effect of the earth's rotation on the velocity light at Clearing, Illinois.

1925-1927   Makes velocity of light experiments at Mount Wilson.

1927   *Studies in Optics* published.

1929   Retires from University of Chicago; moves to Pasadena, California; repeats Michelson-Morley experiment at Mount Wilson.

1930   Undertakes measurement of velocity of light in a vacuum tube.

1931   Dies in Pasadena, May 9.

FOR FURTHER READING

Born, Max, ed. *The Born-Einstein Letters.* Translated by Irene Born. New York: Walker, 1971.

Cohen, I. Bernard. *Roemer and the First Determination of the Velocity of Light.* New York: Burndy Library, 1944.

Jaffe, Bernard. *Michelson and the Speed of Light.* Garden City, N.Y.: Doubleday, Anchor Books, 1960.

Michelson, Albert A. *Light Waves and Their Uses.* Chicago: University of Chicago Press, 1903; paperback ed., Phoenix Science Series, no. 509, 1961.

_____. *Studies in Optics.* Chicago: University of Chicago Press, 1927; paperback ed., Phoenix Books, 1962.

Millikan, Robert A. *The Autobiography of Robert A. Millikan.* Englewood Cliffs N.J.: Prentice-Hall, 1950.

Newcomb, Simon. *The Reminiscences of an Astronomer.* Boston: Houghton Mifflin, 1903.

Reingold, Nathan, ed. *Science in Nineteenth Century America: A Documentary History.* New York: Hill & Wang, 1966.

Strutt, Robert John. *John William Strutt, Third Baron Rayleigh.* London: Arnold, 1924.

Swenson, Loyd S., Jr. *The Ethereal Aether: A History of the Michelson-Morley-Miller Aether-Drift Experiments, 1880–1930.* Austin and London: University of Texas Press, 1972.

Thompson, Silvanus P. *The Life of William Thomson, Baron Kelvin of Largs.* 2 vols. London: Macmillan, 1910.

Williams, Howard R. *Edward Williams Morley: His Influence on Science in America.* Easton, Pa.: Chemical Education Publishing Co., 1957.

Wright, Helen. *Explorer of the Universe: A Biography of George Ellery Hale.* New York: Dutton, 1966.

ACKNOWLEDGMENTS

For help in the preparation of this book, I am particularly indebted to Robert S. Shankland, Ambrose Swasey Professor of Physics at Case Western Reserve University and author of several distinguished papers on Michelson's work, who kindly edited my account of the experiments; and to Professor Loyd S. Swenson, Jr., Historian of Science at Houston University and author of *The Ethereal Aether: A History of the Michelson-Morley-Miller Aether-Drift Experiments, 1880–1930*, who helped me to reconstruct the historical background and edited an early draft of the book. My thanks go also to Dr. Gerald Holton, professor of physics at Harvard University, with whom I have had the temerity to differ on certain views, for his wisdom and advice in the face of my stubborn filial bias; to Thomas J. O'Donnell, faithful assistant for the last twelve years of my father's life; to Professor William Crew, for contributing passages from the diary of his father, Henry Crew; to Professor Charles H. Townes for permission to quote his views on Michelson's contribution to modern physical trends; to Joan Warnow and the staff of the Niels Bohr Library, at the American Institute of Physics, where I have spent so many pleasant hours; to Admiral Ernest Eller, former Director of Naval History, Earl W. Thomson, Senior Professor Emeritus, and E. J. Cook, Senior Professor of the Science Department, United States Naval Academy; and to Christa Kirsten, Director of Archives, National Academy of Science, East Berlin.

D. T. McAllister, curator of the Michelson Museum, Naval Weapons Center, China Lake, California, and members of his staff, including Mrs. Georgia Cabe, collected the documents without which the book would have no historical accuracy and checked to see that they are correctly quoted here. For this enormous task all words of gratitude are totally inadequate. The responsibility for any remaining errors is mine alone.

I am also indebted to Winifred McCulloch, Joan Pittman, Marcia Kelly, and Ann Higgins for invaluable assistance; to my cousins Henry Meyer and Arthur McEwen Smith for information; and to Michelson's granddaughters by his first marriage, Paula and Rosamund Meeres, for letters dictated by their mother Elsa Michelson Meeres, which gave me insights into aspects of my father's life I could not have known about otherwise. Finally, I am grateful to my sisters, Madeleine Mueller and Beatrice Foster, for sharing their memories of our childhood.

Grateful acknowledgment is also made to the following publishers, institutions, and individuals for permission to use or quote specified material:

The McGraw-Hill Book Company, New York, N.Y.: diagram on page 71, adapted from F. A. Jenkins and H. E. White, *Fundamentals of Optics*, copyright 1957 by the McGraw-Hill Book Company

Prentice-Hall, Inc., Englewood Cliffs, N.J.: quotation on page 184 from Robert A. Millikan, *The Autobiography of Robert A. Millikan*, copyright © 1950 by Prentice-Hall, Inc.

ACKNOWLEDGMENTS

Algemeen Rijksarcheef (E. van Laar): letter from H.A. Lorentz to Lord Rayleigh, page 131

Estate of Albert Einstein: Einstein speech, pages 335–36

U. S. Naval Academy Museum: Einstein letter, page 6

Aage Bohr: letter from Niels Bohr, pages 301–302

G. V. R. Born: letter from Max Born, pages 256, 258–59

Melville Bell Grosvenor: Letter from A. G. Bell, page 96–97

Lily Hasselberg: letter from K. B. Hasselberg, pages 238–39

Thomas C. Mendenhall: letters from AAM to T.C. Mendenhall, pages 244, 246–47; Mendenhall speech, page 183

Margaret Hale Scherer: letters from G. E. Hale, pages 181–82, 228–29

Beatrice Gale Valentine: Letter from Henry Gale, page 290

INDEX

INDEX

INDEX

Mall, F. P. 144, 163–67
Mascart, Éleuthère Élie Nicolas, 86–87
mathematics, AAM's use of, 132, 159, 184, 251–52, 259–60, 284
Maxwell, James Clerk, 73–74, 82, 100, 106, 136
Mayer, Alfred Marshall, 64, 66
measurement, astronomical, 146, 154–157, 161, 271, 274–77
measurement, standards of, 6, 136–41, 171–72, 174–77, 187
"Measurement of the Velocity of Light in a Partial Vacuum," 338
Mendenhall, Thomas Corwin, 104, 108, 161, 182, 183, 209, 244–47, 298–99
Menzel, Donald H., 341
metals, elastical behavior of, 282
Meyer family, 13, 15, 19
Michael, Arthur, 144, 158
Michelson, Albert Abraham
  "the artist in science," 6, 98, 185, 205, 206, 221, 321–22
  birth, 12
  blackmail threat, 135–36, 147
  childhood and youth, 15–22
  conservatism, 182, 315–16
  death, 337–38
  diffidence, 5, 7, 98, 214, 277
  experiments. See Betelgeuse, diameter of; ether-drift experiments; Jupiter, satellites of; measurement, standards of; metals, elastical behavior of; Michelson-Morley experiment; optical glass experiments; rigidity of the earth; velocity of light
  finances, 76, 95, 112, 121, 227, 271, 328, 330
  independence of thought, 9, 31–33, 282
  intuition, 31–33, 252, 260, 333
  inventions. See binoculars, naval; comparer; echelon spectroscope; harmonic analyzer; interferometer; ruling engine; telemeter
  migration to U.S., 13–14
  nervous breakdown, 111–15; 147
  nightmares, 225
  patriotism, 203, 235, 261–62
  personal appearance, 3–4, 98, 184, 204, 226
  personal interests: billiards, 226, 248, 274; boxing, 19, 30, 33–34, 174; chess, 249; music, 19, 33–34, 59, 224, 270; painting and drawing, 30, 249, 250; sailing, 30, 38, 219–20, 268; tennis, 97–98, 226, 256
  personal relationships: with colleagues, 112, 145, 147, 173, 189, 210, 249–50, 264; with family, 3–4, 8–9, 114, 148–49, 214, 219, 268, 315–16; with students, 40–41, 98–99, 150, 185, 283–86
  significance of his work for modern science, 6, 155, 237, 253–54, 256, 275–76, 341
  temperament, 9, 114, 115, 121, 147–48, 160, 214, 293
  religious views, 106–7, 180, 294
  work habits, 112, 148, 150, 156, 158, 223, 282
Michelson, Albert Heminway (son), 57–58, 149, 174, 239–40, 242, 247, 258
Michelson, Beatrice (daughter), 3–4, 221–22, 254–55, 256, 265, 273
Michelson, Benjamin (brother), 19, 119, 162, 223
Michelson, Bessie (Mrs. Arthur McEwen; sister), 19, 119, 162
Michelson, Charles (brother), 22, 36, 119–20, 162, 323–24
Michelson, Dorothy ("Dody"; Dorothy Michelson Livingston; daughter), 3–5, 7–9, 221–23, 254–55, 265, 276, 293–95, 333–34
Michelson, Edna Stanton (second wife), 214–21, 224–25, 242–42, 257–59, 291, 294, 328–30, 339

(373)

Michelson, Elsa (daughter), 8, 81, 85, 88, 96, 149–50, 174, 242
Michelson, Johanna (sister), 12
Michelson, Julie (sister), 19, 118, 119
Michelson, Madeleine (daughter), 3–5, 221–22, 254–55, 258, 265, 293, 295
Michelson, Margaret Heminway (first wife), 42–46, 63–65, 81–82, 88–89, 96, 112–15, 118–21, 133–36, 148–49, 173–74, 178, 213–14, 242–43
Michelson, Miriam (sister), 19, 21–22, 37, 118–19
Michelson, Pauline (sister), 12, 118, 119
Michelson, Rosalie Przylubska (mother), 12, 13, 16, 17, 20, 21, 36, 37, 118, 162
Michelson, Samuel (father), 12, 13, 20–22, 25, 36, 118, 162
Michelson, Truman (son), 63, 149, 174, 242
Michelson crater, 341
Michelson Laboratory, 340
Michelson-Morley experiment, 109, 123–33, 147; demonstrated for students by Paul Ehrenfest, 260; repeated by AAM, 199–203; repeated by Morley and Dayton C. Miller, 228–30; repeated by AAM at Mount Wilson, 271; repeated by Miller, 313–15; repeated by Auguste Piccard, 314; repeated by Charles H. Townes with laser light, 341. See also ether-drift experiments
Michelson Museum, 8
Miller, Dayton C., 212, 227–28, 230, 313–15, 321
Millikan, Robert A., 184–85, 245, 263, 264, 285–87, 292, 336
Minkowski, Hermann, 253, 259–60
Morley, Edward, 100–101, 107–13, 116–18, 123, 128–30, 135–41, 145–48, 228, 234
Moulton, Forest, 251–52, 265, 328–29

Mount Hamilton. See Lick Observatory
Mount Wilson Observatory, 140, 230, 267, 270–77, 281, 292, 328
Murphy's Camp, 13, 15–20, 118

National Academy of Sciences, 57, 64, 95, 244–45, 263, 297, 300, 314
National Bureau of Standards, 208–10
National Research Council, 263
Nautical Almanac Office, 54, 64–66, 73
Naval Coast Defense Reserve, 264–67
Naval Weapons Center (Naval Ordnance Test Station), 8, 266, 340–41
Nef, John Ulrich, 144, 152, 164–67
Newall, H. F., 206
Newcomb, Simon, 54–57, 62, 63–66, 75–76, 93–95, 101–4; 161, 181, 196
Newton, Isaac, 68, 140, 253
Nichols, Edward L., 210, 241
Nichols, Ernest Fox, 298
Nobel, Alfred, 232
Nobel Prize, 232–41
Noyes, Alfred, 272

O'Dell, Mary, 134–35
O'Donnell, Thomas J., 277–81, 290, 296, 309–10, 331–33, 340
"On the Application of Interference to Astronomical Measurements," 159
"On the Modifications Suffered by Light on Passing Through a Very Narrow Slit," 64–65
"On the Velocity of Light in Carbon Disulphide," 103
optical glass experiments, 266
Optical Society of America, 320–21

Paris Exposition of 1900, 208
Pavillon de Breteuil, 137, 174–75
Pearson, Fred, 185–86, 223, 239, 241, 244, 264, 279–81, 305–7, 331–33, 337–38
Pearson, Julius, 185–86, 193, 239, 244

74252